Comparative and International Research in Education

Comparative and international research in education is being transformed and revitalised by changing geopolitical relations, the acceleration of globalisation, major advances in ICT and paradigmatic shifts across the social sciences. This multidisciplinary book critically examines the implications of these changes for those engaged in such work worldwide. Ground-breaking and insightful, it draws on the latest research within and beyond the field to give a comprehensive overview of contemporary developments and emergent trends.

Drawing upon the authors' extensive international experience, the text:

- re-assesses the diverse and multidisciplinary origins of this field of study;
- documents the increased orientation towards research;
- explores the changing nature of the problems and issues faced by both new and experienced researchers;
- articulates a coherent and well-informed case for a thorough reconceptualisation of the field as a whole.

The book argues eloquently for increased cultural and contextual sensitivity in educational research and development in order that comparative and international studies might make a more effective contribution to educational theory, policy and practice worldwide. This multidisciplinary work will be welcomed by theorists and researchers in education and the social sciences, as well as teachers, policy-makers and anyone concerned with improving dialogue and understanding across cultures and nations.

Michael Crossley is Reader in Education in the Graduate School of Education at the University of Bristol, and Director of the Research Centre for International and Comparative Studies in Education.

Keith Watson is Emeritus Professor of Comparative and International Education, and a former Director of the Centre for International Studies in Education Management and Training at the University of Reading.

For Anne, Martin and Sam
and
Sheila, Joanna, Adrian, Pippa and Katy

Comparative and International Research in Education

Globalisation, context and difference

Michael Crossley and Keith Watson

RoutledgeFalmer
Taylor & Francis Group

LONDON AND NEW YORK

MT

First published 2003 by RoutledgeFalmer
11 New Fetter Lane, London EC4P 4EE

Simultaneously published in the USA and Canada
by RoutledgeFalmer
29 West 35th Street, New York, NY 10001

RoutledgeFalmer is an imprint of the Taylor & Francis Group

Typeset in Palatino by GreenGate Publishing Services
Printed and bound in Great Britain by
Antony Rowe Ltd, Chippenham, Wiltshire

British Library Cataloguing in Publication Data
A catalogue record for this book is available from the British
Library

Library of Congress Cataloging in Publication Data
A catalog record for this book has been requested

ISBN 0–415–19122–X

11/03/05

Contents

Foreword   vi
Preface   x
Acknowledgements   xii
Abbreviations   xiii

1   Introduction   1

2   Multidisciplinarity and diversity in comparative and
    international education   12

3   Difficulties in conducting comparative and
    international research in education   32

4   Globalisation, context and difference   50

5   Changing research agendas: Issues and priorities   70

6   Educational research, global agendas and international
    development co-operation   84

7   Reconceptualising comparative and international
    research in education   116

8   Context and culture in educational research and
    development   134

References   143
Index   172

Foreword

This book is a major contribution to the field of comparative and international education. It has been co-authored by two distinguished figures, who write with authority and clarity, and who present conceptual insights which add creative and intellectual vitality to the field at a time of major change and development. Specialist libraries may already have many books concerned with comparative and international education. The present work goes far beyond its predecessors by integrating insights from an impressive range of literatures, and by exploring the implications of many newly emergent issues and themes. These include contemporary philosophical and epistemological debates about the nature, role and impact of contrasting research paradigms, and worldwide concern about the relationship between educational research and efforts to improve policy and practice. The book challenges many of the traditional boundaries and assumptions that have come to characterise even this multidisciplinary field. The commentary is articulated in a way that demonstrates the potential of an increased 'bridging of cultures and traditions' – be it between theory and practice; different disciplinary or professional foundations; paradigmatic orientations; studies of the North and South; or past and present scholarship.

A coherent case is made by the authors for a deep and fundamental reconceptualisation of comparative and international research in education. This is formulated in the light of a keen awareness of the international impact of intensified globalisation, and of the implications of poststructuralist challenges to educational research and socio-economic policy worldwide. Emergent issues that are highlighted include the rise of new technologies; the marketisation of education; the impact of an assessment and accountability culture; and the globalisation of powerful educational policy agendas.

At the heart of the book is a well-informed analysis of the uncritical international transfer of educational theory, policy and practice. This is well illustrated and reflected in the discussion of the changing role of multilateral agencies, and in the related exploration of the implications for global democracy of the new architecture of international development. Crossley and Watson point out that the improvement of links between educational research and the economic and humanitarian needs of the twenty-first century requires deeper understanding of culture and context. This task, they argue, demands stronger attention to the implications of difference, to improved cross-cultural dialogue, and to reflexivity and sustainability. It also requires attention to political factors and to power differentials in international efforts to promote new forms of partnership and new modalities in research. The book thus has significant theoretical, methodological, substantive and organisational implications for the future of comparative and international research in education.

Among other important features are the ways in which this book is firmly grounded in history. Crossley and Watson present an insightful summary of the core features of the field and of key developments in previous decades and centuries. The book appositely quotes the distinguished historian Eric Hobsbawm, who in 1994 lamented that most young people at the century's end 'grow up in a sort of permanent present, lacking any organic relation to the public past of the times they live in'. A similar remark may be made with reference to comparative and international education: too many contemporary researchers lack awareness of the history of the field, and of the insights and evolution in the thinking of their forebears. Were these scholars and practitioners to have a stronger sense of history, they would understand more fully the reasons for the current contours of the field. As Crossley and Watson so well demonstrate, they would also find much wisdom in earlier analyses – wisdom that itself holds potential for the future.

Part of this history of the field concerns the distinctive features of, and relationships between, comparative education and international education. The fundamental characteristic of comparative education, of course, is comparison. This does not necessarily mean cross-national comparison, and indeed an increasing volume of exciting comparative work is being conducted within countries. International education, in contrast, by definition requires a crossing of national boundaries. However, the label has been used to mean different things in different settings. In some contexts, the term international education is used to describe the process of educating people to see themselves as international citizens in other nations. In other settings, which are more closely within the domain of the present book, the term international education describes educational work which practitioners and scholars undertake in countries other then their own. This use of the term often distinguishes such applied work from the more theoretical research traditions which are characteristic of comparative education. Historically, the label international education has often been used to describe the work of scholars from industrialised countries who have studied education in less developed countries. Such scholars have not always used the methodological tools, paradigms and insights of the comparative education constituency, which has traditionally been more concerned with the industrialised countries of Europe and North America.

In some parts of the world, the twin fields of comparative and international education have been formally linked in the names of professional societies. Thus in the USA, the Comparative Education Society (CES), which had been established in 1956, was renamed in 1969 as the Comparative and International Education Society (CIES). Similarly, in 1979 the British Comparative Education Society (BCES) was renamed the British Comparative and International Education Society (BCIES). Subsequently the BCIES merged with another body to become the British Association for International and Comparative Education (BAICE). Crossley and Watson have respectively been Chairperson and President of BAICE, and are major figures in its ongoing organisational leadership. Their own careers have exemplified the processes of cross-fertilisation between the more academic-oriented arena of theoretically-informed comparative education and the more practitioner-oriented field of international education; and the present book is one of the fruits of that cross-fertilisation.

In addition to their firm bases in the United Kingdom, both authors have extensive experience and deep awareness of the cultures and traditions of other parts of the world. From this awareness has come the observation that the distinctions between comparative and international education outlined above have not been held universally. At the global level, the CIES and BAICE are two constituent societies of the World Council of Comparative Education Societies (WCCES), which was created in 1970 and which brings together 30 national, regional and language-based societies in the field. The World Council has not considered it necessary to add 'International' to its own title; and indeed only five of its 30 constituent societies have the word in their titles.

This observation links well to a fundamental point about the diversity of approaches to comparative and international research in different parts of the world. Despite the impact of globalisation, scholarly traditions remain far from homogeneous. Thus, one major message of this book is that within the overarching field of comparative and international education are many sub-fields which adopt different research paradigms, assumptions and orientations. This is partly because of the different contexts within which scholars and practitioners operate, which itself is allied to the literatures available in different languages, to varied traditions of academic discourse, and to differing values and geo-political influences. It is also connected to the practical and conceptual roles of comparative and international education, which vary across different countries, cultures and communities. Thus Crossley and Watson refer in this book to comparative educations, in the plural, as well as to the overall field of comparative and international education.

Viewing this matter positively, diversity within the field promotes vigour and encourages debate. This is the perspective that is convincingly present here, and the authors highlight the importance of the growth of international dialogue in the last few decades. However, Crossley and Watson are also keenly aware of the shortcomings of much contemporary research. They observe that too many comparative and international studies are poorly conceived, are insufficiently rigorous, and lack adequate sensitivity to contexts. In part, this is a legacy from the division between the more theoretical and the more applied dimensions of the field; but in some situations it arises from the political agendas of the stakeholders and/or their sponsoring agencies.

Further, the accommodating nature of the field can be seen as a weakness as well as a strength. Thus, renewed growth of the field has led many researchers to describe their work as comparative or international, even if those involved have little relevant experience and training in the methodological and cross-cultural sensitivities associated with the field.

In the light of such issues, Crossley and Watson reassess the future trajectory for comparative and international research in education. They note that the rise of the Internet and the proliferation of publication outlets have greatly expanded access to information, and they observe that the forces of globalisation have increased the interest in international trends among policy-makers, practitioners and theorists. This is therefore a critical, insightful and constructive book that is especially sensitive to the centrality of differing views in advancing this re-emergent field and in improving our understandings of the contemporary world. A core motif of the book is that, using the wording from Chapter 4, the field 'may now be entering a new, creative and forward-looking period of development – but one that may also better represent a diversity of forms and a constructive bridging with the valuable traditions of the past'.

Michael Crossley and Keith Watson are to be applauded and thanked for this book, which brings together so many insights in such a challenging and illuminating way. The book will itself be at the forefront of the next wave of revitalisation in the field, and will be appreciated by both students and seasoned scholars from a very wide range of professional backgrounds, disciplines and countries.

Mark Bray
Chair Professor of Comparative Education
University of Hong Kong

Secretary General
World Council of Comparative Education Societies

Preface

> The world is never static. Even in periods when everything appears to remain the same, streams of change, however small, exist. But in some periods myriad streams of change all flow into a giant river of transformation. Change becomes apparent when the different currents 'encounter' each other and the obstacles in their paths ... All the streams of change that have been flowing quietly and even slowly during the century are now overflowing their banks.
>
> (Miller 1991:i)

In this book we recognise that the processes of globalisation are advancing simultaneously with a rich variety of poststructuralist challenges to the nature and form of much social and educational research – and to related developments in educational policy and practice. Indeed, throughout the book, we suggest that the tensions that are emerging between the ideas and developments that underpin globalisation on the one hand, and the theoretical perspectives that prioritise difference on the other, generate what may be the most fundamental of all intellectual challenges of the present day. It is this combination of perspectives that inspired the sub-title of the book itself, and that informs the content and title, 'Globalisation, Context and Difference', of Chapter 4. The concept of context has, however, long been of central importance to the multidisciplinary field of comparative and international education; and, for us, it holds increased significance for the quality and relevance of future educational research and educational development worldwide.

In the light of these issues and developments, and drawing upon our own international experience – in contexts as diverse as the small states of the Caribbean and the South Pacific, the post-industrial economies of Australia, the USA and the United Kingdom, and the highly populated nations of China and Pakistan – we demonstrate how and why culture and context increasingly matters. In doing so we critically explore the current and future potential of comparative and international research in education. The history and traditions of this field, we suggest, deserve renewed consideration in times when the uncritical international transfer of educational policy and practice is increasingly evident – and ever more possible with the advent of modern information and communications technologies.

Experience within and beyond the field, however, also points to the need for deep and fundamental change, and for major reconceptualisation in terms of the theoretical, methodological, substantive and organisational dimensions of comparative and international research in education. This book therefore originates from our efforts to consider how this might be done, in ways that improve the field's ability to contribute to both the improvement of educational policy and practice and to the advancement of theoretical scholarship within education and the social sciences, and beyond. Central to our thesis is respect for cultural and intellectual diversity, combined with an argument for the vastly improved bridging of cultures and traditions – be they intellectual, disciplinary, professional, paradigmatic, regional, human or other.

The analysis, perhaps inevitably, reflects our own specific interests, backgrounds and experience although we have tried to capture and reflect upon the diversity and complexity of the field as a whole. We do not intend this to represent a fully comprehensive or complete analysis, especially given our commitment to the potential of a diversity of perspectives and views. We do, however, hope that our construction of issues and changing priorities will prove to be helpful for others, and will be seen as a creative and challenging contribution to the ongoing revitalisation of the broad field of comparative and international education. Linking with the humanitarian dimension of the field, we further hope that our attention to issues of power, reflexivity, and cross-cultural dialogue, will play a part in increasing global awareness of the issues involved in fostering improved international understanding, in our increasingly complex, turbulent and interconnected world.

Michael Crossley
Bristol

Keith Watson
Reading

Acknowledgements

Many people have contributed to the development of the ideas that underpin this book, in the United Kingdom where the text was written, and in the different places that we have worked throughout the world. The book reflects many rewarding years of theoretical, methodological and practical engagement with the field of comparative and international education. As such, we would like to acknowledge the influence of the many current and former colleagues and students, in the North and the South, with whom we have been fortunate to work. It is such international experience that has helped to shape our own understanding and respect for the impact of differing cultural and intellectual perspectives upon educational research and educational development. In particular we would like to acknowledge the stimulation, insight and support generated over the years by our colleagues on the editorial boards of the two journals *Comparative Education* and the *International Journal of Educational Development*; colleagues and students at the University of Bristol, Graduate School of Education; and in the Faculty of Education and Community Studies at the University of Reading. Similarly, ongoing work with members of the National Executive Committee for the British Association for International and Comparative Education (BAICE) has proved an invaluable source of insight and understanding about the nature and scope of the field itself. In this regard, we also remember our friend and colleague, Edmund King, with much affection. In preparing the manuscript for publication, Keith Holmes, Anne and Martin Crossley and Mark Bray were generous in providing, at different stages, helpful feedback upon sections of the text. Pat O'Brien at the University of Bristol, Margaret King at the University of Reading, and, especially, Margaret Lole in Bristol, provided excellent secretarial support when needed. We are also grateful to the co-editors of the journal *Compare* (Caroline Dyer and Rosemary Preston), and the publishers Carfax, for permission to update and build upon an article in Chapter 7, which was first published by Michael Crossley as 'Reconceptualising Comparative and International Education' in Volume 29, Number 3 of that journal.

Finally, our sincere thanks go to Hywel Evans, Anna Clarkson and all at the Routledge offices in London for their consistent and helpful support throughout all stages of the conceptualisation, development and completion of the book.

Abbreviations

ADEA	Association for the Development of Education in Africa
AIDS	Acquired Immune Deficiency Syndrome
ASEAN	Association of South East Asian Nations
BAICE	British Association for International and Comparative Education
BATROE	British Association of Teachers and Researchers on Overseas Education
BBC	British Broadcasting Corporation
BCIES	British Comparative and International Education Society
BRAC	Bangladesh Rural Advancement Committee
CERC	Comparative Education Research Centre
CESE	Comparative Education Society in Europe
CHOGM	Commonwealth Heads of Government Meeting
CICE	Current Issues in Comparative Education
CIDA	Canadian International Development Agency
DAC	Development Assistance Committee (OECD)
DANIDA	Danish International Development Assistance
DFID	Department for International Development (United Kingdom)
DSE	Deutsche Stiftung für International Entwicklung (German Foundation for International Development)
EBRD	European Bank for Reconstruction and Development
EFA	Education for All
ETEG	Education and Training Exports Group
EU	European Union
FAVDO	Forum of African Development Organisations
GATS	General Agreement on Trade in Services
GNP	Gross National Product
HICs	High Income Countries
HIPCs	Highly Indebted Poor Countries
IB	International Baccalaureate
IBE	International Bureau of Education
IBO	International Baccalaureate Office

IEA	International Association for the Evaluation of Educational Achievement
IIEP	International Institute for Educational Planning
IMF	International Monetary Fund
INSCED	International Standard Classification of Education
JICA	Japan International Cooperation Agency
LDCs	Less Developed Countries
MDGs	Millennium Development Goals
MLAs	Multilateral Agencies
NAFTA	North American Free Trade Agreement
NEPAD	New Partnership for African Development
NGOs	Non-Governmental Organisations
NICs	Newly Industrialised Countries
NORAD	Norwegian Agency for Development Co-operation
NORRAG	Northern Policy Research and Advisory Network on Education and Training
ODA	Overseas Development Administration, United Kingdom (now DFID)
ODA	Overseas Development Assistance
OECD	Organisation for Economic Co-operation and Development
OPEC	Organisation of Petroleum Exporting Countries
SACHES	Southern Africa Comparative and History of Education Society
SADC	Southern African Development Community
SAP	Structural Adjustment Policies
SIDA	Swedish International Development Co-operation Agency
SWAPs	Sector Wide Approaches
TNCs	Trans National Corporations
TVET	Technical and Vocational Education and Training
UNDP	United Nations Development Programme
UNESCO	United Nations Educational, Scientific and Cultural Organisation
UNICEF	United Nations Children's Fund
USA	United States of America
USAID	United States Agency for International Development
USSR	Union of Soviet Socialist Republics
WCCES	World Council of Comparative Education Societies
WCEFA	World Conference on Education for All
WTO	World Trade Organisation

Chapter 1

Introduction

At the outset of what has been called the 'Global Century' there is much evidence of a revitalisation of the field of comparative and international education that few would have envisaged even a decade ago. The impact and implications of intensified globalisation and rapidly changing geopolitical relations underpin much of this revitalisation, as do dramatic advances in information and communications technology, paradigmatic challenges and developments across the social sciences, and the relative ease of international travel that has come to characterise our times.

A research orientation

A research orientation is evident in this revitalisation and in the emergence of related research centres and research training initiatives. These trends are well documented by directories such as those produced by Dyer and King (1993) and Altbach and Tan (1995); and by related reviews of organisational developments, institutional capacity and the growth of national comparative education societies (Bray 1998; Tjeldvoll and Smehaugen 1998; Schweisfurth 1999; Wilson 2003). To this we can add evidence of the buoyant expansion of the World Council of Comparative Education Societies (WCCES), the emergence of new specialist journals, the research impact of international development agency involvement in the South, and the growing influence of large scale, collaborative research initiatives. Indicative of such developments are the various African Education Research Networks (Mwiria and Wamahiu 1995), the vibrant Northern Policy Research and Advisory Network on Education and Training (NORRAG) (King and Buchert 1999), the European Union funded PRESTIGE (Training and Mobility of Research) initiative (Phillips and Economou 1999), and the globally influential International Association for the Evaluation of Educational Achievement (IEA) (Postlethwaite 1999).

International interest in the latter, large-scale, comparative studies of educational achievement, and in the methodologies employed in their design, is often motivated by concern for system differentials in performance – notably, as revealed in school subject league tables. Intensified global economic and educational competition has thus helped to heighten the prominence of comparative and international research – and involved a wider range of stakeholders in both the research process and in the interpretation of findings (Goldstein 1996). So too has the international application of related studies concerning school improvement and school effectiveness; inspired by the apparent 'lessons to be learned' from the economic transformations and educational achievements of Pacific Rim states, such as Taiwan and Singapore (Levin and Lockheed 1993; Reynolds and Farrell 1996; Teddlie and Reynolds 2000). Indeed, the high profile and controversial nature of such studies have been instrumental, in themselves, in involving a wider range of formerly mainstream educationalists in comparative and international research. Alexander (1995), for example, has challenged the school effectiveness studies by extending his contextually grounded work on primary education in the United Kingdom to new multi-level studies of culture and pedagogy in England, France, India, Russia and the United States (1999, 2000). From a more macro-oriented stance, well known analysts such as Ball (1998a) have also begun to apply their own distinctive, and theoretically inspired, policy perspectives within a comparative framework, and sociologists, including Green (1997) and Dale (1999, 2000a and b, 2001), are increasingly exploring comparative implications as they engage directly with the processes and mechanisms through which globalisation affects national systems of education. Planners, funders and consumers of education are, moreover, increasingly expressing keen interest in international and comparative studies as they seek ways of dealing with the implications of competitive league tables, market forces, multiple innovations, and demands for ever more cost effective ways of increasing access and improving the quality of educational provision. This resurgence is visible, at all levels, within and beyond the framework of formal national systems of education – and it encompasses, for example, non-formal provision, adult and continuing education, distance and lifelong learning, community projects and a diversity of private sector initiatives.

More broadly speaking, it is pertinent in the post-September 2001 era to emphasise renewed worldwide preoccupation with the need to improve cross-cultural dialogue and understanding. Such goals, as we shall argue later, have long underpinned the rationale for much work in the field of comparative and international education. They were especially prominent in studies carried out following the two world wars, but the centrality of the humanitarian dimension of the field has remained visible in its consistent engagement with concerns that include, for example, development studies, health related initiatives and the implications of HIV/AIDS, work with refugees and migrants, liberation theory and peace education. Adding renewed stimulus, world leaders today can be observed, with some urgency, to be calling for international development issues to be more clearly seen as priorities for all in society to engage with – as we try better to understand the causes of international conflict and work towards a 'safer world'. This was, for example, a core theme in a speech delivered by the Secretary of State for

International Development in the United Kingdom, in March 2002 (Short 2002). In this global context, implications for the rethinking of development strategies, and for comparative and international research in the fields of education, development and beyond, cannot be underestimated. Other pertinent issues could be mentioned, but these examples are clearly indicative of the contemporary widening of interest in the potential and processes of comparative and international research in education worldwide.

The present volume is designed both to contribute to, and further stimulate, this resurgence of interest and activity, at what is clearly a strategically important time for research and scholarship that transcends national and cultural boundaries. In doing this, however, it is argued that comparative and international research in education must also be fundamentally reconceptualised in ways that better articulate and demonstrate its continuing relevance for the future (Crossley 1999; Watson 1999b). The field's diverse history and traditions, for example, deserve both celebration and challenge – while its multidisciplinary origins and nature position it well for further advancement in a world in which the socio-cultural analysis of global trends and developments requires concerted attention.

The case for such reconceptualisation is developed within a conceptual framework that recognises that the processes of globalisation are advancing simultaneously with a variety of poststructuralist challenges to the Enlightenment project, positivistic science, modernisation theory and rationalism itself (Howard and Lewis 1998; Peters 2001). Tensions between the ideas and developments that underpin globalisation on the one hand, and theoretical perspectives that prioritise difference on the other, it is argued, generate what may be the most fundamental of all intellectual challenges of the present day. The implications of this for comparative and international education are profound because concern with global trends, the dilemmas of international transfer, and the concepts of cultural and contextual difference lie at the very heart of both the traditions and the aspirations of the field. Indeed, capturing the contemporary discourse well, Arnove and Torres (1999) portray the re-emergent intellectual agenda for comparative education as one that, most pertinently, focuses upon the 'dialectic of the global and the local'.

Our own perspectives on these core issues have developed from extensive professional and academic experience in different capacities and contexts across the globe. This cumulative experience consists of periods of long-term work and residence in Australia, Papua New Guinea, Kenya, Bangladesh, Poland, Iran, Thailand and the United Kingdom. It includes intensive periods as researchers, consultants and teachers in countries such as Belize, St Lucia, Botswana, Tanzania, Canada, the USA, India and China; and senior professional and administrative responsibilities within, or for, a wide range of universities, international agencies, professional associations and non-governmental organisations. We also bring together a range of different intellectual traditions, substantive interests and areas of professional expertise. These include specialist interests in research and evaluation capacity for development, globalisation and education, education in small states, language policies in ethnically and linguistically plural societies, educational policy, planning and administration and – most pertinently here – theoretical and methodological developments in the field of comparative and international education.

The present volume thus draws upon a combination of theoretical analysis, critical reflection upon practical and professional experience, and extensive engagement in empirical research in a wide variety of professional and cultural contexts worldwide. This combination of theory, methodology, policy and practice also underpins much of the reconceptualistion thesis advanced throughout the present work. We therefore argue that, to a great extent, a more effective bridging of the worlds of theory and practice lies at the heart of contemporary efforts to improve both the quality of educational development and the quality and impact of educational research itself. These arguments are developed more fully in subsequent chapters in ways that build cumulatively upon the previous work of both writers (see, for example, Watson 1980, 1982; Crossley 1984, 1990; Crossley and Broadfoot 1992; Crossley and Vulliamy 1997a; Watson 1998; Crossley 1999; Watson 2001a; Crossley and Jarvis 2000a, 2001).

Conceptual framework

In the light of the above, and given the extent of contemporary challenges to the nature and impact of both social and educational research, this book is designed to develop a meta-level analysis directly related to the socio-economic transformations, intellectual shifts and educational priorities that characterise the outset of the twenty-first century. This is intended as a stimulus and benchmark for others to build upon in shaping what is emerging as a new period of development for the field of comparative and international education as a whole. In saying this, we acknowledge the teleological dangers and limitations of attempts to demarcate phases of development in any arena. The reconceptualisation proposed here therefore argues for a more cumulative building upon the valuable traditions of the field, while articulating a challenging and future-oriented critique that is informed by contemporary social and intellectual developments.

The book is structured around three theoretically and methodologically oriented conceptual themes. First, we present an historically informed review of the nature and evolution of the combined field of comparative and international education, from its nineteenth-century foundations to the present day. In doing so we explore the differing origins and foundations of diverse comparative and international traditions; identify the changing motivations and purposes that have generated various periods of growth; chart major paradigmatic shifts of emphasis; and examine the nature of the challenges that currently command critical attention. This historical perspective is largely focused upon Chapter 2, although it plays an important part in shaping our overall and contemporary critique.

Second, a critical analysis is undertaken of the implications of the literature relating to globalisation, post-modernism and post-colonialism for the future development of comparative and international research in education. This is initially articulated in Chapter 4, but the emergent themes are applied in the broader analysis through to the conclusions.

Third, throughout the book an assessment is made of the significance of the current, and internationally prominent critique of educational and social research, with particular regard to its relevance for (i) the improvement of educational policy and practice and (ii) the theoretical and methodological advancement of future comparative and international research and development initiatives.

In developing the overall framework for the book, from Chapter 3 onwards we examine the changing nature of problems encountered within the field. Ideas derived from the various theoretical and methodological analyses are also applied to an identification and examination of the substantive issues and priorities that have dominated the research agenda during the past decade, and to those that we believe will continue to command attention well into the twenty-first century. This incorporates a critical review of recent developments and problems encountered within the field – and further consideration of the professional and intellectual implications of the globalisation and other theoretically-inspired debates. Particular attention is given to the impact of globalisation and changing geopolitical relations upon the nature and role of influential bilateral and multilateral development assistance agencies. We examine how such bodies have influenced the research process, their part in the shaping of educational policy worldwide, and how they have impacted upon varied educational contexts and systems in practice.

In doing this, we address specific geopolitical changes that have taken place in major regions of the globe such as East Asia, Southern Africa and Eastern Europe. The book thus examines the impact of rapid socio-political change upon dramatic educational transformations worldwide, and demonstrates how new research priorities, challenges and opportunities have opened up as a result. This is linked to a discussion of pertinent and contemporary research studies and, in Chapter 6, to a more focused examination of the implications of changing priorities and agendas in the arena of international development co-operation. As indicated above, this is informed by the analytical framework generated by the globalisation, post-modern and post-colonial debates – and by our evolving critique of the uncritical international transfer of education policy and practice. Indeed, at the heart of the rationale for the book lies our concern with the dilemmas generated by the increasingly rapid, and uncritical, transfer of educational theory, policy and practice from one context to another. Moreover, we argue that the complexities of this issue have become increasingly problematic as multilateral and bilateral development agencies have sought to collaborate in the formulation of internationally agreed educational policy agendas. While many benefits can, indeed, be derived from such co-ordinated efforts, these have often been achieved at the expense of important contextual considerations. Dadey and Harber (1991) and Harber and Dadey (1993) have, for example, shown how many of the findings of Western school effectiveness research do not apply well in African contexts. The same can also be seen to apply to much of the Western literature on curriculum change, decentralisation, teacher professionalism and school autonomy (Crossley 1984; Thaman 1993; Harber and Davies 1997; Reimers and McGinn 1997; Buchert 1998). In the course of later chapters we examine a number of these substantive topics in greater depth. Here, however, we first draw attention to the more fundamental need for all those engaged in comparative and international initiatives to accord such issues and contemporary challenges the disciplined and critical attention they deserve worldwide. This clearly underpins our own proposals for the reconceptualisation of comparative and international research as outlined further in the section below, and as articulated more fully in Chapters 7 and 8.

Context matters

Perhaps it should not come as a surprise that, when faced with the turbulence of successive waves of economic and social change, policy-makers, practitioners and consumers of education, alike, look to the successful experiences of others for guidance and advice. We have already noted, for example, how policy-makers in the United Kingdom have purposefully examined the experience of Pacific Rim nations, in the light of their reported 'superior performance' in international surveys of educational achievement (Reynolds and Farrell 1996). Much can certainly be learned from comparisons with the work of others and from the international experience, but many distinguished comparativists have long pointed out that major problems lie in any simplistic transfer of educational policy and practice from one socio-cultural context to another. To cite Sir Michael Sadler's (1900:49) seminal lecture, appositely delivered at the turn of the last century:

> We cannot wander at pleasure among the educational systems of the world, like a child strolling through a garden, and picking off a flower from one bush and some leaves from another, and then expect that if we stick what we have gathered into the soil at home, we shall have a living plant ...

Many are familiar with Sadler's socio-cultural and interpretative perspective, but it justly deserves re-consideration here as we increasingly recognise the importance of cultural influences on learning, and assess the future potential of the field as a whole. Indeed, it is especially pertinent in a global era where economic imperatives, neoliberalism, and positivistic assumptions currently dominate much social policy – and where the diverse challenges of, for example, post-modern and post-colonial perspectives help to highlight the extent of contested terrain, and the (multi)cultural forces and factors that underpin human progress (Mazrui 1990; Morrow and Torres 1995; Cowen 1996a; UNESCO 1998a; Welch 1999; Peters 2001). As argued elsewhere, (Crossley 1999; Crossley with Jarvis 2001a and b), context matters – and comparative and international research in education is especially well placed to demonstrate this. On the other hand, while the field of comparative and international education has many professional and intellectual traditions that deserve both recognition and celebration, it must also face concerted internal and external challenges if it is to prove to be of continuing worth and influence for the future. Chief of the field's traditional strengths are its multi-disciplinary character and 'time honoured commitment to policy-oriented research relevant to the world around it' (E.J. King 1997:90). These and other strengths upon which we can build are considered in subsequent chapters – here, however, it is first pertinent to pursue the contemporary critique a little further – to show how this underpins the rationale for the proposed reconceptualisation process and for the thesis of the book itself.

A rationale for reconceptualisation

New developments and challenges to the established traditions of comparative and international research in education are becoming visible on many fronts but, to date, their cumulative impact and potential has not been coherently articulated in a way that directly examines the implications and complexities of globalisation. The time, however, is ripe for a comprehensive re-assessment of the field as a whole. This is demonstrated well by the many strategically significant arguments for change that can be marshalled to build on those already outlined above.

First, the timing is most propitious, following both the 100th anniversary of Sadler's (1900) lecture, and the start of a new century. For many analysts of trends the end of a century, and especially of a millennium, provides a useful opportunity to take stock, although we emphasise here that the year 2000, in itself, is a Eurocentric perception. Societies such as China or India, whose civilisations go back several millennia, or the Islamic world, which also has its own calendar, do not accord the year 2000 the same significance as do Western nations. This was not their millennium. Such a fundamental difference points to the limitations of any field, but it is especially significant and revealing in studies concerned with cross-cultural issues, and those that have been dominated by Western theoretical perspectives, methodologies, literatures and personnel. As Bray (1998) points out, recent years have seen the greatest growth of professional interest in comparative education occur beyond the English speaking world – in countries with increasingly large and vibrant comparative education societies, such as China and Japan. He goes on to note how development agency involvement in research has also stimulated calls for renewed growth throughout the South.

> This includes the UNESCO Principal Regional Office for Education in Asia and the Pacific, which during the 1980s and early 1990s had declined in visibility but which is making renewed efforts to play an active role. It also includes the Asian Development Bank, which has emerged as a major figure in the education sector. Thus considerable work is being conducted outside universities as well as within them.
>
> (Bray 1998:8)

Second, the influence of intensified globalisation and changing geopolitical relations has profound implications for the nature of our discourse and for the ongoing relevance of many previously taken for granted terms and conceptual distinctions. The continuing appropriateness and utility, for example, of distinctions between the 'first' and 'third' worlds, and between 'developed' and 'developing' countries, are clearly increasingly problematic in the post-colonial era – and following the dramatic decline of the Soviet Union. Indeed, many post-colonial writers challenge the implicit values, analytic assumptions and over-generalisations that underpin such 'dualistic' classifications in principle (Tikly 1999). The same can be said for commonly used generic terms such as 'Western', 'Northern' and 'the South'. While recognising the intellectual limitations and dangers of such terminology, we argue here that our aim to engage with a wide spectrum of contemporary debates (and varied stakeholders) – as our reconceptualisation thesis demands – is still often facilitated by their use. We therefore prefer to adopt a critical stance, in sympathy with the post-colonial critique, wherever possible; however, throughout the text, we retain use of more commonly applied terminology and distinctions where it is pragmatically necessary to communicate with as wide a range of readers as possible. In the light of these developments it is, nevertheless, clear that any contemporary reconceptualisation must find more effective ways of incorporating difference, and divergent cultural perspectives into the basic canon of comparative and international research and scholarship.

Third, the contemporary Western critique of mainstream educational research points to problematic divisions between the professional cultures of research, policy and action (Crossley and Holmes 2001). Critiques are being generated within professional circles as well as by governmental agencies, policy-makers, funders, practitioners and a wide spectrum of other stakeholders (Hargreaves 1996; Kennedy 1997; Furlong 1998; Hillage 1998; Tooley and Darby 1998). In this politically charged debate, calls are being made for educational research to be more cumulative and authoritative – to be more directly relevant, useful and accessible to both policy-makers and practitioners – and to be more cost effective as budgets tighten and accountability is ever more emphasised. Comparative and international research faces similar challenges (Heyneman 1995; Crossley and Jarvis 2000b), and must find ways of bridging the professional cultures that have often separated academic theorists from the work of those more directly engaged in matters of policy and practice. Ways in which this might be achieved are explored later, but here it is perhaps more pertinent to note that, in the United Kingdom, 1997 saw indications of positive organisational developments in the formal inauguration of the British Association for International and Comparative Education (BAICE).

This significant and symbolic advance came about from the merger between two formerly distinct professional associations, the British Comparative and International Education Society (BCIES) and the British Association of Teachers and Researchers on Overseas Education (BATROE). This new start reflects many of the widespread professional concerns that we have identified here. In particular the merger represents the further bringing together of two distinctive communities – those that have tended to specialise in detached, comparative study (often of Western industrial nations), and those whose primary interests lie in 'international' educational policy and practice and active involvement in the direct experiences of developing countries (see also Wilson 1994). While both sides of the combined field have frequently been concerned with educational reform, it is often the case that those who have traditionally perceived themselves as 'comparativists' saw their work as less directly practical in nature, than that of the 'internationalists', and as more of an academic, research-based activity. Since such rapprochement holds multiple potential for the future of research, policy and practice worldwide we will return to this issue and to the history of the field and its implications in more detail later. In doing so, however, it should be noted that a more global history of comparative education also emerges in our analysis, highlighting the ongoing significance of complexity and diversity.

The above arguments are all the more pertinent given that many large-scale educational reforms of recent decades – in many different contexts – have been markedly less successful than intended. There is therefore an urgent and current need to take stock of what has happened, where, and with what results, if we are to contribute to the generation of improved understanding and greater success at the level of implementation. As Watson (1999b:235) points out there are now:

> ... too many pressures from governments and aid agencies for research to be focused on the present and for the immediate future rather than taking a longer time perspective. Our time frames are too short ... Comparative historical experience of what has been tried elsewhere and with what success or failure, such as in the fields of community education or the vocationalised curriculum, is rarely called upon in policy recommendations, often with depressing consequences.

While there is therefore a need for comparative and international research to bridge the theory–practice divide, there is also a strong case for a reconsideration of the potential to be gained from the renewed application of historical research perspectives. As Hobsbawm (1994:3) observes:

> The destruction of the past, or rather of the social mechanisms that link one's contemporary experience to that of earlier generations, is one of the most characteristic and eerie phenomena of the late twentieth century. Most young men and women at the century's end grow up in a sort of permanent present, lacking any organic relation to the public past of the times they live in.

To some extent this critique points to the need for comparative and international education to re-value connections with its own intellectual past – 'to re-establish its unique role in providing comparative historical insights for future policy action' (Watson 1999b:235). More recently, for example,

Kazamias (2001:439) has made an impassioned plea for 'reinventing the historical in comparative education' as a means of tackling what he sees as its 'humanistic impoverishment'.

In a related way there are equally significant dangers that too much contemporary comparative and international research remains blind to important theoretical and methodological issues and debates that have characterised the field in the past (Rust *et al.* 1999; Torres 2001). This is a particularly sensitive and pertinent issue for researchers new to cross-cultural work, and given the recent exponential growth of international consultancy work that is increasingly carried out by personnel with little formal training in the pitfalls of undertaking comparative and international studies (see the arguments raised by Noah 1986; Crossley and Broadfoot 1992; Preston and Arthur 1996). As Cowen (1999:73) points out, while comparative education is currently attracting renewed attention, it is also 'going through a dangerous moment' with the re-emergence of 'cargo-cult' assumptions about the transferability of policy and practice, and the 'advocacy discourse of politics'.

Finally, it is pertinent to return to the growing influence of globalisation and modern information and communication technologies on the nature and concept of education itself. Is, for example, formal education as we currently know it the best means for educating the millions of people – young and old – currently denied access? Given the rapid development of new technologies, the growth of private sector initiatives and the changing role of the media, much potential for new forms of teaching and learning is emerging in what is now increasingly seen as the learning society. Thus Broadfoot (1999a and b) and Jarvis (2000) both argue for a further broadening of scope in our frames of reference, to include all forms of learning, in any redefinition of the field of comparative and international education. This we also endorse and pursue in our subsequent review of the field, and in our proposals for the future.

Conclusion

In conclusion it is argued that the outset of the twenty-first century is a particularly apposite time for a critical, reflective and forward-looking review of comparative and international research in education. There is already much evidence of a revitalisation of the field, stimulated by intensified globalisation, rapid geopolitical change and a broadening of interest from the mainstream educational and social science research communities. In this book we argue that if the potential of these developments is to be fully realised, a fundamental reconceptualisation of comparative and international research in education is essential – and that this process has theoretical, methodological, substantive and organisational implications. In the following chapters we further develop and articulate this reconceptualisation thesis in the light of an analytical framework derived from the relevant literature relating to globalisation, and to post-modern and post-colonial perspectives on the significance of context, culture and difference. To paraphrase Miller's (1991:i) words, quoted at the outset; so many streams of thought have now begun to come together that their collective 'encounter' makes such 'transformational' change an urgent priority for all engaged in comparative and international research in education worldwide.

In the sections above we have begun to set the analytical scene by introducing the rationale for critique and change. This is now continued in Chapter 2 in a way that focuses upon an exposition and critical review of the history, nature and evolution of the field itself. While this begins to document diversity and major shifts in substantive lines of enquiry, it also helps to demonstrate further our overall conviction that, in these times of increasingly rapid and global change, there is a greater need for disciplined, comparative and international research in education than ever before.

Chapter 2

Multidisciplinarity and diversity in comparative and international education

As indicated in the previous chapter, comparative education in one form or another has a long history. International education's emergence as a distinctive field of activity is more recent. The purpose of this chapter is to show in what ways these and other related fields of study have evolved, merged and intertwined; what the major strands of enquiry have been; and why there is, today, a need to re-consider the nature and focus of contemporary comparative and international research in education. In engaging with such issues the more orthodox history of the field is first explored. In critiquing this, however, increased attention is given to the diversity of intellectual foundations that underpin contemporary work, and to the cross-cultural implications of this analysis for the reconceptualisation thesis. The chapter does not, however, consider the challenges and developments of the later decades of the twentieth century – leaving these for exploration in subsequent sections of the book. The fact that this diverse and multidisciplinary field has repeatedly changed and adapted according to the context and the times is, nevertheless, testimony to the pertinence and resilience of its varied foundations and traditions.

Comparative and international foundations

The early foundations of comparative education have been described as 'travellers' tales' because they consisted of little more than observations about how young people were educated or trained in different societies (Kazamias and Massialas 1965; Hausman 1967; Jones 1971; Trethewey 1976). For example, the ancient Greeks and Romans admired the discipline of Spartan education. The Romans marvelled at the debates in ancient Persia concerning what future government employees should learn and how they should be assessed. Indeed, there is a remarkable contemporaneity about many of these specific topics! The Italians of the early medieval period were intrigued by the tales brought back by Marco Polo (1254–1324) of how the Chinese taught their children and administered their vast country (Latham 1958). The *Codex Mendoza* reveals how Mexican children had a differentiated curriculum for boys and girls in what would now be classified as the primary years (Dore 1976, 1997). Ibn Batuta (1304–1368), a well documented traveller from Morocco, wrote fascinating accounts of society in much of fourteenth-century Islamic North Africa and the Middle East. However, these various works provided general social vignettes and did not comprise serious or systematic studies of education in other societies.

Brickman (1960) has described these early developments and insights as the 'prehistory' of comparative education, yet they reveal that man's ongoing curiosity about what happens in different parts of the world has very deep roots. To some extent this explains why, in an age of increased global pressures for uniformity, the differences and diversity of communities continue to attract serious attention. Going beyond Western constructions of the field's history that have, to date, dominated the English language literature, more truly global foundations and traditions are thus increasingly visible today. Wilson (2003) and Bray (2003), for example, draw attention to these multiple origins of the field, and highlight significant Chinese and Japanese historical foundations and antecedents.

The roots of comparative education as an academic field, however, are generally acknowledged to go back only to the beginning of the nineteenth century, as, also, do the origins of international education. Because these two parallel and somewhat complementary sub-fields have traditionally had different foundations and purposes (Epstein 1992, 1994; Wilson 1994, 2003), their approaches to research have often been predicated on different sets of assumptions. These differences can generate both confusion and misunderstanding. Moreover, since the two fields have become so closely entwined that they are now often seen as one, it is even more pertinent for their different foundations to be well understood by those engaging in such work today.

In the Western literature it is widely claimed that systematic comparative education had its origins with Marc-Antoine Jullien's proposal in 1817 that governments should provide statistical information concerning different facets of their education systems (Jullien 1817). This would include data on educational finance, student enrolments at different levels of the system, numbers of teachers and so on, in order 'to deduce true principles and determined routes so that education would be transformed into an almost positive science' (cited in Fraser 1964:20). Jullien is certainly acknowledged for first using the term 'comparative education' – and for many Western writers, he is seen as the founding 'father' of this dimension of the field. Over a century later Jullien's vision came closer to reality with the creation of the International Bureau of Education (IBE) in Geneva in 1925. This was followed in the post-World War II period with the annual production of collections of international statistics on education by bodies such as the United Nations Educational, Scientific and Cultural Organisation (UNESCO), the United Nations Development Programme (UNDP), the Organisation for Economic Cooperation and Development (OECD) and the World Bank. Such annual reports and statistics have now become essential tools for analysts, policy makers and practitioners in comparative and international education (see for example UNESCO 1993, 1995, 1998b; OECD 1995, 1998 and b; World Bank 1998, 1999/2000; UNDP 1999, 2000, 2001). The growth of international data collection also led academics such as

Anderson (1961), Holmes and Robinsohn (1963) and Noah and Eckstein (1969) to try to establish comparative education more firmly as a positivistic (social) science. This was to have major implications for the nature and form of much analysis in the field, especially as many national policies at that time were based on the belief that educational reforms introduced in one country could be transferred to another with little regard to the different national contexts. However, as Halls (1977:82) argued in challenging the dominance of such thinking:

> The truth is that if we borrow macro-concepts from other systems their application in our own system is almost bound to fail. The most telling example of this is where implantation was forcibly imposed, as in the colonial territories.

The origins of international education, on the other hand, can be traced back to César Auguste Basset, another Frenchman, who in 1808 called for scholars who were free from national preconceptions and who could observe education outside France with the intention of making recommendations for the reform of the French education system. This was just then beginning to evolve as a result of the Napoleonic Code and the creation of the Université de France. For many researchers international education gradually came to mean looking at education systems within the socio-economic, political and cultural context of a particular country, a far cry from the positivistic trends pursued by Anderson (1961) and Noah and Eckstein (1969). However, differences also emerged in the way international education came to be seen, and in the USA, especially following World War II, international education became closely associated with study tours to different countries, and with the express purpose of improving international understanding and awareness of other cultures and societies. More recently some writers have begun to use the term to describe the work (and study of) 'international schools' across the globe, schools which might be located in any country but whose student intake may come from a wide range of nationalities. In many cases these students will take the International Baccalaureate or the European Baccalaureate (Peterson, 1977; Jonietz and Harris 1991), will be prepared for employment anywhere in the world, and will be expected to develop an understanding of different cultures, as well as good relations with people of different nationalities and languages (see also Hayden and Thompson 2001). Indeed, in 2002 a new journal with this more specific focus was launched, titled the *Journal of Research in International Education*, by Sage publications in collaboration with the International Baccalaureate Organisation (IBO).

Further differences emerge because of the characterisation, as noted in Chapter 1, of comparative education with academic analyses of education in the industrialised world, both East and West, and international education with more applied studies carried out in developing countries (see Holmes, B. 1965; Wilson 1994). As we have already seen, both traditions have, to some extent, been brought together under the overarching umbrella of the composite term 'comparative and international education'. This was illustrated, for example, by the pre-BAICE redesignation, in 1979, of the British Comparative Education Society as the British Comparative and International Education Society (BCIES), modelled on the earlier 1969 reformulation of the Comparative and International Education Society (CIES) in the USA (Kay and Watson 1982; Watson and King 1991). However, it needs to be recognised that, while this merger of the twin fields has major intellectual implications for all involved in such work, in conceptual and organisational terms it is not a universal phenomenon. Many European countries have thus not seen a need to change the title of their 'comparative' societies. The same is true, for example, of the comparative education societies of China, Hong Kong, Japan and Taiwan and, indeed, of the World Council of Comparative Education Societies (WCCES). In Southern Africa there is also a strong historical connection in the character and focus of the Southern Africa Comparative and History of Education Society (SACHES).

To return to the core argument being developed here, however, Epstein (1994) suggests that because many scholars have lost sight of the differing roots of the main arenas within this multidisciplinary field of study, confusion has prevailed in much of the recent literature. This is apparent in the following comments from leading writers in the field of comparative education. Arnove (1982:464), for example, in seeking to justify a 'world systems' approach, argues that 'world systems analysis restores the international dimension to the field of comparative and international education ... by providing ... a framework that is essential to an understanding of educational developments and reforms ... that are simultaneously sweeping many countries of the world'. R.M. Thomas (1990), writing from a different perspective, argues that the work of bilateral and multilateral agencies and many non-governmental organisations (NGOs) is applied 'international comparative education'. Paulston (1994:925) generates further possible confusion when he suggests that 'international' education is ' a new branch of comparative education' which addresses the problems of educational planning, development and theory construction in macro-studies of education and social change, especially in the 'Newly Industralised Countries (NICs)'.

The significance of this debate extends well beyond logistics and semantics because, for the best part of a couple of centuries, it has underpinned two very different approaches to the study of education in different societies. These, as we have noted, can be seen as the more detached academic approach often characteristic of the 'comparativists', and the more directly applied work conducted under the 'international' banner. It is true to say, however, that some pioneers in the field, most notably Sadler, were able to operate equally well in both the theoretical and applied arenas (see Higginson 1979, 1995). Indeed, in his work as Director of the Office of Special Inquiries and Reports within the then United Kingdom Department of Education (to which he was appointed in 1895), Sadler always strove to ensure that any comparative study with which he was involved was both sensitive to cultural context and had an emphasis on the practical application of his findings. Reflecting on the purpose of his Office, he had this to say in 1903. The chief purpose of comparative research is:

(1) ... to collect, summarise, and publish various kinds of educational experience, with a view to getting what is sound and true from a number of discrepant opinions; (2) informing the nation how it stands in regard to educational efficiency as compared with other nations; (3) promoting, as far as possible, general consent and agreement as to the wisest and most fruitful line of development in national education (cited in Higginson 2001: 384–385).

It is little wonder that Sadler is often remembered as a farsighted and clear thinking figure and that, in the words of Magnussen (1990:1284), 'He made his office a powerful research bureau and virtually founded the study of comparative education in the process'. Sadler was keenly aware of the need to consider the context for each education system. This made each system unique, and helped Sadler to recognise how questionable it is to transfer educational models and policies from one system to another. As we shall see below, his views were shared by many other pioneers of comparative education.

Returning therefore to the basic distinctions between the comparative and international traditions, Epstein's (1994:918) analysis helps to clarify the picture further. He thus maintains that, comparative education 'is primarily a field of study that applies historical and social science theories and methods to international problems in education' and, as a result, 'is primarily an academic and interdisciplinary pursuit'. On the other hand, he argues that 'international education fosters an international orientation in knowledge and attitudes' by bringing together teachers and scholars in academic exchange or interchange. He goes on to say that whereas 'comparativists ... are primarily scholars interested in explaining why educational systems and processes vary and how education relates to wider social factors and forces... ', international educators, on the other hand, 'use the findings derived from comparative education to understand better the educational processes they examine and thus to enhance their ability to make policy relating to programmes such as those associated with international exchange and understanding' (Epstein 1994:918). We now look at the nature of some of the most pertinent early work in more detail, before further exploring the purposes given for comparative and international education, as traditionally articulated in the field's own core literature.

Definitions and purposes

The elements of confusion surrounding the terms comparative and international outlined in the previous section pervade the differing definitions that have appeared over the years. They also reflect the particular concerns of the individual authors, demonstrating how identified priorities are related to the standpoint of the commentator – be they, for example, researchers, teachers, policy-makers or practitioners. Starting with Sadler's much quoted address delivered in Guildford in the United Kingdom in 1900, he justified comparative education in the following terms:

The practical value of studying in a right spirit and with scholarly accuracy, the working of foreign systems of education is that it will result in our being better fitted to study and to understand our own.

(Sadler 1900, cited in Higginson 1979:50)

This theme of 'being better fitted to understand our own' has been a hallmark of comparative education for much of the past century. So also has the aim of trying to explain differences. This can be seen from the comments of another of the early pioneers, Isaac Kandel, who stressed explanation and analysis as key features. Kandel wrote:

The chief value of a comparative approach to educational problems lies in an analysis of the causes which have produced them, in comparison of the differences between the various systems and the reasons underlying them, and finally in a study of the solutions attempted.

(Kandel, I.L. 1933:922)

Hans (1959b:56), on the other hand, was at pains to stress the reformative element of comparative studies:

Comparative education is not only to compare existing systems but to envisage reform best suited to new social and economic conditions ... Comparative education quite resolutely looks into the future with the firm intent of reform.

This was very much the thrust of King's work (see, for example, King, E.J. 1964, 1968, 1976, 1979a), though as the popularity of his best-selling book *Other Schools and Ours*, which went into five editions, testifies, he never lost sight of the need to see education within its particular social, cultural and historical context (King 1979b). This view was shared by Bereday (1964:5) who took the focus of social and cultural contexts as his main thrust when he said that 'comparative education seeks to make sense out of the similarities and differences among education systems'. Mallinson (1975:275) wrote in a similar vein when he argued that 'the highest goal of comparative education must be to describe, explain and compare educational systems in terms of their cultural totality'. He elaborated this in the following terms:

By the expression 'comparative study of education' we mean a systematic examination of other cultures and other systems of education derived from those cultures in order to discover semblances and differences, and why variant solutions have been attempted (and with what result) to problems that are often common to all.

(Mallinson 1975:10)

More recently, R.M. Thomas (1998:1), has stated that:

> In its most inclusive sense, comparative education refers to inspecting two or more educational entities or events in order to discover how and why they are alike and different. An educational entity in this context means any person, group or organisation associated with learning and teaching. An event is an activity concerned with promoting learning.

Thomas thus takes the debate away from being simply concerned with the comparison of education systems to the comparison of any educational activity, and Bray and Thomas (1995) extend and represent such thinking most effectively in multi-level diagrammatic form. Their framework for comparative education analysis thus demarcates seven geographic/locational levels, ranging from the individual to world regional, six non-locational demographic groups and seven aspects of education and society. In calling for multi-level analyses they argue that 'many studies neglect discussion of the ways in which patterns at lower levels in education systems are shaped by patterns at higher levels, and vice versa' (Bray 1999:212).

The above arguments relate well to the views of several other writers in the field. For example Farrell (1979), argues that:

> ... there can be no generalising scientific study of education which is not the comparative study of education (1979:1)[since the latter ...] attempts to study a class of phenomena usually called education which seeks to explain the complex web of inter-relationships which can be observed within education systems and other kinds of systems.
>
> (1979:5)

Raivola develops a similar case, suggesting that no general theory or hypothesis can be developed from the study of one situation alone. Thus 'all research that seeks to offer general explanations must be comparative' (Raivola 1985:261). This is a theme that other more contemporary commentators are increasingly advancing, including Phillips (1999:15) who maintains that:

> It is, after all, in the very nature of intellectual activity to make comparisons. Comparing is a fundamental part of the thought processes which enable us to make sense of the world and our experience of it. Indeed, it can be argued that only by making comparisons can we properly defend our position on most questions of importance which require the making of judgement.

Finally, Postlethwaite's (1988:xvii) definition and his distinction between the comparative and international dimensions of the combined field, add a valuable degree of clarity to the debate. This is both useful, and largely consistent with the position that we adopt in the present volume. He writes:

> Strictly speaking to 'compare' means to examine two or more entities by putting them side by side and looking for similarities and differences

between or among them. In the field of education, this can apply both to comparisons between and within systems of education. In addition, however, there are many studies that are not comparative in the strict sense of the word which have traditionally been classified under the heading of comparative education. Such studies do not compare, but rather describe, analyse or make proposals for a particular aspect of education in *one* country other than the author's own country. The Comparative and International Education Society introduced the word 'international' in their title in order to cover these sorts of studies.

Despite the various definitions noted above, major dilemmas remain because the combined field can be seen to be so all-embracing that it is almost impossible to pin it, and its parameters of study, into any neat description. Writing from the early 1980s researchers such as Arnove *et al.* thus argued that the field of comparative and international education was characterised by much methodological debate and diversity of opinion relating both to its subject matter and orientation. They went on to say that comparative and international education is thus 'a loosely bounded field held together largely by a belief that education can serve and bring about improvements in society and that lessons can be learnt from developments in other societies' (Arnove, *et al.* 1992:3). Kelly (1992:21) went even further in her analysis of the state of the field by maintaining that:

> Comparative education remains an ill-defined field whose parameters are fuzzy. No simple theory or method guides scholars and the importance of culture and historical specificity continues to be debated ... The field has no centre, rather it is an amalgam of multidisciplinary studies, informed by a number of different theoretical frameworks.

This, therefore, is a complex, multifaceted field that is both difficult to define and challenging to engage with. Greater clarity, however, surrounds the purposes and reasons for comparative and international education that have typically been identified in the literature. These are certainly easier to identify and have traditionally been seen as to:

1   gain a better understanding of one's own education system;
2   satisfy intellectual and theoretical curiosity about other cultures and their education systems; and better understand the relationship between education and the wider society;
3   identify similarities and differences in educational systems, processes and outcomes as a way of documenting and understanding problems in education, and contributing to the improvement of educational policy and practice;
4   promote improved international understanding and co-operation through increased sensitivity to differing world views and cultures.

In later chapters we reconsider this long-standing rationale in the light of more contemporary developments, the expectations of different stakeholders, and our own critical analysis. Here, however, it is pertinent to conclude, by noting that much of what has come to be seen as the traditional canon of writing within the field – sources such as those cited above – currently stems from largely Western sources and personnel. This is, however, only a partial picture and one that, as we look to the future, warrants further challenge in its own right. Moreover, for many, this construction is closely associated with somewhat dated mid-twentieth-century traditions of comparative education – conceptualised largely as area studies (Foster 1988) and encyclopaedic teaching about the nature of education in other countries – often within programmes for teacher education and training. While this perspective reflects the persistence of a fixed, and often inaccurate and unhelpful, historical snapshot, it does draw attention to the importance of current and future work more clearly articulating the nature and potential of contemporary changes and developments. These are all issues that we return to later, as we go beyond the historical foundations reviewed here.

A multidisciplinary field

In the light of the above it is argued that comparative and international education is certainly a diverse, multidisciplinary and ever-changing field to which contributions from many disciplinary perspectives have long been welcome. Literature on the field's evolution clearly demonstrates the early dominance of historical and philosophical approaches to research, although more positivistic epistemologies have clearly also long underpinned important developments. Similarities, for example, exist between the positivistic assumptions made in the early work of Jullien, and more recent 'scientific' advances in the post-World War II era. In identifying periods that represent the development of the field, authors such as Trethewey (1976) and Brickman (1966, 1988) point to historical phases that can be broadly classified as those of (i) travellers' tales, (ii) cultural borrowing, (iii) cultural context and (iv) empirical social science. We will return to the implications of this for more recent periods of time later, but from this historical perspective, phase (or strand) one is characterised by the unsystematic travellers' tales that we have already noted. Phase two is perhaps best represented by the nineteenth- and early twentieth-century preoccupation with the 'borrowing' (or imposition) of metropolitan models of education in the colonial territories of the South – the direct transfer of policy and practice from one cultural context to another. Phase three, often seen (in Europe and North America) to begin at the start of the twentieth century, is closely associated with Sadler's critique of uncritical international transfer, and his advocacy of the systematic study of education within its socio-cultural context. It is here that the historical and philosophical approaches and related epistemological frameworks rose to prominence. These, in turn, were later challenged by the more positivistic emphasis that underpinned the post-

World War II dominance of the empirical social sciences and disciplines such as political science and economics.

In later chapters we will note how more recent developments within the field both add to, and challenge, this type of phases representation. For the time being, however, this remains helpful in sketching out basic changes in emphasis during the broad span of the field's history. From the outset, nevertheless, we recognise that the demarcation of phases oversimplifies many issues that will later assume greater significance in our own analysis, and raises many questions about the details of both the process and substance of comparative and international research in education. For example, the phases are not necessarily linear or consistent across time, cultures or individuals. Moreover, throughout the history of the field many have asked if there is such a thing as 'the' correct comparative method, and whether researchers should be concerned with one or many countries and systems. The pursuit of the ideal comparative method thus characterises the influence and the writings of B. Holmes (1965, 1979, 1981). On the other hand, and writing in the same era, E.J. King (1979b) was notable for challenging the influence of positivistic science and for rejecting the direction of comparativists to any one 'correct method'. To cite Kay and Watson's (1982:133) pertinent interpretation of King's standpoint:

> ... we must get inside the skin of other people as nearly as we can. We must learn the 'language of life' as far as possible. We must 'make sense' of their conditioning and concerns in their idiom ... a holistic contemplation of a national education system could be compared with the aesthetic appreciation of a work of art: the complete experience is of more value than the discussion of the parts which compose it.

While King had a major influence during the post-World War II period, he clearly did not seek to make comparative and international research 'scientific'. Nor did he pursue law-like generalisations, arguing that improved cultural integrity is of paramount importance for the field. In many ways this demonstrates a clear and ongoing link with the interpretive and hermeneutic foundations that inspired earlier writers such as Sadler and Kandel. Indeed, Kandel, himself, described comparative education as the continuation of the history of education into the present (Kandel 1959).

A variety of research approaches may thus be seen to operate within periods most characteristically represented by one dominant paradigm or group of disciplines. Our own use of any notion of phases is therefore pursued with considerable caution, but in a way that, hopefully, highlights dominant trends in an accessible way.

Other complications in reviewing the history and nature of the field result from questions relating to matters of substantive focus. Should, for example, researchers be concerned with formal systems and their interaction with society, politics, the labour market and other aspects of socio-economic development, or should more emphasis be placed on non-formal education,

or sub-sectors such as primary schools, secondary education, teacher training, technical and vocational training or higher education? Should
comparativists be concerned with the processes of education in different
societies: what happens within the schools or the classrooms; the
teacher–learner interaction; the way in which the curriculum is constructed
or conducted; or the ways in which a school is organised? Or should they be
more concerned with the measurable outcomes of the system: examination
results; numbers of graduates; or the numbers going into different branches
of the economy? Should the unit of analysis be the nation-state, as has traditionally been the case, or should this be smaller to focus on practice – or
wider in scope to include whole regions like the European Union (EU), the
Southern African Development Community (SADC) group of countries, the
Association of South-East Asian Nations (ASEAN), or East Asia? If it is to be
the latter, is the concern to identify similar trends or problems, or to examine
key issues across a whole region of countries? Alternatively, should comparative study be only related to the present or to a particular historical period,
or can different historical periods be examined simultaneously, as demonstrated by Phillips (1994)?

The point being advanced here is that all of the above have, at different
times, been seen as legitimate areas for comparative and international research
in education over the years, and each position has been vigorously defended.
Much thus depends upon the standpoint of the commentator and the purposes
of the various investigations. This diversity, nevertheless, has generated a wide
range of critics. There are those, like Farrell (1979) and Psacharopoulos (1990),
who have argued that there has been too much concern for theoretical considerations and not enough emphasis on the practical lessons to be learnt. Others,
like Halls (1990), Rust et al. (1999) and Torres (2001), maintain that too many
studies have been overly descriptive and have lacked a substantial theoretical
foundation. As noted in Chapter 1, Rust also argues that there is currently too
little knowledge about the early pioneers in the field, and that insufficient
attention is given by new researchers to the ongoing implications of important
methodological debates that were pursued by past generations. This would
accord with Hobsbawm's (1994:3) observation that too many commentators
are now growing up 'in a sort of permanent present' with little or no historical
perception. This is a view shared by other writers, such as Cowen (1996b), and
underpins the rationale for the historical dimension of this volume itself.

Evolution of the field

In this section we return to the evolution of the field by examining in more
detail the changes of emphasis reflected across the main periods of historical
development. In doing this we relate, albeit cautiously, to the four phases
identified above, but also go more deeply into an examination of specific initiatives and changes in distinctive strands of enquiry. We begin briefly with
work characteristic of the phases of cultural borrowing and cultural context,
but pay most detailed attention to the later institutional growth of the field

and to developments in the initial post-World War II period that was, in many contexts, dominated by the influence of the empirical social sciences.

Promoting cultural borrowing

For most of the nineteenth century and the early part of the twentieth, many writers in the field of comparative education, regardless of whether they saw their roots in the comparative or the international traditions, were primarily concerned with what came to be known as cultural borrowing. Thus Horace Mann, Secretary of the Board of Education in Massachusetts in the USA from 1848, studied education in Prussia, France and England with the express intent of borrowing those ideas that he felt could most easily be transplanted to the USA. He is often called the father of American public education as a result. Ushinsky, whose study of Prussian education led to faltering reforms in Tsarist Russia, and Matthew Arnold, whose examination of education in France, Germany (especially Prussia) and Holland pointed up the deficiencies of education in England, and had a direct influence on the 1870 Education Act in England and Wales, were also in the mould of cultural borrowing. Although since Sadler many others have argued that it is not possible to borrow educational policy and practice from one context and transfer to another with any real hope of the transplant being successful, many governments and international agencies still do not appear to recognise this today. Cultural borrowing has thus continued in practice as decision-makers adopt such perspectives and seek directly to transplant models of, for example, school choice, school improvement, higher education governance and finance, non-formal provision or vocational qualifications from one system to another.

Understanding cultural context

Under the influence of Sadler, for much of the early part of the twentieth century many researchers in the field of comparative and international education became more critical of such assumptions, and were increasingly concerned to show that an education system could only be understood in the light of a particular culture and society. As Sadler was at pains to point out, 'what happens outside the school is more important than what happens inside because it shapes and influences what takes place inside' (cited in Higginson 1979:52). Writers in this genre were Kandel, Hans, Bereday, Mallinson and E.J. King. Not only did they stress that it was essential to understand the language of a particular society in order to appreciate the underpinning philosophy of the school system, but there was also a concerted attempt to understand the 'forces' (Kandel), 'factors' (Hans), 'national character' (Mallinson) and 'cultural philosophy' (King), that had helped to shape an education system. Until the 1960s, including the pre- and post-World War II periods, there was, perhaps understandably, a preoccupation with conflict and ideological competition. Much of Kandel's work, for example, aimed to highlight the superiority of democratic systems over totalitarian ones, and his book titled *Studies in*

Comparative Education (1933) is still regarded as a classic in this regard. All of the above mentioned authors, however, were largely descriptive and historical in their approach (see, for example, Hans 1959a). They saw their role as encouraging international understanding and helping to bring about educational reform by showing what was happening in different countries. Their *modus operandi* was comparison, their framework for study was the nation–state, and their cultural perspective was decidedly Western.

It was during this early period that the establishment of a number of seminal university courses specifically designed to teach comparative education studies was achieved. Amongst the leading organisations were Teachers' College at Columbia University, New York, and Syracuse and Michigan State Universities in the USA; the University of London Institute of Education in the United Kingdom and other centres throughout Europe (Cowen, 1980). Wilson (2003) notes that the first Western textbook, titled *Comparative Education*, was published by Peter Sandiford in London in 1918. There were other important developments associated with the creation of specialised yearbooks and journals. Most notable of these were the *Education Yearbook* (1924–44); the *World Yearbook of Education* (which was founded in 1932 and, apart from a few missing years, is still regarded as a key annual work for the analysis of educational developments throughout the world); the *International Review of Education*, founded in 1931; and the *International Yearbook of Education*, founded in 1933. By the late 1930s, therefore, the field of comparative education was firmly established on both sides of the Atlantic but its scope was still rather limited and it consisted essentially of historical attempts to understand and explain how and why a particular system of education had developed along the lines it had. Further afield, as Hayhoe (2001) and Bray and Gui (2001) emphasise, the parallel development of a specifically Chinese comparative literature had also emerged, with origins around the start of the twentieth century. There are also other pertinent histories of the field that have yet to receive appropriate attention, as we will argue later in this volume.

Organisational developments and the dominance of the empirical social sciences

World War II was to prove a watershed in more ways than one, though it was not until the late 1950s and 1960s that its impact on the field of comparative and international education was to become so noticeable. The creation of many international bodies concerned with rebuilding a world shattered by war; the desire on the part of individual governments to redesign their education systems to take into account the changed social climate; and the beginnings of the end of the European colonial empires were all to lead to a ferment of ideas about education's role in social and economic development. Along with this came renewed interest in educational experiments and reforms in different countries.

In 1956, the Comparative Education Society was formed in the USA, to be redesignated the Comparative and International Education Society (CIES) in

1969. In Europe the Comparative Education Society in Europe (CESE) was created in 1961, with individual countries forming their own national sections. Japan followed suit in 1964 with the creation of its own national society, while in Vancouver, in 1968, an International Committee of Comparative Education Societies was convened with the express purpose of furthering interest in the field. This led to the establishment of the World Council of Comparative Education Societies (WCCES) in 1970, with a remit to bring together representatives from around the world for a World Congress to be held every few years. Significantly, of the five societies that initially established the WCCES, two were from Asia – the Japanese Comparative Education Society and the Korean Comparative Education Society.

Several of what were to become the leading comparative and international education journals also appeared during this period: *Comparative Education Review* (1957); *Comparative Education* (1964); and *Compare* (1968). More recently, in 1979, the *International Journal of Educational Development* was launched with the main purpose of bringing comparative and international education research perspectives to bear specifically on the educational problems facing less developed countries (Watson 1990). Subsequently the serial *Oxford Studies in Comparative Education* was founded in 1990 – indicating the growth of the field itself within that university. These, however, are all initiatives originating in the Western world. Reflecting wider organisational growth, more recent times have seen the emergence of other journals worldwide, often emphasising comparative and international research or dealing with educational development in specific countries and regions. Illustrative examples include the *Comparative Education Review* (Beijing), the *Papua New Guinea Journal of Education*, the *Journal of Comparative Education and International Relations in Africa*, the *Revista Española de Educación Comparada* (Spanish Comparative Education Review), and the *Journal of Education and Development in the Caribbean*. According to Altbach and Tan's (1995) global inventory of programmes and centres in comparative and international education, by the mid-1990s there were at least 28 national societies and other regional bodies, and specialist comparative programmes were taught in 71 institutions situated in every continent of the world. This, moreover, was only a partial world survey, despite the authors' intention to be more global in scope. Bray (2003) more recently records the further growth of the WCCES to comprise 30 societies by 2002, along with its ongoing expansion and the regular publication of selected World Congress proceedings.

While the post-war ferment of ideas and creativity led to much organisational development and the establishment of numerous journals and societies, there emerged an equally creative debate relating to methodology and focus. This led to the development of new strands in the way in which comparative and international research was conducted. Because much of the work carried out during the cultural borrowing and cultural context phases was largely historical, descriptive and explanatory, it faced much criticism from the new generation of post-war educational planners. Farrell (1979:4), for example, argued that much of this work was 'of little use to or little used by policy makers'. In the light of such criticisms new approaches were formulated that more directly reflected the influence of the empirical social sciences. The early critics – Anderson (1961), Bereday (1964, 1967), Noah and Eckstein (1969) – emerged from the positivist school of social sciences developing in the USA. Such writers argued that the previously dominant historical and cultural approach lacked scientific rigour because it failed to draw causative links between schools and society, and especially with the labour market. They therefore focused upon the connections between education and society, to see if it was possible to identify 'laws' governing this relationship. Bereday's approach was undoubtedly the most complex, and it is questionable if it has ever been successfully applied, but all were forerunners of the later applied aspirations and intentions of bodies such as the World Bank and UNESCO. Their work also coincided with the growing concern for studying the outcomes of education, rather than the internal workings of schools or universities as institutions.

In the United Kingdom, B. Holmes (1965) sought to refine the scientific model by creating what he called the 'problem' approach to comparative education. Greatly influenced by Karl Popper's concept of 'critical dualism', Holmes believed it was possible to establish 'laws' governing school–society relationships, if it could be shown that where certain conditions existed then certain outcomes could be predicted. On this basis he argued that it was possible to transfer educational policies and educational practices from one society to another where the problems were very similar. Difficulties in identifying 'problems' (whose problems?) and in translating this method into context-sensitive practice underpin subsequent critiques raised by writers such as E.J. King (1968) and Kay (1981).

A rather different approach to the above debate was taken by Anderson (1961). He wanted to see if it was possible to develop theories of school–society relationships that could be tested in different contexts and that might generate general 'rules' that could be of use to policy makers and planners. He also believed that it was important to undertake in-depth studies in more than one country. Perhaps his most enduring contribution to the evolution of the field is that he did not see either the nation-state or national school systems as the main focus of research. He therefore argued that it was just as legitimate to explore social stratification or educational achievement in the light of political philosophies or against economic growth, as it was to look at any other aspect of education. Researchers would thus isolate certain variables for observation and analysis. According to Kelly *et al.* (1982), Anderson's work had a profound influence on the development of comparative and international research in this period, and led to further significant advances in the field.

Adopting a political science perspective, other writers at this time argued more strongly than before that one could only understand a nation's education system, and the ways it was administered, if there was a clear understanding of the underlying political philosophy. Thus any appreciation of education in the USSR or Eastern Europe was not possible without knowledge of Marx's thinking and the development of Lenin's application of this philosophy. Likewise it was argued that one could only understand education in the USA with reference to the early founding fathers, such as Jefferson and Franklin, or education in China with reference to Mencius and Confucius as well as to Mao and Marx. Influenced by such thinking, a series of books on education, culture and politics in Eastern Europe (Grant 1969), France (Halls 1976), West Germany (Hearnden 1974, 1976), and the USA (King, E.J. 1976) began to appear in what many now see as a high point of visibility for the Anglo-American constituency of the field.

Further advances were, however, to be made during this phase of develop-ment by social scientists who were both keen to generate empirical data and committed to the application of new development perspectives – initially that of modernisation theory. By the 1950s and 1960s the dominant paradigm influencing the field, and much social science thinking about education, was that of structural-functionalism, out of which came various shades of mod-ernisation theory. These assumed that because education systems were part of the social, economic and political structures of a nation then investment in education would bring about enhanced economic growth. Education was also increasingly recognised as a means of socialising the younger generation into the norms and values of the country of their birth, of preparing them for the labour force and for their position in society. Evidence for the role of schooling in modernisation came from the way certain countries – Turkey (Kazamias and Massialas 1965), the Soviet Union (Grant 1969), Japan (Dore 1974), China (Price 1977; Gu 2001) – were seen to have deliberately used their education systems to foster this process. Many other writers, economists of education in particular, were also arguing in favour of investment in education for eco-nomic as well as modernisation purposes (see, for example, Vaizey 1962; Harbison and Myers 1964; Hanson and Brembeck 1966; Hunter 1969). As the process of de-colonisation began to accelerate, others began to argue in favour of educational investment as the quickest and most reliable means of national development, by which was meant not only economic growth but also changed attitudes to work, industrialisation and social development (Beeby 1966; Adams and Bjork 1969; Adams 1971; Inkeles and Smith 1974; see also Watson 1988 for a detailed list of others). This brought in many researchers, human capital theorists and international agency personnel who would not explicitly have seen themselves as in the vanguard of advances in compara-tive and international education.

Within a few years this perspective was also being rigorously challenged for a number of reasons. First, because many Western societies were becoming transformed by immigration into ethnically, religiously and linguistically plural societies, the traditional functional patterns of education were seen to hold true no longer. Second, the launching of the first space satellite, *Sputnik*, by the USSR in 1957, and the defeat of the USA in Vietnam in 1975 were sym-bolically important. Such events shattered, at least for a time, the illusions fostered by the Western powers that Western democratic systems of govern-ment, and hence education systems which fed into these, were necessarily the best, or indeed, the only way forward to economic and social development. Third, and perhaps the most compelling reason, was the fact that, despite much educational investment in developing countries, much of it financed by foreign aid, the gap between high-income countries and low-income countries, measured by a whole range of indicators, was seen to be growing rather than diminishing. Economic growth was, at best, very uneven. In many countries equality of opportunities was a mirage. As for democracy taking root and new attitudes being inculcated, the evidence for this was very mixed. If anything, political and social unrest were growing and modern schooling was viewed increasingly as an instrument for maintaining the inequalities within and between societies. By concentrating on the social, political or economic impact of education, rather than on its pedagogic, academic and cognitive outcomes, others also argued that much educational research had failed in its primary task of writing about, and encouraging governments to engage in, educational reforms (Paulston 1976; Apple 1978). New approaches were seen to be needed for the comparative analysis of education systems (see, for example, Cummings and McGinn 1997).

By far the most damning, and consequently influential, criticisms of the modernisation school came from critical theorists who argued that the effect of promoting the Western functionalist view of schooling was to lead, not to greater economic freedom and growth, but to economic and educational dependency. Moreover, it was argued that many comparativists had been too concerned with the industrialised world: Europe, North America, Japan and the USSR. When Anglophone writers had taken an interest in the less developed countries of the South, their insights and observations were seen to have been largely based on the English speaking countries of Africa and Asia, thus ignoring, and remaining ignorant of, others that were not English speaking. French, Spanish, and other European writers did take into account Francophone and Lusophone contexts, and, importantly, some of their contributions significantly helped dependency theory emerge as a major alternative strand of comparative enquiry. Paulston (1994) describes such neo-Marxist critics as 'radical functionalists' because they argued that modern education was repressive, highly selective to ensure the dominance of the existing political and social élites, and wasteful insofar as those who did not succeed in the system were condemned to menial tasks. Writers in this vein included Fanon (1968), Freire (1971), Carnoy (1974), Bowles and Gintis (1976) and Althusser (1990).

Marxist and neo-Marxist critiques of the 1960s and 1970s thus generated a range of new theoretical perspectives to help explain education's role in society, and these had a major influence upon comparative and international research in education at this time. For example, correspondence theory argued that education and employment opportunities were not only closely inter-related but that school structures and curriculum options help to maintain society's social and economic structures.

Acknowledging the above criticisms, from the 1970s increased attention began to be paid to the study of the educational problems of less developed countries from a greater variety of theoretical perspectives. These studies were partly historical, exploring the impact of colonialism on society, administrative structures, schooling, language and literacy, and partly contemporary, seeking to explain why, in spite of massive investment, and the huge expansion of education, many new nation-states were falling further behind the high-income countries. Indeed, the de-colonisation process created so many new states that this factor, in itself, generated new interest in comparative and international research – and new national units for analysis. British East Africa, for example, became Kenya, Uganda and Tanzania – and throughout the rapidly expanding Commonwealth 12 new small states (with less than 1.5 million people each) were founded between 1965 and 1977 alone (Crossley and Holmes 1999:11). Critical analyses and their conclusions highlighted the naïve neo-colonial transplantation of education systems in the colonies, a form of cultural borrowing but one that was imposed and therefore unwillingly accepted. The dominance of colonial languages (Watson 1993a), colonial curricula (Mangan 1993), foreign textbooks and examinations, and links with metropolitan universities all led, it was argued, to an educational dependency as insidious as colonialism itself (Altbach 1971, 1975, 1977; Carnoy 1974; Altbach and Kelly 1978, Altbach, Arnove and Kelly 1982; Arnove 1980).

Inspired by changing times, and much of the same critical theory, related challenges to the dominance of the empirical social sciences rapidly emerged in diverse forms that ranged from gender studies to critical ethnography, cultural studies, legitimation theory and the post-modern critique (see, for example, Burns and Welch 1992 for an Australasian perspective). These are, however, major themes that are more appropriately addressed in the following chapters, as we move beyond our historical analysis and deal with more contemporary issues and developments.

Conclusions

In the light of this historical review, it is argued that while empirical social sciences can be seen to have played a dominant role in reshaping the nature of much of the immediately post-war comparative and international research in education – notably in the Anglo-American literature – the more recent history of the field has been characterised by concerted challenge and considerable epistemological and theoretical diversity. Some of these more contemporary trends were initially stimulated by the impact of increased interest in the relationship between education and national development – and by the work of writers living and working in the South. Others reflected the widening of the research constituency, and the influence of specialists from different disciplines. This more contemporary history and its impact on the field is the focus of subsequent chapters. It is apposite here, however, to note that any conception of phases for the development of the field must certainly highlight the profusion of late twentieth-century challenges to the dominance of the empirical social sciences. Writing in 1997, Mitter thus saw five paradigmatic phases through which he believed the field had passed. He identified the 1980s as the 'post-modern revolt' and the 1990s as a period characterised by 'universalism versus cultural pluralism' (Mitter 1997:401). While this usefully acknowledges recent trends in some contexts, our own historical review draws attention to the dangers and limitations of the demarcation of all broad forms of categorisation. In particular, such thinking can mask the ongoing diversity of perspectives that has long invigorated the variety of the many different comparative and international educations that have jostled for dominance throughout each stage of the field's history.

In concluding this chapter it is, therefore, argued that, although the assumptions of the empirical social sciences have had a marked and lasting impact upon the historical evolution of the field, reactions to the dominance of such approaches to research, and to the positivistic epistemologies that underpin related theoretical frameworks, have, in turn, inspired much of the contemporary intellectual landscape that we must now engage with. Without encroaching too far upon ground to be covered in detail later, it is pertinent to foreshadow how, in challenging the post-war dominance of empiricism, leading comparative and international researchers came to pioneer critical advances in, for example, development studies, multicultural and multilingual research, gender studies, post-colonialism, and world systems analysis. Thus, for example, by the 1970s the study of education and international development had become well established as a legitimate specialisation within the broader multi-disciplinary field. With regard to gender, although there had been a rapid increase in studies of the impact of education on gender stereotyping and job opportunities in the Western world, there had been remarkably little systematic work done on a comparative basis until writers such as Kelly and Nihlan (1982) and Kelly (1984) pointed this out. Their complaint was that hitherto much comparative work ignored the role of education in reproducing gender inequalities and in encouraging male domination in society and the economy. Subsequently there have been numerous cross-cultural studies, as well as in-depth country analyses, undertaken so that gender issues are now also very much a specialist sub-section of the field. While this is not universal in its application and impact, it points to the diversity of international perspectives, is a revealing and culturally sensitive issue in its own right, and is an arena that now increasingly acknowledges the dangers of both male and female marginalisation (Miller 1991). Given the international community's expressed concern to equalise the opportunities available to all throughout the world, especially in those parts of the globe that have been adversely affected by poverty, it is clear that challenging, and critically informed, comparative research on education and gender is continuing to advance rapidly (see, for example, King and Hill 1993; Brock and Cammish 1994, 1998; Swainson 1995; Kutnick et al. 1997; Sutherland and Cammish 1997; Stromquist 1997, 1998).

The emergence of the debate relating to world systems analysis is perhaps most appropriate in an illustrative capacity here, given the centrality of the more recent intensification of globalisation to our contemporary analysis of the field. The main thrust of the world systems thesis is that global social, economic and political linkages need to be better understood since these have an increasingly powerful bearing on any individual country – and its education system. Early comparative work of this nature was carried out by Arnove (1980) and Ramirez and Boli-Bennett (1982), anticipating the growing convergence of educational systems, the perceived commonality of many problems and the similarity of trends in related policy and practice. Given increased recognition of the powerful role played by international agencies in shaping influential educational debates, global frameworks of analysis have thus assumed enhanced explanatory power and legitimacy (Jones 1992; Samoff 1993; Ilon 1994; Watson 1995; Cummings and McGinn 1997). These are therefore all issues that we will look at in considerably more detail in later chapters.

From the above discussion it can be seen that while the twin fields of comparative and international education have different roots, origins and purposes, they also have a great deal in common. Moreover, together, there is much to suggest that each tradition has much to offer the other. As a combined and multidisciplinary field of enquiry, comparative and international education has a rich collective history, a diversity of purposes and foundations, a global institutional network and a distinguished and well-established literature. The evolution of this multidisciplinary field well demonstrates its responsiveness to both changing geopolitical relations and to advances in disciplinary and paradigmatic thinking. Chief of the distinctive concerns that are visible across the various strands and phases of the field's development are sensitivity to cultural context (at macro, societal and micro institutional levels) and critical concern with the international transfer of educational policy and practice.

Because comparative and international research in education is influenced by many different intellectual, disciplinary and professional foundations it cannot lay claim to any one single theoretical or methodological perspective that sets it apart from other areas of educational or social science research. Perhaps not surprisingly, therefore, the history of the field demonstrates as many vigorous debates about theories and methods as it does about changes in substantive areas for sustained enquiry. The complexity that such multidisciplinarity generates remains a perpetual challenge for those engaged in research, as we shall argue in the next chapter. It is, however, also the source of much of the creativity and enthusiasm that has so well sustained growth and renewal throughout the field's substantial and distinguished history.

Chapter 3

Difficulties in conducting comparative and international research in education

Throughout the history of the field that we have documented in Chapter 2, there has emerged a growing body of literature on the difficulties typically faced in conducting comparative and international research in education. See, for example, selected contributions in Noah and Eckstein's (1998) retrospective account of *Three Decades of Collaboration*, and Watson's (2001a) recent edited collection titled *Doing Comparative Education Research: issues and problems*.

Many of these issues relate to fundamental problems faced by all educational and social science researchers concerning epistemological, paradigmatic and broadly methodological dilemmas (Usher 1996; Crotty 1998). Other issues relate more directly to distinctive problems encountered by those working specifically within the field of comparative and international education. Many philosophical and epistemological conceptions of problems encountered in carrying out specifically comparative and international research are closely related to the generic methodological literature, but there are other uniquely comparative dilemmas. To date, however, such work has attracted only somewhat specialist and periodic attention, and where this has been the case, it has stemmed largely from personnel working in the more theoretically-oriented 'comparative' constituency (see, for example, Schriewer with Holmes 1988; Schriewer 2000). Pragmatic issues and problems have, nevertheless, been addressed by a wider variety of personnel, and especially by those working in the more 'applied' arenas. Thus, in practice, much of the most accessible literature stemming from the field itself has traditionally conceptualised research problems and difficulties more in terms of the practicalities and logistics of doing comparative and international research.

Writers on such themes draw attention to, for example, problems of conceptual equivalences, the sources and accuracy of statistical data, or the logistics of international fieldwork. Such practicalities are, indeed, of considerable importance in cross-cultural research and they rightly deserve attention, especially in times of rapid change when the value of the cumulative experience of previous generations can easily be overlooked.

In this chapter, we therefore pay initial attention to the more pragmatic and practical conceptions of the problems encountered by researchers working within the field. Consistent with the broader thesis of the book, however, we also go further, to examine the significance of more fundamental theoretical and methodological problems and implications that emerge from this review, as we connect with recent intellectual debates and critical perspectives. Contemporary geopolitical and paradigmatic changes, we argue, make it ever more imperative that comparative and international research more effectively bridges the worlds of theory and practice; and better acknowledges the implications of differing world views, cultural perspectives and values upon the research process. At the heart of this lies the challenge posed by post-structuralist critiques at the meta-theoretical level (Peters 2001). Despite their own limitations, such critiques generate insights that demonstrate the theoretical *and* applied potential of research paradigms and strategies that more effectively acknowledge the significance of cultural differences; recognise the role of power and values in shaping international debates on educational and social policy; prioritise diversity and the dynamic relationship between agency and structure; and challenge the dominance of positivistic notions of the research process itself.

This, we argue, suggests the need for a wider conceptualisation of the nature and scope of the problems to be faced by those carrying out comparative and international research in the future. This, in turn, highlights the significance of the relationship between research methods and research methodologies (see related distinctions made in Crossley and Vulliamy 1997b), and draws attention back to the dilemmas generated by the legacy of the division between the more theoretical and applied dimensions of the field itself.

When concluding this chapter we therefore advance this argument further, to explore the implications of reconceptualising our understanding of the difficulties and problems encountered during the conduct of comparative and international research. Moreover, this is done in a way that links directly to the broader arguments for change that are pursued in subsequent chapters. This, we suggest, has implications for the theoretical frameworks we adopt, for the substantive priorities we address, for the ways in which we carry out research, and for the broad nature, organisation and scope of the field. We therefore build upon the arguments that emerge from this initial discussion of difficulties and problems, not only in concluding this chapter, but also throughout the subsequent sections of the volume itself.

Problems stemming from complexity

In setting the scene here, it is perhaps pertinent to begin on a general note that foreshadows the broader dilemmas faced by all comparative and international researchers in the field of education. To begin with, it has long been recognised that the multidisciplinary nature of the field generates especially significant problems in terms of the organisation and management of potentially vast amounts of information – relating to a wide range of cultural contexts. When combined with the equally wide range of disciplinary perspectives and methodological paradigms, the related challenges generate complex problems for the individual researcher. Indeed, the potential conflict or 'jostling' of different perspectives, and the inevitable paradigmatic clashes are clearly visible in our previous account of the historical evolution of the field. A degree of personal specialisation for any individual is therefore necessary to avoid what Foster (1998:1) wisely refers to as 'the bane of the field, the universal expert'.

To some extent the complexities noted above also highlight what some see as an institutional weakness of the field – the absence of tight disciplinary boundaries that can leave it exposed to confusion about its defining characteristics, to the attrition of personnel and to the appropriation of the research agenda. Certainly these are all issues that we deal with as the case for reconceptualisation is advanced throughout the present book.

Perhaps even more pointedly, basic theoretical and methodological debates have repeatedly raised the central problem of how we might best learn from comparative and international research. Can we, for example, legitimately move 'toward a science of comparative education' as advocated by Noah and Eckstein (1969); to what extent can we seek out generalisable statements or universal principles in education and the social sciences (Alexander 2001); and how can we deal with the potential and limitations of the 'borrowing', 'lending', and 'imposition' on the international transfer of educational theories, policies and practices? These are all distinctive problems that have long been faced by specialists working within the field – and they continue to raise new challenges for experienced and new researchers to the present day.

Political motivations

Even in an age of globalisation, and despite the growth of international and regional organisations, considerable store is still placed by many audiences on national, comparative analyses. Governments like to see their countries in a comparative perspective with other similar, or neighbouring countries – a trend that was encouraged by the early IEA studies in the late 1960s and which has continued to this day (Goldstein 1996; Postlethwaite 1999). When the comparisons have proved unfavourable, as for example for the USA in the 1980s, they have led not only to national soul-searching as illustrated by the publication of *A Nation at Risk* (National Commission on Excellence 1983), but also to ongoing policy changes. Something similar happened in England and Wales in the mid-1970s when the country was adversely compared with other European states in terms of skills training and literacy (Department of Education and Science 1975). This led to the so-called Great Education Debate of the late 1970s and to the major restructuring of the educational system that followed during the 1980s and 1990s (Lawton 1992).

Traditionally the early 'humanitarian', literary and historical approaches to comparative research ignored all but a few statistical data, partly because they were often unavailable. This was the case even though Marc-Antoine Jullien, who, as we have already noted, as the founder of systematic comparative education had advocated the establishment of a centre for gathering international educational statistics (Jullien 1817). Not until the establishment of the International Bureau of Education, under the auspices of the old League of Nations, were his ideas realised. The implication, as we explain elsewhere, was that early writers in the field, like Matthew Arnold, Isaac Kandel, Nicholas Hans, Joseph Lauwerys, George Bereday and Vernon Mallinson used remarkably few statistics and other 'hard' data in their analysis of education systems. As a result their comments were often highly personalised and rather sweeping. These authors were mainly concerned with the macro-level of education systems, the use of official government information, and what other data was available, plus, where possible, personal visits.

Following World War II, and more especially from the late 1950s and 1960s as more and more countries gained their independence from colonial powers and placed education high on the national agenda for investment and expansion, the need for improved statistical data for planning purposes increased considerably. This so-called age of optimism or age of expansion (Weiler 1978; Watson 1988) coincided with the development of key international bodies, most notably UNESCO and the Organisation for Economic Co-operation and Development (OECD) in Paris, the UNESCO Institute of Education in Hamburg, the World Bank in Washington and the International Institute for Educational Planning (IIEP), also in Paris. As indicated earlier these bodies began systematically to collect education statistics and other data on an international basis and for comparative use. Comparativists and writers in the field of international education, as well as many governments, thus now make much use of this available and influential material.

These developments thus coincided with quite a marked shift in comparative studies from the dominance of the historical, explanatory approach to the more substantial use of statistical information and quantitative data analysis that came to be known as the 'scientific approach'. As noted in Chapter 2, this shift of emphasis had its origins in the USA and is associated with writers such as Noah and Eckstein (1969), although other scholars, most notably Anderson (1961) and Coleman (1965) also sought to draw generalisable conclusions by emphasising the examination of official data from across a large number of countries. As more and more newcomers came into the field, greater use began to be made by comparativists of material published by the international agencies. Unfortunately, not everyone researching comparatively was, or is, well enough aware of the pitfalls of relying unquestioningly on this type of data. These and other related issues are, therefore, further explored later in this chapter.

Moreover, such are the benefits of attracting international students into higher education, or of undertaking short-term consultancies abroad – both, for example, are increasingly seen as avenues for bringing in additional revenue to hard pressed institutions – that there are now many involved in comparative and international activities who have little or no background knowledge of the field, or of the theoretical and methodological debates of former years. As Rust et al. (1999) have recently observed, many of those engaged in such work who claim to be comparativists are unaware of the key literature, let alone the different research perspectives that have been used. This makes the identification of the many inherent difficulties that have long been recognised increasingly important today.

Bias and accuracy of data

One of the most frequently acknowledged problems that needs to be recognised by those carrying out comparative and international research is that of bias. This may be based on personal prejudices, implicit values or preconceptions. It may also stem from the ways in which existing data are formally presented. In other words bias can be both personal and 'official'. We are all conditioned by our upbringing, culture, education, environment, our status in society and our perceptions of how others view us, as well as by our political, social and religious values and attitudes. All researchers, but especially those involved in research across cultures or across national boundaries, need to be aware of such potential biases and assumptions, their past 'baggage' if preferred, that they bring with them. Inevitably this will influence how they view the 'other,' and how they document the similarities and differences that they perceive in different cultures. Such biases are not always easy to recognise, let alone overcome. Attitudes to specific countries in Europe may be influenced by an older generation's views on, say, Germany or France, or by first reactions on visiting one of these countries; there may be deeply held ideological views about Russia and her former territories or there may be an antipathy to American cultural dominance, based either upon experience, or upon others' criticisms. Today, for example, this may be seen in some of the standpoints taken by the critics or supporters of globalisation and America's perceived role in this process.

Questionable assumptions, perhaps, most often influence debate and perceptions about the less developed world, especially relating to Africa, and are as much based on lack of knowledge or selective reading as they are shaped by experience. See, for example, the critique of such misrepresentation presented by Daloz and Chabal (1999) in their challenging book titled *Africa Works. Disorder as Political Instrument*. It is difficult enough to overcome potential biases when working in a familiar context; it is even more difficult when the researcher is trying to understand a new cultural context without spending long periods of time in the field observing, listening and trying to get behind the way the society operates on different levels – finding out what is culturally or socially acceptable and what is not. This means that fleeting visits, or brief consultancy trips, do not allow sufficient time to understand, let alone speak with authority on, local contexts. As argued later, here are the seeds of the rationale for working in more depth, alongside local researchers with a knowledge of their own context (IJED 1985; Crossley 1990). Yet too many international initiatives lack an adequate local contextual perspective, precisely because they do not sufficiently appreciate the underlying assumptions upon which that society is based. This is reflected in the earlier critique of Reynolds and Farrell's (1996) research on school effectiveness. Another example would be some of the studies commissioned by the United Kingdom's Department for International Development (DFID) which have been strongly criticised by Hoppers (2001) for being based too strongly on the agenda of the commissioning agency and biased according to Northern research paradigms (McGrath, 2001a and b). This argument will be developed later in Chapter 6 when we focus more directly upon possible new directions for educational research and international development co-operation.

Bias also works in other ways. Government statistics, publicity brochures and official publications often seek to portray a system, or a country, in the most favourable light. In doing this, figures may be officially massaged if it is perceived that this will be politically advantageous. Recent evidence of this comes from the critique of figures relating to the AIDS epidemic in Uganda (Parkhurst 2001). Because both the Ugandan government and the World Bank have tried to show Uganda's battle against AIDS in a positive light, it has been argued that only those figures which do this have been published. While the merits of the various arguments in this case remain open for debate, researchers must clearly guard against the use of official documents as their first, and sometimes only, source of information, and be aware of the need for a cautious 'health warning.' The old Soviet Union was notorious for generating problems such as this. As John Dunstan, a specialist in Soviet affairs, once wrote: 'Facts, figures, information are developed or discarded, changed or falsified, if it is felt that this is beneficial to the cause of the Party' (Dunstan 1978:36). Certainly the old Soviet authorities had few qualms about rewriting the school curriculum as political figures, like Stalin or Kruschev, fell from favour. Other authoritarian regimes have done much the same over time. But it is not only authoritarian governments that seek to massage the figures. The current British government is frequently accused of distorting official statistics in order to show that it is meeting its targets, whether these are related to improvements in the reading and mathematical skills of primary-age pupils, improvements in the treatment of patients in hospitals, success rates in school examinations or the amounts of public funding available to schools, hospitals and universities. Sometimes official agencies have been forced to admit that there are errors; but such discrepancies can often be sidestepped and put down to the technicalities of different ways of collecting data.

More pertinently, in the international arena, if a country is wanting to attract overseas development assistance the state may show the economic or educational picture to be worse than it is; if it is wanting to impress foreign investors or its own electorate it will portray things to be better than they really are. Regarding educational data it also needs to be recognised that this is sometimes difficult to acquire, simply because of a lack of experienced personnel, appropriate infrastructure or effective communications. Information is thus often 'made up' so as not to leave too many blank spaces in formal data columns. This is particularly true in poorly resourced countries, where, for example, head teachers often do not have the time, the staff or the support to find and provide the school enrolment data requested, from which the Ministry of Education will eventually compile an 'authoritative' annual report.

Moreover, in such conditions of austerity, Ministries may not have enough field officers, either at the regional or local levels, to follow up those schools or other agencies which do not respond. On the other hand there are other countries whose data collection is not only exemplary, but is, perhaps, so zealous that it often produces more information than can be used. Getting the balance right between establishing efficient management information systems, and 'filling the gaps' because some participants have not responded to government questionnaires is thus one of the major problems currently facing educational planners throughout the developing world (Hallak 1990; Chapman and Mahlck 1993).

Other problems arise where several ministries are involved in providing education; they provide their own databases without necessarily feeding these into the collective education statistics. In several countries the Ministries of Agriculture, Defence, Health, Rural Development and even Sport might be providers of education. As a result, trying to ascertain the educational expenditure of the country as a whole may prove to be very elusive. This used to be a particularly acute problem in the Soviet Union, but it applies just as much to large federal countries such as Brazil, India and Nigeria where regional/ provincial/local governments relate to different ministries that have responsibilities for providing different levels of education.

Thailand provides an interesting example of such overlaps. Some years ago there were as many as 17 government and para-government agencies involved in providing education and development initiatives in the rural areas. At central ministry level different divisions operated as if they ran their own private fiefdoms with little regard for the other divisions. While doing doctoral research in Thailand, one of the present authors thus found significantly different statistical data provided by government ministries, UNESCO and other agencies while all purporting to refer to the same thing (Watson 1973). All involved in comparative education studies need to bear these concerns in mind. They also raise the question of the reliability of the conclusions drawn by researchers when they have done little more than look over the official statistical evidence provided by international agencies, without delving into how these figures were arrived at. More disturbingly, both UNESCO and the World Bank are sometimes in danger of decontextualising their own information and extrapolating unrealistic trends from such data.

Focus for research

At the outset of any comparative or international study researchers need to be especially well aware of what they are looking for, and why. Is it for academic interest only? Is it to identify trends? Or is it for the purposes of reforming their own or other systems of education? The latter has long been cited as one of the main justifications for researching comparatively. Or is it to test a set of hypotheses? Unless there is clarity of purpose in this complex, multidisciplinary field, it is likely that much unnecessary material will be collected to the detriment of disciplined enquiry. A clear focus, especially regarding which aspect(s) of education are to be studied, for what purpose and in what way, will do much to help clarify the research parameters and hence the selectivity of the information sought. The issue of for whom the research is being conducted is also crucial in this respect, since this has a bearing on the units of analysis; the timescale; the priorities to be decided upon; whether or not the research is to be undertaken individually or as part of a research team; and the theoretical and methodological paradigms employed.

Tensions between global and local priorities

Issues raised in this next section are fundamental to the core spirit of comparative and international research in education. In recent years there has been a growing tendency for policy-makers worldwide to identify global problems and to seek to implement global solutions as if one model fits every situation. Many writers argue that this underpinned much of the approach of the World Bank during the 1990s with its strategies for higher education (World Bank 1994), proposals for general education below the tertiary level (World Bank 1995), and structural adjustment policies throughout much of the developing world (Samoff 1993, 1996a; George and Sabeli 1994; Ilon 1994, 1996; Watson 1996a and b; Chossudovsky 1997; McGinn 1997). Critical voices have thus expressed many pertinent and enduring concerns about such approaches. Common problems may exist in different countries but solutions can rarely be found in the application of a common model across different cultures, regions and political regimes regardless of whether the administrative framework or professional expertise or local culture is capable of introducing, or adapting such reforms (see, for example, Buchert and King 1995, 1996; IJED 1996a: Harber and Davies 1997). While educational reform through school improvement is one area that has been subject to this type of approach and critique, it also applies to much of the literature on decentralisation and local finance as well as that on local community involvement in running and managing schools. Over the years such over-generalised ideas have been advanced by various international organisations without due consideration for local differences. Chapman *et al.* (2002) have shown the fallacy of such strategies with reference to rural Ghana; Cheng (1997) in the case of China; and R.C. Riddell (1997) with reference to Africa as a whole. Sadly these are just a sample of critiques of global 'solutions' being applied uncritically in diverse local contexts.

To understand an education system other than one's own in real depth ideally requires a long period of time spent within that 'other' context, or at least numerous repeated visits until the researcher has an instinctive feel for what makes that society tick: why decisions are arrived at in the way they are; who the powerbrokers are and so on. As Sadler (1900) reminds us, every system of education is shaped by its local, historical, economic, cultural and social context. It cannot truly be understood without this fundamental principle being acknowledged. As Lauwerys (1959) argued, only then can the underlying philosophy of an education system be understood. Education, in short, cannot be decontextualised from its local culture, though this is so often the case when less disciplined (but often influential) cross-cultural analyses are carried out across many different countries. UNESCO's World Education Reports (1993, 1995, 1998b) have, for example, identified trends in education across many systems, and while they have acknowledged national differences, they have failed to go far in helping us to understand the reasons for the different contextual nuances. For example, the United Kingdom was often compared unfavourably with other European countries because of its low enrolment of children aged three or four, yet these comparisons overlooked the fact that state provision began at age five, and frequently included the rising fives, whereas in much of Europe formal schooling does not begin until six or even seven years of age. More recently there has been a closing of the gap of school provision at an early age across Europe. Similarly, the lower percentage of the age group entering British higher education was often adversely compared with the entry rates to higher education in the USA, France and Germany, with scant regard taken of the fact that the dropout rates in all those countries were far higher than in Britain. If one looked at completion rates instead of entry rates, the gap became very much smaller. With the determination of the United Kingdom's New Labour government to expand both nursery provision and higher education, the differences between enrolments in the different European countries are also becoming less marked. The relatively unstructured school curriculum in England also used to be compared unfavourably with the more centrally controlled national curricula prevailing in most of her continental neighbours; but this has also changed with the development of a National Curriculum for England and Wales, and the paradoxical explorations of less centralised models within Europe, during the 1990s. The continuing importance of understanding the relationship between national culture and the curriculum is, therefore, most appositely demonstrated by writers such as Broadfoot and colleagues in their comparative studies of European education (Broadfoot *et al.* 2000).

The focus of the school curriculum, or the place of the teacher in an education system, can thus only really be understood by an appreciation of the underlying philosophy or purpose of schooling in different societies. This, it has long been argued by comparativists, is best achieved by an extended stay within a country, preferably with a knowledge of the local language(s), or by working alongside local researchers. Unfortunately, an extended timescale for researching and understanding any country, its cultures, social and political interactions, its taboos and customs is a 'luxury' that few can afford (McGrath 2001a and b). This points to further problems relating to the commissioning of research and to related questions of power and control.

Conflicting agendas

Much comparative and international research is now commissioned by governments, international organisations or private educational charities. These each have their own agendas and often want to commission consultants or researchers for their own ends, either to propagate a particular theory or to advance a set of policies (Samoff 1993, 1996a). As Preston and Arthur (1996,

1997) have pointed out, this can often lead to a conflict of interests and professional compromises, especially if the researchers unearth findings that are not acceptable to the commissioning agency or to the host government. Researchers might thus feel compelled to pursue particular lines of inquiry, but be prevented from doing so because of constraints over which they have little control. Consultancy priorities are especially likely to be determined by whoever is pulling the purse strings; or there may be a conflict of interest between the external funding agency, if it is a national or international aid organisation, and the host government. The researchers may then be caught in an ethical dilemma as to which body they should be answerable to. Sometimes researchers may, as a result of undertaking such work, find themselves supporting particular groups against the views of the funder. Dove (1980) highlights this in the context of teachers and community schools, especially in rural communities, where teachers might find themselves at odds with the central government over, for example, language or ethnic policy. This, as she demonstrates, can lead to researchers finding themselves aligning with the teachers. Aikman's (1995) work with Amazon communities helps to show that these are widespread and ongoing issues. Perhaps the biggest danger stemming from this lies in the way that researchers from the North may become unwitting agents of Northern 'knowledge control' and policy transfer (Samoff 1996a and b; Habte 1999; King and Buchert 1999; McGrath 2001a; Watson 2001b; Hoppers 2001). The main loser in this increasingly common scenario for educational consultancy and research is the academic and professional credibility of the work undertaken.

So much for difficulties facing individual researchers, but few scholars now operate entirely independently. Funding agencies often prefer comparative and international studies to be undertaken in teams, or with counterpart(s) within the countries under study. While such strategies have many advantages, Osborn (2001) and Phillips and Economou (1999) have highlighted the difficulties encountered in undertaking collaborative research across Europe; Shaw and Ormston (2001) have discussed the misunderstandings which occurred in introducing a reform package into Russia; and Lewin and Stuart (2002) and Stuart and Lewin (2002) touch on the difficulties of conducting a highly complex, interdisciplinary research project across five different developing countries, mainly in Africa but also including the Caribbean.

Equivalences and misconceptions

As the above writers note, not only are there 'political' and personality difficulties to be worked through, but language can generate major dilemmas for comparative and international researchers. Even if there is an agreed working language in which the terms being used might appear at face value to be the same, words can have very different meanings in different contexts. The term 'school' has, for example, different meanings in the USA from its use in most European countries. At one level there is a common usage, but at another it is more usual in the USA to talk about students at college or university as going to 'school'. This is not so in Europe. Even defining primary and secondary schools is fraught with potential difficulties because of the differing age ranges involved in the different levels in different countries. Again students 'graduate' from various levels of school in the USA, whereas only university students are seen to 'graduate' in most European and African countries. Familiar terms like 'community,' 'participation,' 'management,' 'decentralisation,' and 'professor,' also take on subtly distinct meanings in different cultural and political contexts. It is essential, therefore, that all who are involved in any form of collaborative research ensure that they understand what each participant means by the terms being used, even if this might involve hours of careful negotiation before the detailed research gets underway. This partly explains why it is so dangerous for systems, especially in the developing world, to accept the recommendations of bodies like the World Bank and UNESCO at their face value, because the latter have too often been based on thinking, concepts and rationales largely developed in Western contexts; and which might not be easily adapted into, say, francophone Africa or the Islamic Middle East. Today, even these terms are culturally laden, as we have noted previously.

In concluding here, it is therefore clear that problems of equivalence are both central to comparative and international research and multi-dimensional in nature. Indeed, our own analysis closely parallels Warwick and Osherson's (1973) useful categorisation that distinguishes between conceptual equivalence, equivalence of measurement and linguistic equivalence. These are clearly problematic issues that are of enduring significance in comparative research across the social sciences.

Limitations of statistical data

Linking back to earlier sections in this chapter, regardless of how official statistical data have been compiled there are a number of additional caveats which need to be carefully recognised in comparative and international research. First, raw statistics ignore the human and cultural dimensions of a society, which for many comparativists, are at the very heart of what they are studying. Raw data do not, as we have seen, reveal the underlying philosophy or rationale of an education system which help to explain anomalies, or reasons for differences with other systems. What they may tell us, for example, are details about enrolments (and even these might be misleading if they provide gross enrolment figures and not the net enrolment figures); or wastage rates (without looking at the underlying causes); or progression from one level to the next (without commenting on the policy on grade retention or annual examinations). These might be helpful but they can also be misleading if they are compared with data from another system where an entirely different set of background information would be needed to explain their figures.

Second, the GNP and per capita income data, that are used by agencies such as the World Bank and UNDP to classify the countries of the world, are typically national data and are essentially aggregated. They therefore ignore regional variations and ethnic and linguistic disparities. Indeed, language differences and problems rarely seem to enter official international data sets, as if these have no bearing on academic performance or economic development or attitudes to education or healthcare. Moreover, any existing data that are used for internal purposes might be significantly different from those that are published by the various international agencies.

Third, much of the above is predicated on the belief that the key data source on population figures – the national census – is accurate. This cannot necessarily be guaranteed. Over a million people did not complete the 1991 British census because, by being unregistered, they could avoid paying the unpopular community charge, or poll tax as it was known. Malawi had no census between 1966 and 1987. China had no census between 1953 and 1983, and even now there are doubts about the accuracy of the country's national census. In many countries, Bangladesh and Pakistan being but two examples, there are no accurate figures for births and deaths, particularly in the remote and rural areas. Nigeria's population figures have been notoriously inaccurate. The 1973 census there had to be abandoned because of irregularities, and the 1983 census was grossly inflated in certain provinces because the larger the population the greater the federal subsidies. These inaccuracies contributed to planning chaos when it came to introducing Universal Primary Education (UPE) in Nigeria (Okoro 1979; Bray 1981). In Ethiopia and several West African countries the census figures have frequently had to be estimated, either because certain areas have proved inaccessible for census officials or, for cultural reasons, people have avoided answering personal or sensitive questions about the numbers in a family or in the village.

If the basic population figures are erroneous, other data which are based on these figures are, at best, questionable, and this poses distinct and significant problems for comparative and international education research in such contexts. As the Nigerian UPE example illustrates, it is also very difficult to plan for the expansion of education provision without an accurate idea of the age group population, its likely growth rate and any understanding of regional density. This is why school mapping has become such an important tool for educational planners in developing countries today. It can be very difficult to calculate the population growth rates accurately, the Gross Domestic Product, the average per capita income, and the percentage of the population engaged in agriculture or in other areas of the economy. Researchers in education, and throughout the social sciences, thus need to recognise where there are elements of uncertainty in the data used. Indeed, some years ago Puryear (1995) highlighted the problems of acquiring accurate educational statistics, especially by bodies like UNESCO which rely so heavily on member states providing the organisation with the basic information. At the end of the 1990s Heyneman (1999a:65) therefore observed:

... in the field of education, UNESCO data must be treated with caution or worse, they must be assumed to be untrustworthy. Consequently, it is

possible that the results of research on education and economic development by the World Bank, as well as many academic institutions using
UNESCO statistics, are unreliable.

On a positive note, Heyneman did suggest that the statistical data provided
by the Organisation for Economic Cooperation and Development (OECD)
were somewhat better because the OECD countries had the resources and
infrastructure to ensure greater reliability. Considerable improvements are
also now being made to standardise the information being sought, as well as
to improve the accuracy of the figures presented. The development of the
International Standard Classification of Education (INSCED) should also
gradually improve both the access to, and the reliability of, educational data
for comparative purposes (Carr-Hill *et al.* 2001; Lievesley, 2001).

Even so there is still a long way to go. Two of the most notorious areas for
acquiring accurate data, whether for comparable purposes or not, are those of
literacy and non-formal and adult education. Apart from different interpretations of what constitutes literacy, or a literate person, which varies from
country to country, there are problems relating to which language a person
might be literate in or in which they function on a daily basis. In Thailand a
person is regarded as literate if they have enrolled in primary school for at
least two years, whereas in the Philippines a person who is literate has been
defined as: 'a good citizen who should be able to read with understanding
newspapers, bulletins, advertisements, tax notices and letters and should be
able to write an ordinary letter' (UNESCO 1971:22).

Many countries use school enrolment figures, or examinations data, to
arrive at relevant totals but these can prove unreliable if children have
dropped out of school before they have reached grades 5 or 6 when there is a
possibility of achieving levels of permanent literacy. Even then, as Rogers
(1992) cogently argues, unless there are materials produced in local languages
which can help to sustain that literacy, it does not take many years before
there is a lapse into semi-literacy. Samson's (2001) study of the situation in
Addis Ababa in Ethiopia illustrates this point well. Samson argues that there
is ample evidence of semi-literates being classified as literate, whereas she
found that many of these individuals were in effect illiterate, and this was
only in the area of urban Addis Ababa. The situation in the rural areas may be
even more alarming. Wherever there are multilingual situations and the collection of literacy data is in one, or at the most two, languages, figures are
likely to be distorted. This was the case in colonial Vietnam. Before the French
insisted on teaching and using French for educational purposes the literacy
rates in Vietnamese schools were relatively high. However, with the introduction of French medium schooling, many Vietnamese opted out and by the
time the French were forced out of the country those rates had dropped significantly. No more than 10 per cent of the population were reported to be
literate in French (Kelly 1978).

In the area of comparative adult and non-formal education the situation
has become even more complex, as Carr-Hill *et al.* (2001) have been at pains to

explain. Not only has there been continuing uncertainty as to what constitutes non-formal education since the term was first introduced in the early 1970s, but there has been no agreement across countries as to who, or what, should be included in statistical data covering the area of non-formal education, nor where the dividing line between formal and non-formal education should come. The result has been a considerable degree of confusion. Hopefully this will be resolved by further work in the next few years.

There is little room for complacency about the figures for formal school enrolments either. Some international figures for the United Kingdom, for example, refer to the whole country, some to England and Wales, which internally have traditionally been linked together, some to Great Britain, which traditionally has referred to the mainland only, thereby excluding Northern Ireland. If such a situation can arise in a context which has good access to data, how much more problematic must data collection be in large countries such as Brazil, China, India, Nigeria and Indonesia where communication links between the central government and outlying regions are often far from easy. Anyone familiar with Sub-Saharan Africa cannot fail to be aware that while the Ministries of Education have official lists of schools and teachers and pupils, many of these schools do not exist as buildings. Rather they are made up of groups of children sitting in the open air under trees, at least during the dry season! Some of the problems that arise from such situations have been usefully identified by Croft (2002) in Malawi as part of her research for the Multi-Site Teacher Education Research Programme (MUSTER) recently co-ordinated by the University of Sussex in the United Kingdom (see Lewin and Stuart 2002).

Perhaps some of the biggest difficulties in collecting official statistics and using them for international comparative research arise from differences in the length of schooling for different age groups, as argued earlier, and in ensuring that one is comparing like with like. For example UNESCO, World Bank and OECD figures take primary school enrolments as running from ages 6 to 12; secondary enrolments as from 12 to 18; and tertiary enrolments as from 18 to 23. However many countries begin primary school at 5 or 7, secondary at 11, 12 or 13, while tertiary education might begin at 17, 18 or 19 or even later. To arrive at realistic and meaningful data which can accurately be used for comparisons is thus fraught with difficulties.

Problems related specifically to research in developing countries

While many of the above issues have general currency for comparative and international research in education worldwide, there are other problems that apply more specifically to the developing world. These are considered in a little more detail below.

Poorly developed infrastructure

Since many developing countries are located in the equatorial and tropical regions of the world, they experience specific problems of environmental context which are less problematic elsewhere. Many countries in Africa and South Asia suffer from poor soils and scrub vegetation; in South-East Asia and large parts of Latin America there is dense jungle or inhospitable mountain ranges while in the Middle East and North and Northwest Africa it is desert that predominates. These environmental features become particularly problematic once the urban areas are left behind. Distances between centres of population may be considerable. Many places are inaccessible by public transport, even when this is fairly reliable. Roads may be badly maintained or even non-existent apart from dirt tracks or laterite highways.

Researchers, whether they be insiders or outsiders, may thus have to travel long distances, in the heat and on foot. Lodgings may lack basic facilities. Access to computers, the internet, telephones or other means of telecommunication may be non-existent because of an absence of electricity. It is revealing to note, for example, that 80 per cent of the world's population has no access to basic infrastructure facilities that are regarded as commonplace in the industrialised world – and that there are reported to be more computers in New York alone than in the whole of Africa (DFID 2000).

Infrastructure problems might also relate to the postal system, basic administration and law and order throughout the country. All these can hamper researchers in the field on a practical level. Far more problematic, and something that has a direct bearing on the successful development of poverty research and poverty alleviation programmes in many countries, is a weak or poorly developed bureaucratic system. This often means that there are not enough trained personnel on the ground to ensure that government policies are implemented, or that research and evaluation can be actively supported.

Limited levels of public research

Although there are some beacons of successful research initiatives within the South, and there have been successful links established between Northern research institutions and Southern counterparts, it remains true to say that much educational research carried out in developing countries is either done by Northern researchers, or takes place under the aegis of a Northern research consultancy or funding body. In medical research alone barely 10 per cent of funds are spent on those diseases which affect 90 per cent of the world's population (DFID 2000). Both Samoff's (1993) and Buchert's (1998) studies of educational reforms in the South show how these were dictated, or directed, by Northern aid agencies; while Samoff's (1996b) analysis of the contents, procedures and personnel involved in over 240 educational surveys conducted in Africa between 1990 and 1994, demonstrates that, apart from some nominal representation of local researchers, the work was almost entirely conducted by expatriates (see also Leach 1994). Habte (1999) has, therefore, rightly called into question the international community's commitment to developing a viable research capacity in the South. The need for this was advocated as long ago as 1985 in a special issue of the *International Journal of Educational Development* (IJED 1985). At the heart of this dilemma are familiar issues relating to funding, resources, human resource development and access to specialist training. However, as we shall argue later, more political questions of dependency, power and control also emerge if any change is to be globally influential and locally sustainable.

Limited funding

While the lack of funding for educational research is a significant problem in most societies, it is particularly acute in developing countries which are desperately short of money for basic system functions. In such contexts research can be seen as a luxury that cannot be afforded. Even in situations where there are active local researchers, they are frequently hampered by their working conditions which place excessive demands on their time so that little is left that might be channelled into productive research. Such situations can fuel sensitivities and political opposition to outsiders receiving support, further limiting the possibilities for positive capacity development.

Language complications

The majority of the world's nations are multi-ethnic and multilingual. This highlights the importance of language skills for cross-cultural researchers. While comparativists have long recognised this principle, it is also clear that few researchers can realistically expect to be fluent in more than one or two of the necessary languages, let alone understand the nuances of the different languages or ethnic groups within a country. It is therefore of vital importance that researchers working in such multicultural contexts should, at the very least, recognise the implications of these issues, and familiarise themselves with local customs and aspects of the language which might lead to confusion or misunderstanding. Robinson's (1994, 1996a and b) studies of language use at the grassroots level in different parts of Africa, for example, well illustrate the problems for aid donors of working at central government level who expect their proposals to be understood by different levels of administrators further down the system. Counterparts at this level might well, and probably do, operate in a local vernacular as opposed to the national language. Certain terms, concepts and ideas familiar to those at the centre who work with, or through, the international community might have entirely different meanings in such different language settings. Thus, while researchers might be able to bypass some of the levels of administration, they are nevertheless confronted with these different linguistic assumptions and understandings the further away they operate from the centre. Chapman and colleagues (2002) recently found this while working with local primary school communities in Ghana, and their work could be helpful to others dealing with such issues in the future.

The changing nature of research problems and priorities

Running throughout the above discussion it can be seen how apparently practical and logistical research problems are so often impossible to disentangle
from more substantial issues relating to culture, values, ethics and power.
Here it is argued that contemporary changes in geopolitical relations, combined with the implications of the intensification of globalisation, have
heightened the significance of such relationships to the extent that the very
conceptualisation of problems in comparative and international research is
itself in need of fundamental change. Further inspiring this critique is recognition of the challenges raised by the variety of poststructuralist frameworks
for the analysis of education. Such thinking points to the need, increasingly
acknowledged across the social sciences, for a more critical reconsideration of
the relationship between policy and practice, and between theoretical studies
and applied research (Crossley and Holmes 2001). Too often, as illustrated by
the division between the comparative and international dimensions of our
own field, the discourses and priorities of academic theorists are pursued in
ways that fail to relate effectively and accessibly to matters of educational policy and practice. On the other hand, this hiatus also inhibits policymakers and
practitioners from valuing and engaging with potentially helpful theoretical
perspectives and insights.

The relevance of these meta-level issues for the reconceptualisation of
research problems in comparative and international education is paramount
here. As our discussion already demonstrates, underpinning many of what
are, at first sight, practical and logistical problems, can be found more substantial dilemmas that existing theoretical work can play a valuable role in
understanding. Problems relating to cultural bias, for example, can often be
more effectively addressed in the light of theoretical work on the legitimation
of educational knowledge, or from the perspective of recent scholarship on
cross-cultural knowledge transfer and 'dialogue among civilisations' as
demonstrated by Hayhoe and Pan (2001). Similarly, writers such as Hickling-
Hudson (1998) usefully demonstrate how post-colonial frameworks can
challenge pervasive ethnocentrism that can seriously inhibit very practical
efforts to advance genuine research partnerships between the North and the
South. Turning the rhetoric of 'partnership', 'collaboration' and 'co-operation'
into improved research practice thus has a potentially powerful ally in the
arena of theoretical scholarship. For those involved in research capacity building, in the North and the South, this holds much future potential. Given the
pertinence of this for our own work we pursue these themes in some detail
later in Chapters 6 and 7.

To take a different set of priority issues, sensitivity to culture and context
also underpins the increasingly successful application of qualitative research
strategies in the field of comparative and international education. Case study
(Crossley and Vulliamy 1984), action research (Stuart *et al.* 1997) and critical
ethnography (Rockwell 1991), for instance, have all proved helpful in contributing to improved educational policy and practice in developing countries

– despite the ongoing dominance of positivistic assumptions and paradigms in the agendas of powerful development agencies and government bureaucracies. Much more, however, needs to be done if we are to maximise the benefits of differing perspectives, or, for example, if the applied potential of critical theory, such as that which inspired Freire (1971, 1982, 1996) or Chambers (1994, 1995), is not to be limited to the work of 'alternative' pressure groups or the advocacy efforts of non-governmental organisations (NGOs). For the benefits of such theoretical perspectives to be maximised, we argue that the range and the quality of the dialogue across professional cultures must also be improved, and for this to happen the nature and scope of the discourse itself must change.

This brings us back to the primary need to broaden our understanding of the nature of the difficulties and problems that confront contemporary advances in the field of comparative and international education. In doing this, we return to the implications of our argument for more effective bridging between the worlds of theory and practice – the discourses, personnel and cultures – in ways that will enhance our understanding of the contemporary problems and priorities that we all face in the twenty-first century. To a significant extent this suggests the need to focus increased critical attention on the ways in which comparative and international research is conducted, by whom, and for whose benefit. The nature of this task thus requires more direct attention to research processes than has hitherto been the case.

In the following chapter we therefore extend the present discussion of difficulties and problems faced within the field into the theoretical and methodological arena, and examine more closely the implications of this for our understandings of the concepts of globalisation, context and difference.

Chapter 4

Globalisation, context and difference

The analysis of the nature and evolution of comparative and international education presented so far demonstrates how the field has repeatedly responded both to changing geopolitical realities, and to theoretical and paradigmatic shifts within the humanities and social sciences. Such changes are reflected in the efforts that have been made over the years to identify phases of development for the field as a whole. While we recognise that there are significant teleological and intellectual limitations with such categorisations, they can provide helpful analytical frameworks especially for newcomers interested in an introduction to shifts in broad historical and epistemological trends in a chosen field. We will therefore return again to the dilemmas of the chronology of distinctive phases for comparative and international education in later chapters. Here, however, it is first pertinent to explore, in more depth, how late twentieth century and contemporary geopolitical and intellectual developments fundamentally challenged the current scope and nature of the field; the appropriateness and continued legitimacy of the dominant forms of empirical social sciences; and, what Samoff (1992) calls the hegemony of the 'intellectual-financial' complex in much globally focused educational research and international development work in general.

It is to the nature of these contemporary challenges that we now turn our attention in the light of the impact of intensified globalisation and the related theoretical literature. In doing so we consider the implications of such developments with particular reference to the significance of post-modern and post-colonial perspectives that highlight the importance of contextual and cultural difference.

This adds further weight to our thesis that the field must be fundamentally reconceptualised in ways that enable it to be more effective in recognising and dealing with the substantive and intellectual challenges of the emergent twenty-first century. The analysis also suggests that the field itself may now be entering a new, creative and forward-looking period of development – but one that may also better represent a diversity of forms and a constructive bridging with the valuable traditions of the past.

Challenge and continuity

While the field of comparative and international education is well placed for the study of contemporary relationships between globalisation and cultural context, it is argued here that this will, nevertheless, generate significant conceptual and intellectual challenges for all involved. At the heart of these challenges, as noted by Dale (2000a), are the field's traditional focus on the nation-state as the principal unit of analysis, and the continued dominance (and reassertion) of positivistic social science in much of the contemporary intellectual canon. Having said this, our review of the historical evolution of the field well demonstrates how interpretative frameworks, critical theory and world systems perspectives have long influenced some of the most distinguished research agendas. Returning to our historical analysis, Cowen (1996b:153), for example, documents how Sadler's seminal work at the turn of the last century embodied a combination of intellectual challenge and a concern for policy and practice that was both contextually sensitive and critical of the search for universal principles that was inspired by his more positivistic predecessors.

In more recent decades, we can also see how the application of conceptual advances in development economics further demonstrate how the field has continued to look beyond national boundaries, strengthened its multidisciplinary orientation and adopted various combinations of world systems analyses and critical theory. Thus, dependency theory, as articulated by writers such as Frank (1967), Fanon (1968), and Cardoso (1972), was systematically applied by comparativists in the 1970s and, as Little points out, this perspective:

> ... focused on underdevelopment rather than development, viewing it as a necessary outcome of systematic exploitation and manipulation of peripheral economies by central economies ... a process which created and maintained cultural and educational dependency.
>
> (Little 1999: 30)

Comparative and international research has thus made significant contributions to critical and theoretically informed scholarship through, for example, the pioneering work of researchers such as Carnoy (1974), Bowles and Gintis (1976) and Bourdieu and Passeron (1977). This trajectory of work challenged structural functionalism, often adopted neo-Marxist frameworks and, as was the case across the social sciences, led to early moves away from the nation-state as the central unit of analysis. Indeed, Little goes on to say that:

> By the 1980s and 1990s much of the discussion of dependency had been replaced by concepts of economic and cultural globalisation. But the analytic imperative remained the same – the need to look beyond national boundaries for explanations of educational change, and the inclusion of that broader vision in the construction of purpose and value in education by actors on the ground.
>
> (Little 1999:30)

While this continuity with the globalisation debate is revealing – and pertinent for our own analysis – it, nevertheless, remains clear that much of the
second half of the twentieth century saw many valuable interpretative, cultural and critical perspectives ignored or marginalised by the increasingly
dominant positivistic social science paradigm and the rationalist, modernisation theory that it underpins. To cite Cowen (1996b:152):

> Thus the work of Hans and Schneider, drawing centrally upon history,
> was not refuted: it was merely avoided in the search for a relevant sci-
> ence. Similarly, the culturalist motif in the work of Ulrich (1964),
> Lauwerys (1967), Nash *et al.* (1965), Halls (1973), Mallinson (1975) and
> King (1979) became overwhelmed by the search for scientific rigour and
> precision. The dominant paradigm, for research, became positivist eco-
> nomics and positivist sociology, particularly in the USA. The work was
> done and much of it was done well, within its own terms (Noah and
> Eckstein, 1969). Comparative education as a university subject flourished.
> But there was a price.

Cowen also argues how preferences for structural-functionalist sociology with
' ... a positivist orientation towards policy' also separated much Anglo-
American inspired comparative education from European sociology, Marxist
perspectives and Latin-American theoretical critiques of the modernist project
(Cowen 1996b:152). This, revealingly, also highlights linguistic, cultural and ideological divisions that, we suggest, continue to compartmentalise and limit the
broader advancement of the field to the present day. Other more contemporary
examples of important challenges to the mainstream paradigm, that we will
consider in depth later, include the increasingly influential, qualitative research
movement within the field (Heyman 1979; Masemann 1990; Crossley and
Vulliamy 1997a), work on multi-level and cultural analysis (Broadfoot *et al.*
1993; Bray and Thomas 1995; Alexander 2000), applications of critical theory
(May 1994; Arnove and Torres 1999), critiques of the neo-liberal project
(Colclough 1997; Lauder and Hughes 1999; Apple 2001; Dale 2001) and work on
the implications of post-modernism and post-colonialism for the field as a
whole (Rust 1991; Paulston 1996; Cowen 1996a; Masemann and Welch 1997;
Tikly 1999).

Returning to the contemporary critique, at this stage it is increasingly clear
that the emergence of globalisation as a focus for much research and scholarship, the dominance of marketisation and neo-liberal policy initiatives, and
widespread international interest in 'performativity' and 'effectiveness', highlight the limitations of the nature and scope of many firmly established
approaches to comparative and international research in education. A sustained reconsideration of the field and of the appropriateness and legitimacy
of some of the most influential theoretical and methodological frameworks is
therefore increasingly important. Before developing our analysis further,
however, we turn next to a more detailed consideration of the concept and
implications of globalisation itself.

Conceptions of globalisation

The literature on globalisation has grown rapidly throughout the last decade, though many argue that, while the concept itself is nothing particularly new, it represents a dramatic acceleration of international trade made possible by improved transport and communications. 'Globalisation' is thus a complex and highly contested term – and one that is widely used but open to multiple interpretations. This is partly because it is as relevant to geographers, economists and others as it is to specialists in international relations and education (see, for example, Green 1997; Watson 1998; Radice 1999; Sklair 1999), thus generating numerous confusions and misunderstandings that can further complicate the debate. There are, however, certain common themes in the literature that warrant attention and clarification. Some writers have also found it possible to demarcate broad 'tendencies' or conceptions of globalisation that can prove helpful for application in the analysis of contemporary educational trends.

At the most basic level the popular view of globalisation represents rather ill-defined and questionable notions of the exponential spread of a common world culture, with the prospect of societies converging and becoming very much the same in nature and operation. Certainly, the term figures prominently in all manner of discussions world-wide. As Giddens (1999:1) points out, 'no political speech is complete without reference to it', business leaders, policy-makers and journalists increasingly focus their attention on its implications and, as a concept, it 'has come from nowhere to be almost everywhere'. Research studies also commonly portray globalisation 'as the widening, deepening and speeding up of world-wide interconnectedness in all aspects of contemporary social life, from the cultural to the criminal, the financial to the spiritual' (Held *et al.* 1999:2).

Beyond this there is wide disagreement relating to the origins, mechanisms, significance and implications of the concept – though a vibrant debate is clearly visible in the already substantial literature. For Held *et al.* (1999) the various perspectives on globalisation can be classified into three tendencies or broad schools of thought. These are represented as the hyperglobalists, the sceptics and the transformationalists. This is a useful classification for it helps to reveal the nature and origins of the different lines of thought, and of some of the most significant sources of present confusions and misconceptions. In brief, the hyperglobalists see globalisation as defining a new world era dominated by the influence of the global marketplace. The Japanese business analyst Keniche Ohmae (see Ohmae 1995), for example, argues that nations have already lost much of their sovereignty, that the power of politicians is significantly reduced and that the era of the nation-state has come to an end. This perspective prioritises economic motivations and processes along with neo-liberal marketisation. Moreover:

> ... many hyperglobalists share a conviction that economic globalisation is
> constructing new forms of social organisation that are supplanting, or

that will eventually supplant, traditional nation-states as the primary economic and political units of world society.

(Held *et al.* 1999:3)

Both neo-liberals who support marketplace principles, and neo-Marxists who
oppose such developments, work within the hyperglobalist framework.
Many also point to the breakdown of the traditional North–South divide
arguing that a new global division of labour is now emerging with radical
implications for the changing futures of all involved (see Soudien 2002).

The sceptics, on the other hand, argue that globalisation is in large part an
exaggerated myth (Hirst and Thompson 1996). Moreover, they maintain that
the hyperglobalist tendency ignores evidence that demonstrates the historical
continuity of powerful international influences, underestimates the continuing impact of the nation-state and disguises a more significant regionalisation
of the world economy dominated by the three trading blocks of Europe, Asia-
Pacific and North America (Held *et al.* 1999:5). The sceptics therefore suggest
that the world economy is now less connected that it was during, for example,
the colonial and cold war eras. Globalisation is thus challenged as a freemar-
ket ideology, perpetuated by the opponents of state intervention in
socio-economic affairs. The intensification of worldwide trade is further criticised as a new phase of Western imperialism promoted by dominant, and
primarily self-interested, national governments – often working in collaboration with multilateral organisations. Vocal challenges are, for example,
articulated by groupings of poorer economies against the 'corporate culture'
of the World Trade Organisation (WTO). The criticism that surfaced at the
WTO Conference in Seattle in 1999, and at numerous subsequent events,
vividly illustrates the significance and impact of such thinking. Thus, from
the sceptics' perspective, globalisation is linked to the perpetuation of the economic dependence and marginalisation of the poorer nations of the South.
Moreover, they also argue that such inequalities undermine the very notion of
the global civilisation envisaged by the hyperglobalists – and, as Huntington
(1993) posits, this is more likely to foreshadow worldwide fragmentation into
competing and antagonistic groups of civilisations.

Finally, the transformationalists, including Giddens (1990,1998), accept
that contemporary globalisation processes are indeed unprecedented, 'such
that governments and societies across the globe are having to adjust to a
world in which there is no longer a clear distinction between international
and domestic, external and internal affairs' (Held *et al.* 1999:7). From this perspective the new instant, transnational and computerised economy is without
parallel or precedent. Unlike the hyperglobalists or the sceptics, the transformationalists do not envisage any particular future world scenario, but they
pay more attention to globalisation as an historical process, that affects all
societies and their many dimensions. Nor do they envisage global convergence and homogenisation – but they do see new configurations of global
power relations, and a recasting of:

... traditional patterns of inclusion and exclusion between countries by forging new hierarchies which cut across and penetrate all societies and regions of the world. North and South, First World and Third World are no longer 'out there' but nestled together within the world's major cities.

(Held *et al.* 1999:8)

The transformationalists thus see contemporary globalisation as a unique phenomenon that is requiring nation-states to adapt in ways that allow them to engage more effectively with powerful non-territorial agencies and economic forces. They do not foresee the demise of the nation-state, but they do believe that national governments must be transformed in ways that recognise the dramatically increased influence of global agencies and agendas on all societies worldwide.

The contested intellectual terrain of globalisation is clearly visible from the above discussion, but so too are the economic motivations and foundations (Wallerstein 1974) that all three schools of thought recognise. Indeed, emphasising the economic dimension Jones (1999:18) argues that it is fundamentally important to remember that globalisation, as we know it today, is derived from the '1980s ascendancy of a particular form of capitalism, championed in North America and parts of Western Europe (notably the United Kingdom) as the attainment of the century old ideals of the free trade liberals'. It is also possible to see that writers engaged with all three theoretical tendencies recognise how advances in information and communications technologies have helped to make intensified globalisation feasible in the last decades of the twentieth century. Indeed, in *The Rise of the Network Society*, Castells (1996) sees knowledge and knowledge transfer as an integral part of the new capitalism. Reflecting on the globalisation process, he predicts that relationships between individuals and communications networks will eventually become more important than traditional ties to community. This is a view shared by Schluter and his team at the Jubilee Centre in Cambridge, in the United Kingdom, who, along with Hobsbawm (1994), believe that the breakdown of relationships with neighbours and communities, largely as a result of job mobility and ease of personal tele and electronic communications across the globe, is having a deleterious effect on traditional values and social coherence (Schluter and Lee 1993). In this scenario increased personal mobility and information and communications technologies can thus be seen as the tools for the creation of a new economic order – and, as Jones (1998:145) points out,' globalisation as we are experiencing it would not be possible without them'.

While globalisation has typically been portrayed as an economic and technological phenomenon, there is also much within the literature that demonstrates how it has fundamental political and cultural dimensions and implications. Robertson (1992), for example, argues that although economic issues are of major importance, in matters of transnational relations cultural factors often play a more significant role in determining events in practice. Waters (1995) also notes the inter-relationship between the economic, political and cultural dimensions of globalisation. Reflecting elements of the process thesis held by the transformationalists, he, nevertheless, envisages great diversity in a globalised era. This can be seen in the following framework of ideal-typical patterns for economic, political and cultural globalisation that Little (1996:428) has developed from his 1995 publication.

Ideal-typical patterns of globalisation

Economic globalisation
Freedom of exchange between localities with indeterminate flows of services and symbolic commodities
The balance of production activity in a locality determined by its physical and geographic advances
Minimal foreign direct investment
Flexible responsiveness of organisations to global markets
Decentralised, instantaneous and 'stateless' financial markets
Free movement of labour

Political globalisation
An absence of state sovereignty, and multiple centres of power at global, local and intermediate levels
Local issues discussed and situated in relation to a global community
Powerful international organisations predominant over national organisations
Fluid and multicentric international relations
A weakening of value attached to the nation-state and a strengthening of common and global politics

Cultural globalisation
A deterritorialised religious mosaic
A deterritorialised cosmopolitanism and diversity
Widespread consumption of simulations and representations
Global distribution of images and information
              (Sources: Little, 1996:428, adapted from Waters, 1995:94, 123, 157)

Giddens (1999) also emphasises the political and cultural dimensions of globalisation and, as Little's framework usefully illustrates, draws attention to the contradictions and paradoxes that link global processes to the stimulation of local diversity. Giddens (1999:3) thus argues that globalisation is:

> … a complex set of processes, not a single one. And these operate in a contradictory or oppositional fashion. Most people think of it as simply 'pulling away' power or influence from local communities and nations into the global arena. And indeed this is one of its consequences. Nations do lose some of the economic power they once had. However, it also has an opposite effect. Globalisation not only pulls upwards, it pushes downwards, creating new pressures for local autonomy.

In the light of this analysis a rationale for the resurgence of local cultural movements can, paradoxically, be found in the globalisation process and in the weakening of the nation-state. Giddens (1999), for example, links the collapse of the Soviet Union to its inability to compete in the global electronic economy of the 1980s, and to the devastating impact of the new global media upon the ideological and cultural controls exerted by the communist regime. Global forces thus reasserted more local political and cultural movements – albeit within the broader framework that advanced Fukuyama's (1992) conception of neo-liberal, 'end of history' capitalism.

Transnational influences are thus complex and, clearly, not always beneficial. The cultural penetration of economically poor societies by Western consumer products is one commonly voiced dilemma – but the growing disparities that have recently been documented between the world's rich and poor are more deeply troubling (see, for example, DFID 1997; Watkins 2000). So too are the social and economic problems that have resulted from the impact of Western ideologically inspired structural adjustment policies on the role of the state in the South (Stewart 1996; Chossudovsky 1997; Hoogvelt 1997). Globalisation processes can also be seen to influence the West itself through, for example, the reverse colonisation initiated by non-Western cultures, and through migration which has now become a global phenomenon (Castles and Miller 1993; Skeldon 1997). Giddens (1999) uses the example of the Latinising of Los Angeles to illustrate these issues; the controversy over the potential for Taiwanese whole class teaching methods to improve the quality of primary education in England and Wales (Reynolds and Farrell 1996), as noted earlier, provides, however, a more directly relevant example for our purposes – and brings the focus of our analysis appropriately back to the field of education.

Globalisation, international agendas and educational transfer

To date, much research and scholarship on globalisation, as evidenced above, has been carried out within the disciplines of economics, political science, sociology and cultural studies. While this is still a relatively new literature (Radice 1999), it is already vast in scope and is continuing to grow rapidly.

The mainstream field of educational research has focused less direct attention upon the nature and implications of globalisation to date, although recent years have seen significant contributions emerging, most notably related to aspects of policy studies, marketisation and sociology (Meyer *et al.* 1992; Green 1997; Dale 1999; Lauder and Hughes 1999). Dale (1999), for example, is particularly interested in the mechanisms through which globalisation affects national educational systems – arguing that little empirical work of this nature has as yet been carried out. Significantly, this paper is published in a special issue of the *Journal of Education Policy* devoted to the theme of globalisation. In more recent, and linked, studies, Dale (2000b) contrasts differing theoretical perspectives – including that underpinning Meyer *et al.*'s (1992) *World Models and National Primary Curricular Categories* thesis – on the dynamics of the relationship between education and globalisation. Perhaps, even more pertinently for the present discussion, the implications of this line of analysis are beginning to be directly explored for the field of comparative education (Dale 2000b, 2001; Apple 2001). Ball (1998b:117) also addresses, 'the emergence of a set of generic education policies, the globalisation of policy if you like', along with 'the processes of the local translation of generic policies'. As with Dale and other policy analysts such as Whitty *et al.* (1998), however, (apart from consideration of the East Asian Tiger economies), little in-depth attention is given to the experience and impact of globalisation in non-Western contexts. While the implications for the field of comparative and international education are significant, to date this policy genre also rarely engages in any sustained way with the relevant literature and discourse within the field itself. See, for example, the substantial, and valuable, collection of articles on education policy compiled by Marshall and Peters (1999) for the Elgar Reference Collection on Comparative Public Policy. This is a significant and revealing 'cross-disciplinary' relationship that we shall return to in Chapters 7 and 8.

The latter critique is all the more pertinent given the fact that a number of influential researchers explicitly positioned within the field of comparative and international education have, as we have begun to see, also played a significant if still collectively modest part in contributing to the emergence of an educational literature on globalisation (indicative examples are, Little 1996; Ilon 1997; Jones 1998; Arnove and Torres 1999; Watson 2000; Mebrahtu *et al.* 2000; Mundy and Murphy 2001). The 1995 Oxford International Education Conference, a biennial meeting that is of central importance for a wide range of academics, policy-makers and others connected to the United Kingdom comparative and international education constituency, for example, adopted the central theme of 'Globalisation and Learning' in recognition of its emerging importance. The papers resulting from this influential event for the field were subsequently published in a special issue of the *International Journal of Educational Development*, devoted to the same theme, in 1996 (IJED 1996b). Indicating an ongoing emphasis, more recently the Orlando 2002 Conference of the Comparative and International Education Society (CIES) was convened around the theme 'The Social Construction of Marginality: Globalisation's Impact on the Disenfranchised' – and the 2002 Worldwide Comparative Education Forum held in Beijing adopted the title of 'Globalisation and Education Reforms'.

Factors that have helped researchers explicitly located within the field of comparative and international education to play a pioneering role in the study of globalisation, include the multi-disciplinary foundations, character and sensitivities of the field itself – combined with the related personal interests of those involved. Torres, for example, is a sociologist and critical theorist with long-term interests in comparative education. Currently Director of the Latin American Centre at the University of California at Los Angeles, he specialises in the study of Latin American Education (Torres and Puiggrós 1997), and plays an active role in the shaping of the field of comparative education as a member of the editorial board for the *Comparative Education Review*. Torres has thus long drawn upon a range of multi-disciplinary perspectives informed by critical theory (Torres and Mitchell 1995; Morrow and Torres 1995), and by the distinctive contributions to praxis made by influential Latin American scholars of the calibre of Freire (Freire 1971, 1996; Torres 1998). This underpins his work carried out within the field of comparative and international education and his own engagement with the 'dialectic of the global and the local' (Arnove and Torres, 1999).

As we have already argued, linkages between neo-Marxist analyses of education, and dependency theory derived from the Latin American experience, played a significant role in advancing the development of world systems' perspectives in comparative and international education, and in the recognition of global influences upon education worldwide (Hawkins and Rust 2001). Similarly, Little's multidisciplinary background, notably in economics and development studies (1999), underpins her own engagement with the impact of globalisation on education – set firmly within the field, but focusing consistently on her own core research issues relating to assessment and examinations (Little 2000). Indeed, anticipating our following analysis of priorities for future research in the field, much of Little's collective work demonstrates that external examination and accountability mechanisms increasingly amount to one of the most pervasive forms of global influence upon the nature and character of education systems worldwide.

A second set of reasons that have helped to give some comparativists a leading edge in the arena of globalisation relate to the field's traditional study of, and involvement in, activities and agencies designed to promote increased international understanding, and co-operation. As noted in Chapter 2, this rationale was heightened in the post-World War II era as Western nations strived to re-establish their understanding of the economic and political foundations necessary for peaceful development. This is a motif that is visible in the justification for many international agencies and in the work of comparativists such as Zachariah (1990). It is also pursued in a more critical and challenging way by Jones in his studies of multilateral agencies such as UNESCO (1990, 1994a, 1998, 1999) and the World Bank (1992, 1994b, 1997). In assessing the contemporary global influence of international agencies, for example, Jones (1994b:175) observes that 'Differences of local tradition, convention and politics would normally suggest a far greater diversity in educational development than we are currently witnessing worldwide'. Explaining the rationale for his cumulative research trajectory, and the significance of the forces of globalisation in this, he goes on to argue that:

> A starting point, however limited its potential to explain all, can be those actors on the global educational scene who admit an institutional role in exerting global influence on education. Prominent here must be the range of international and regional organisations that include in their mandates the development of education and the promotion of educational change. Their mandates, of course, might be far broader than education alone, but might find in educational change both a means and a sign of effective promotion of those mandates.

For Jones (1998:153), studies that examine the implications of 'unfettered cap-italistic globalisation on multilateral agencies and their agendas in education are crucial, if we are to better understand the dangers to democracy, peace and justice, of an increasingly differentiated and anarchic framework for the conduct of international relations'. Such sentiments are all the more pertinent in the international climate post-September 2001. Related studies of multilat-eral agencies and their impact upon educational policy and practice, include work by K. King (1991a), Mundy (1999), King and Buchert (1999), Watson (1999c) and Crossley and Holmes (1999). While these works further testify to the emergent contribution made to the study of globalisation within the field of comparative and international education, we will return to the substance and implications of their findings when considering the prospects for contem-porary, global research and development agendas in Chapter 6.

Finally, the field's long and critical engagement with the concepts, processes and outcomes of the international transfer of educational policy and practice further helps to position it well for future contributions to research on the nature and implications of globalisation (Crossley 1984; Phillips 1989, 2000). Indeed, throughout this book we argue that the 'question of educa-tional transfer' (Crossley 1984) is a consistently distinctive theme for the field as a whole – and an issue that is becoming increasingly important and prob-lematic with the intensification of the pace and scope of globalisation.

Admittedly, in what Fraser and Brickman (1968) identify as the early trav-ellers' tales and educational borrowing phases of the field, widespread belief in the superiority of Western educational systems reinforced the active export of specific policies and practices – and a less than critical intellectual response. This is perhaps most graphically illustrated with reference to the establish-ment of colonial education systems across the globe in the image of those existing in the metropolitan nations of the colonial powers. So, for example, distinctively British models were transplanted in associated colonial territo-ries, and Spanish and French systems came to be reproduced as an integral part of their own colonisation processes (see, for example, Carnoy 1974; Fägerlind and Saha 1989; Bacchus 1990; Kelly 2000). Today the export, trans-fer, imposition or borrowing of educational policy and practice continues – albeit in more diverse and often subtle ways. The direct export of ideas and expertise also continues to be actively encouraged by, for example, govern-ment bodies such as the United Kingdom's Department of Trade and Industry and the related Education and Training Exports Group. International confer-ences established by agencies such as the British Council also engage in related activities, where overseas visitors to the United Kingdom are invited to consider adopting contemporary policy initiatives for application in their own systems. Clearly there is much that we can all learn from the experience of others, but, as we have well demonstrated, since the days of Sadler the cri-tique of uncritical international transfer has become an increasingly important theme, most notably within the socio-cultural dimension of the comparative and international research literature.

Moreover, much challenging work on this has been carried out with refer-ence to the appropriateness of international development initiatives and the dilemmas of transfer between the North and the South (Crossley 1984; Samoff 1999). Phillips (2000) presents some of the most comprehensive accounts of the broad issues covered in this body of work, and contributes significantly to the conceptual debate. In doing this he also effectively relates the generic arguments to contemporary geopolitical developments across Europe – such as the demise of the Soviet Union – and the specific case of modern Germany. This, moreover, points to new arenas where the dilemmas of educational transfer are now beginning to emerge, to the impact of Western ideologies and models in the reconstituted Eastern Europe and in other states facing rapid transition (Coulby *et al.* 2000; Mebrahtu *et al.* 2000), and to the relationship of such issues to the contemporary processes and mechanisms of globalisation. The rapid intensification of globalisation within recent years has thus brought many challenges to both the disciplines that underpin comparative and inter-national research in education, and to the field itself. While the field has already played a part in the initiation and advancement of the emergent liter-ature on globalisation and education, there is therefore much more to do and this, in itself, highlights the need for more fundamental reconceptualisation. This, as we argue, has implications for the ways in which comparative and international research in education is carried out as well as for the focus of research itself.

At the most fundamental level, the continued dominance of the nation-state as a framework for analysis is increasingly questionable, given the above level of awareness of the influence of global socio-economic factors in all national contexts. Somewhat paradoxically, the existing literature also demonstrates how the significance of local and non-Western perspectives, values and traditions is also heightened in an increasingly inter-connected world (Thomas, E. 2000; Hayhoe and Pan 2001). This in itself, adds to the ever more powerful socio-cultural critiques of positivistic assumptions and para-digms that have dominated educational planning in recent decades – and to the challenge to much related consultancy work and research carried out within and beyond the field of comparative and international education. Farrell (1997), for example, recognises the significance of these challenges for both the nation-state and for the epistemological and theoretical assumptions held by many educational planners, evaluators and researchers. Echoing an increasing number of social scientists, across a wide range of disciplines, he points to the lessons to be learned from a closer investigation of cultural per-spectives and the relevant post-modern literature. For Farrell (1997:313):

This situation requires not simply a Kuhnian paradigm shift but a meta-paradigm shift. Some post-modern writers are beginning to grapple with this problem, but even they have not yet begun, in my judgement, to really grasp the depth of the intellectual disorder we are now in the midst of. They are, however, closer than most, especially those who work from a disciplined multi-truth narrative position and who have not simply used this new label as an excuse for lack of intellectual rigor and a licence for self-indulgence.

It is therefore to the nature and potential of intellectual perspectives that recognise the increased significance of context, culture and difference that we now turn, before drawing the implications of this collective analysis together by focusing upon major factors currently shaping the contemporary comparative and international research agenda.

Context, culture and difference

The failure of many internationally inspired educational development initiatives to be successfully implemented in practice has led our own work, and that by analysts such as Farrell (1997) and Samoff (1999), to give increased attention to the role and significance of local, cultural factors in the process of educational change.

We have also seen how some globalisation theorists recognise that one consequence of the impact of powerful international agendas is, ironically, the stimulation of different local responses. This is visible in Waters's framework reproduced earlier – albeit within broader common parameters. Attention to context, culture and difference is thus, simultaneously with globalisation, increasingly evident in the work of a wide range of academics, and in that carried out by professionals engaged more directly in matters of policy and practice. Crossley and Vulliamy's (1997b) rationale for increased qualitative research in developing countries, for example, illustrates this well. On a wider plane this represents a most significant shift; and an important coalescence of thinking that links qualitative research to earlier historical and interpretive traditions in the comparative field, and to poststructuralist respect for context and difference.

As Farrell suggests, the critique of global meta-theory and the assumptions of enlightenment science have been informed by post-modernist philosophers who have had a profound, if indirect and relatively marginalised, influence across the humanities and social sciences. To cite Usher (1996:28):

> Post-modernism challenges and displaces the abstract, transcendental subject, arguing instead that subjects cannot be separated from their subjectivity, history and socio-cultural location. In the post-modern, there are no Archimedean points, the subject is instead decentred, enmeshed in the 'text' of the world, constituted in inter-subjectivity, discourse and language.

Post-modern perspectives on the world distrust grand theories and meta-narratives while celebrating diversity, difference and the voices of the 'other'. Context and culture, located in both time and space, are given increased recognition, thus Gadamer (cited in Hammersley 1995:14) argues that ' … all knowledge reflects the socio-historical contexts of its production'.

Foucault (1972, 1977), Derrida (1981) and Lyotard (1984) are among the most influential writers who have pioneered post-modern perspectives (Peters 2001). At the heart of their analysis are arguments that maintain that the production and legitimisation of knowledge is as much a socio-cultural process as it is an objective science (see also Habermas 1978, 1990). This informs substantive work on the deconstruction of dominant world views, on discourse analysis and on the relationship between politics, knowledge and power. Apple (1993:46) thus argues that 'What counts as legitimate knowledge is the result of complex power relations and struggles among identifiable class, race, gender and religious groups'. Such analyses arise from and help to stimulate greater awareness of alternative movements and cultures, since knowledge is seen to be socially constructed, socially legitimated and related to time and place.[1]

While many challenges have, in turn, been raised against, for example, the relativism of post-modernism, the epistomological issues it deals with and its critique of positivistic social science are increasingly influential. Recognition of the 'authencity of other voices', for example, resonates well with innovative work carried out by international development workers who acknowledge the importance of understanding different world views and cultural differences at both the macro and the micro-level (see, for example, recent doctoral studies by Levesque 2001 and Ward 2002). Indeed, echoing Foucault, the work of Robinson-Pant (2001) thus suggests how the concept of development itself embodies colonising ambitions to reproduce other societies in its own image. Kempner (1998:456) recognises this, maintaining that:

> The rationalist assumptions of modernism are not capable of guiding educational reform towards a future that is capable of meeting the New Competition while meeting the needs of the least advantaged members of the society. Because the benefits of modernisation are not widely distributed among the social classes, educational reform should be guided by cognitive maps that reject rationalism and Eurocentrism. Such concepts of modernity perpetuate the colonialism of many developing countries not only by the industrialised countries but by their own upper classes.

Within the field of comparative and international education, we have already noted how attention to the potential of post-modern perspectives has, according to Cowen (1996b), come late. However, in 1991 Rust challenged the field to engage with the debate on post-modern ideas, and Paulston (1999:446) points to its liberating potential by noting that, '... letting go of modernity's language, let alone its essentialist and instrumental vision is easier advocated than achieved'. Accepting Rust's (1991) challenge, Paulston (1996, 1999) thus advances social cartography as a framework for future comparative and international studies of education, arguing that:

---

1 This section draws, with gratitude, upon discussions and reviews of literature carried out in collaboration with Keith Holmes at the University of Bristol.

> ... as comparativists we are ... well positioned to ... become social cartog-
> raphers, to compare and map multiple interpretations of social and
> educational life ... we are learning to recognise and include views of the
> Other, thus enlarging the scope of our vision and the diversity, or minute
> particulars, of our representations.
>
> (Paulston 1999:462–463)

The Ninth World Congress of Comparative Education Societies, held in
Sydney, Australia, adopted 'Tradition, Modernity and Post-modernity in
Education' as its core theme; the subsequently published papers draw
attention to the potential and limitations of post-modern perspectives
specifically for the field (Masemann and Welch 1997). Masemann's (1990)
own work, and her acknowledgement of different 'ways of knowing', further demonstrates the less often recognised linkages between the
epistemological and philosophical foundations of the post-modernist critique, and the qualitative research movement that has become increasingly
influential within comparative and international research. Examples of
research influenced by such ideas include comparisons of French and
English primary schools undertaken by Broadfoot *et al.* (1993, 2000), and
the comparatively rare ethnographic studies of education carried out in
developing countries, including Belize, Lesotho, Pakistan and St Lucia, as
reported by the contributors to Crossley and Vulliamy (1997a). Indeed, in
presenting a case for critical ethnography, Maseman (1982) more explicitly
explores how the mutual challenge to positivism, respect for multiple
social constructions of reality, and concern for the other, demonstrate
degrees of common ground with post-modern sensitivities. This is a theme
that Rust (1991:616) develops further in arguing that post-modernists
would:

> ... reject any claim that one way of knowing is the only legitimate way.
> Rather, they would say our task is to determine which approach to know-
> ing is appropriate to specific interests and needs rather than argue some
> universal application and validity, which ends up totalizing and confin-
> ing in its ultimate effect.

In concluding that 'we are witnessing a shift away from universal belief systems towards a plurality of belief systems', Rust (1991:618) gives further
legitimacy both to the qualitative, interpretivist paradigm, and to the post-
modern dimension in comparative and international research in education.

   The limitations of post-modernist literature are, however, also significant;
and help to explain why the implications of this work have often been overlooked or marginalised in the mainstream of educational research as a whole.
Firstly, the aforementioned relativism of post-modern perspectives has been
widely challenged, not least by Watson (1998), with respect to its validity and
utility in dealing with problems of policy and practice in the real world. This
relates closely to the self-indulgence noted earlier by Farrell (1997), and to

the failure of many of its chief proponents to communicate accessibly with a wide enough range of – and here is an irony – 'others' outside a narrow intellectual circle. The paradigm is also seen to be primarily Eurocentric and focused upon conditions and trends in high technology consumer societies (Young 1997). Some writers extend this form of critique to suggest that post-modernism represents an advanced form of cultural imperialism, and others charge that it neglects an appreciation of perspectives from the wider world. This is the view taken by Cowen (1996b:165–166) who argues that:

> Post-modernism, in its comparative dimensions, is impressively parochial: it does not reflect or read the structural socio-economic conditions, ideological projects, educational systems or self-society issues of identity in Japan, Taiwan or South Korea and, still less, China. It cannot easily be extended to understand the state projects for the construction of Islamic identity in Algeria, Iran, Malaysia or Pakistan and it would seem to have little to say about the crisis of state legitimisation and educational reform in Central and Eastern Europe.

For these reasons, in paying attention to research that underpins increased sensitivity to context, culture and difference, we turn also to the application and implications of post-colonial theory.

Post-colonialism itself is heavily influenced by post-modern philosophy and applies the concepts and techniques of, for example, discourse analysis and deconstruction. This perspective does, however, respond to some of the criticisms faced by post-modernism by giving greater attention to issues of culture and identity. This facilitates a more revealing interpretation of changing power relations produced by the processes of education, colonisation and decolonisation (Tikly 1999). Originating in work such as Said's (1978) *Orientalism*, Foucault's modes of analysis are applied to demonstrate how concepts are produced and used in ways that reinforce and maintain power relations. The term post-colonialism first gained acceptance during the 1980s and 1990s and was initially associated with work relating to literary theory and culture undertaken by scholars working from a critical tradition within the Third World. It now encompasses a broader range of work across many disciplines and according to Ashcroft *et al.* (1995:2):

> ... involves discussion of ... migration, slavery, suppression, resistance, representation, difference, race, gender and the responses of the influential master discourses of imperial Europe.

Moreover, as Hickling-Hudson (1998:327) argues:

> Post-colonial theory has specific uses in helping us to think about the nature of societies shaped or influenced by European colonisation and Euro-American imperialism, and of groups in these societies which have experienced these forms of domination as subject peoples.

As noted earlier, attention to knowledge and power relations, as with post-modernism, also helps us to critique globalisation and development studies in ways that more effectively reveal the teleological and hierarchical dangers of binary distinctions, such as 'developed' and' developing' countries, or the 'North' and the 'South'. This, therefore, offers a more coherent theoretical foundation for the critique of the colonially produced nation-state – and of the new forms of imperialism seen by many to be embedded in the concepts of neo-liberal free trade and globalisation. Such perspectives also recognise how economic control, as opposed to the political, now underpins much global power. As with post-modernism, however, post-colonial theorising has signifi-cant limitations relating to the accessibility of the specialist discourse itself – in addition to its own conceptual and analytical problems (see, for example, Hall 1996). It nevertheless has much potential to illuminate social complexities and, in so doing, to help increase our understanding of the relationships between globalisation, context and difference. To cite Hickling-Hudson's (1998:328) account of the potential of post-colonial frameworks again:

> … as an interpretative approach blending history and epistemology in specified locations it is useful in showing how interwoven is the post-colonial present with the colonial past.

Such perspectives help strengthen critiques of the dominance of externally imposed international agency agendas as articulated by writers such as Samoff (1996a, 1999); and arguments for the strengthening of local research capacity in developing countries; for increased collaboration between insiders and out-siders in comparative and international research, and for the participatory development strategies that are increasingly advocated in contemporary pol-icy documentation (Chambers 1995; Crossley and Holmes 2001).

In the light of this cumulative analysis we now move to a reconsideration of the major factors that are likely to influence the current and future agendas for comparative and international research in education. This is designed to help set the scene for Chapter 5, in which the text focuses more directly upon the identification and analysis of substantive issues and priorities for research within the field.

Factors shaping the comparative and international research agenda

Throughout this chapter, and the book as a whole, it is argued that the field of comparative and international education is especially well positioned to play a significant role in the advancement of educational research in an increas-ingly global era. Advantages of the field include its multi-disciplinary and applied foundations, its engagement with a diversity of theoretical frame-works, its traditional concern with the processes and agencies of international transfer and its sensitivity to contextual and cultural differences. In looking to the future, however, it is also argued that the field faces major theoretical, methodological and organisational challenges – and that, across all these dimensions, it must be fundamentally reconceptualised if it is to deal more effectively with the rapidly changing demands of the emergent twenty-first century.

In the light of the foregoing analysis, major factors that currently influence the nature of contemporary comparative and international research in education, and those that are likely to shape future agendas, can be more clearly identified. These we now reconsider, while acknowledging that, in broad scope, many stem directly from a combination of rapidly changing geopolitical relations and contemporary intellectual and paradigmatic developments.

Perhaps most fundamentally, our analysis reinforces the conviction that educational research, and comparative and international studies in particular, must adapt more explicitly to acknowledge the ongoing intensification of globalisation. As Ilon (1997:153) points out:

> Overlooking the pervasive influence of the global economy on local educational conditions renders educational policy impotent. Such policy is at risk of being misdirected, misinformed or simply missed altogether.

The rapid growth of interest in all aspects of globalisation suggests that educational researchers must engage more fully with the diversity of theoretical analyses available. For example, while we have shown that a significant contribution has already been made to the study of the mechanisms and agencies of globalisation, Dale (1999) is right in pointing out that much more needs to be done in this arena, if, to paraphrase Giddens (1999:6), we are to 'impose our will upon them' and 'achieve greater control over our runaway world'.

In a related way, the contemporary challenges to the nation-state as the primary unit of analysis point to the increased importance of alternative frameworks that enable us to deal better with the dilemmas of our times. This is not to suggest that the nation-state itself is no longer viable, or that it no longer has any currency for comparative research. However, concerted attention needs to be focused on the ways in which the place and role of the nation-state in education is 'transforming' under the influence of globalisation.

The increased power and influence of international agencies over educational policy and practice worldwide draws renewed attention to the significance of the critique of international transfer – a critique that is only belatedly acknowledging implications for the uncritical transfer of theory and methodology. We return to these issues later and when reconsidering the implications of paradigmatic shifts below. The exponential growth and impact of modern information and communications technologies adds markedly to the speed and range of the transfer process. This is, in its own right, a new and powerful factor that is re-shaping research agendas worldwide. As the work of Castells (1996) points out, the emergence of a 'network society' has fundamental implications for both the processes and nature of educational phenomenon in the future. Jarvis (2000), for example, depicts the transformations and dilemmas for education that are embodied in various conceptions of the learning society – and the implications of these for new modes of teaching and learning, new opportunities, new forms of inequality and, indeed, new research priorities.

Dramatic socio-political upheavals that characterised the last decades of the twentieth century have set in train major programmes of social and educational reform and reconstruction (McLeish and Phillips 1998; Mebrahtu *et al.* 2000; Griffin 2002). The implications of these highly visible – and often challenging – developments will no doubt continue to shape the scope and nature of much contemporary comparative and international research within, and beyond, the field of education. The demise of the Soviet Union has, for example, generated new motivations for the international transfer of ideas and ideologies, warranting research that offers potential practical benefits as well as theoretical insight and understanding. Moreover, the emergence of many new states, often small in size, vulnerable and marginalised in influence (Crossley and Holmes 1999), demonstrates the paradoxical effects of globalisation in stimulating both socio-political convergence and divergence. The interplay between the global, the national and the local will, indeed, profoundly influence research agendas in the future. To this we should add the impact of the resurgence of cultural and historical studies throughout the humanities and social sciences. This, as we have argued with respect to the implications of post-modernism and post-colonialism, is drawing increased attention to the significance of cultural factors and the concepts of identity and difference in all dimensions of educational research and development.

Such work, as we have shown, reinforces the contemporary intellectual critique of positivistic social science – and of the modernisation theory that has legitimated the nature of much formal international development assistance and related research. While the resurgence of interpretative, historical and critical research paradigms is increasingly visible within diverse academic communities, more positivistic assumptions continue to shape much social and educational policy and the mainstream of educational research and international development assistance. Market forces are thus likely to exert increased pressure upon the research community itself – especially in the consultancy arena (Preston and Arthur 1996; Samoff 1999). Indeed, the growth of tied consultancy work is a factor that may come to be increasingly significant in shaping research agendas worldwide – especially if the privatisation and funding control of the research enterprise increases. In a related way the growing demand from the 'stakeholders' of education for more relevant and policy-oriented research is a factor that will further generate applied research agendas that may bring both potential benefits and problems (Sebah 1999). Market forces, whatever the case, will therefore continue to play a major role in shaping the research agenda. They also deserve close and critical study in their own right, for as McGrath (2001a) points out with regard to international studies, the undue influence of policy-oriented funding agencies can threaten and undermine the independence, quality and very existence of the sort of critical research that is essential if we are to challenge global and ideological orthodoxy. The current commitment of national and multilateral development agencies to a common poverty agenda is illustrative of this dilemma. Indeed, while this is undoubtedly an important theme that will, and should, help to shape ongoing future research agendas, it is an issue that is both laudable for its aspirations, and questionable for its potential to oversimplify and overly dominate some discourses (McGrath 2001a).

Returning to the cross-cultural dimensions of our analysis, we argue that the growth of comparative and international research communities world-wide will further influence and enrich the scope and nature of the field – and in ways that may well help to enhance recognition of alternative cultural per-spectives on the education and identities of marginal groups (see, for example, Aikman 1997). To cite Dimmock's (2000: 289–290) critique of school management theory and policy research:

> There is a clear need for robust cross-cultural comparative research in schooling, school leadership, management and organisation. Developments along these lines are dependent on the emergence of valid cross-cultural frameworks, models and dimensions, research instruments and empirical studies which identify similarities and differences, conver-gences and divergences, and the cultural explanations underlying them between schools in different societies. When the field of educational administration and policy begins to move along these lines, it will be well on the way to developing a sophistication of theory and practice befitting the twenty-first century.

To conclude this chapter, much more could be said, but it is clear that the largely theoretical and methodological factors that we have raised here have major implications for ways in which the field can be reconceptualised, and for the substantive issues and priorities that do, or should, comprise the con-temporary research agenda. Possibilities for reconceptualisation are the focus of Chapters 7 and 8, and implications for the nature and form of substantive issues and priorities are addressed in the next two chapters.

Chapter 5

Changing research agendas

Issues and priorities

In the previous chapters of this book we have identified a range of contemporary challenges facing the field of comparative and international education, and have questioned the ways in which research problems have most commonly been conceptualised. We have also begun to examine the implications of this analysis for the ways in which such research is carried out. In this chapter we build upon these theoretical and methodological perspectives to focus more directly upon their implications for the substantive educational issues and priorities that warrant concerted attention in current and future work. In doing this, we acknowledge that it is both unrealistic, and inappropriate, to attempt to present any form of definitive or comprehensive research agenda for all. Indeed, more in tune with the spirit of the book as a whole, we argue that – especially in times of rapid socio-cultural change – newly emerging issues and priorities deserve clearer articulation and consideration from a wider variety of intellectual and cultural perspectives. We therefore contribute our own assessment of emergent issues and priorities to this broader discourse, to help stimulate further critical thinking, and to encourage others actively to engage in advancing the debate. This is done in a way that is consistent with the evolving critique of the field and with our associated reconceptualisation thesis. We therefore do not attempt to cover every substantive issue that merits contemporary attention, but we do hope our own construction of priorities will both help to illustrate the potential of the broader critique that we develop here, and prove stimulating for others in its own right.

In the interests of clarity and coherence, we group related substantive issues together. This helps to focus our suggestions around a number of potential research themes that best demonstrate the significance of our related theoretical and methodological arguments. In this respect the chapter underpins our argument for a closer 'bridging' between the diverse worlds of educational research, theory and practice. This, in turn, points to what we argue is the increasingly important role of philosophical, epistemological and cultural factors in shaping both research agendas and educational development priorities for the future. Chapter 6 extends some aspects of the analysis begun here, where the issues and priorities raised relate more directly to

changing global agendas and to their implications for international development co-operation.

While a combination of rapidly changing geopolitical relations and paradigmatic challenges may have stimulated the need for change, in earlier
chapters we have noted how the field of comparative and international education now has an expanded audience and a wider constituency of actors to
satisfy. This, in itself, has implications for the shaping of the research agenda –
and generates related tensions concerning the maintenance of theoretical priorities and the advancement of critical scholarship. To cite Apple's (2001:421)
recent contribution to the rethinking of priorities for comparative education:

> As Pierre Bourdieu reminds us, one of the most important activities
> scholars can engage in during this time of economic rationalism and
> imperial neo-conservatism is to analyse critically the production and cir-
> culation of these discourses and their effects on the lives of so many
> people in so many nations.

Elsewhere in the same article Apple goes on to argue that:

> All too often, analyses of globalisation and the intricate combination of
> neo-liberalism and neo-conservatism remain on a meta-theoretical level,
> disconnected from the actual lived realities of real schools, teachers, stu-
> dents and communities. While such meta-theoretical work is crucial, its
> over-use has left a vacancy.
>
> (Apple 2001:421)

It is in this spirit that our contribution to the construction of new agendas and
priorities for the attention of comparative and international research is made.
Firstly, however, we re-connect with our historical review, and reflect upon
what we see as the dominant issues that have attracted most recent research
attention – in the light of the broader historical, contemporary and contextual
factors to which they are related.

Changing issues and priorities

The last two decades of the twentieth century were, in many ways, dominated
by economic concerns that had a major influence upon social and educational
trends and priorities worldwide. The focus of much social science research
thus reflected the nature and tone of the dominant economic discourse, and
the competitive, assessment and accountability culture that it generated.
Indeed, as the challenges raised by the 2002 British Broadcasting Corporation
(BBC) Reith Lectures on the theme of trust (O'Neill 2002) so well demonstrate,
we are today grappling with the human impact and social implications of
what has been called the 'assessment society' (Broadfoot and Pollard 1999).
Work by Broadfoot (1996) and Little (2000a) illustrates the contemporary and
global significance of the latter issues well, and the enduring pertinence of

Dore's 'diploma disease' thesis demonstrates the seminal influence of comparative studies in this arena (see Dore 1976, 1997).

Comparative and international education research priorities that dominated this period across a variety of contexts connected closely, and often critically, with sustained efforts to link education to improved economic competitiveness. In this climate the education policy agenda has been progressively oriented towards training needs, skills development strategies and the promotion of an efficient and adaptable workforce. The term 'human resource development' captures this emphasis well, and illustrates how fundamental changes in professional cultures and values influence both the substance and the language – the discourse – that is adopted. In England and Wales the recent governmental re-branding of its own education department as the Department for Education and Skills (DFES) is, itself, revealingly symbolic. Much attention has, as indicated earlier, also been paid by policy makers, both in the North and the South, to the implementation of educational reforms. This has, in turn, provided a focus for much comparative and international research that examined the imperative for reform, the impact of culture and context on learning, and the similarities and differences in the change strategies applied within and between education systems (Broadfoot *et al.* 1993; Pollard *et al.* 1994; Buchert 1998; Broadfoot *et al.* 2000; Bray and Lee 2001).

The international influence of the performativity culture has been advanced by the rapid globalisation of neo-liberalism and marketisation (Lee 1991; Green 1997; Peschar and Van der Wal 2000; Muckle and Morgan 2001; Mok and Chan 2002), to the extent that the possibility of alternative development models has, for many, been almost eclipsed. The demise of the former Soviet Union, and the subsequent transfer of 'turbo' capitalism into Eastern Europe, for example, helped inspire Fukuyama's (1992) 'end of history' thesis – and underpinned the rapid, but problematic, adoption of neo-liberal educational policies, in transitional societies such as Estonia (Märja and Jõgi 2000), Poland (Elsner 2000) and the former East Germany (Pritchard 2002).

Supporting the broadly neo-liberal market philosophy came increased attention to effectiveness and accountability via new modes of evaluation, performance indicators, the prioritisation of leadership and management training, the previously noted emphasis on examinations and assessment, and the use of comparative league tables. Reflecting such trends are studies by, for example, Dalin *et al.* (1994) on school improvement strategies; research by Reynolds *et al.* on school effectiveness (1994); Levin and Lockheed's (1993) application of school effectiveness research in developing countries, and Harber and Davies' (1997) more critical standpoint taken to the transfer of Western management and effectiveness models to the South. Since comparative league tables have come to feature particularly prominently at the local, national and international levels in recent years, they deserve special mention here.

Indeed, it could be argued that national enthusiasms for school, university and other public sector league tables was stimulated by the assumed potential of international league tables generated by the early IEA studies of school performance. The first of these were conducted and attracted attention long before investment in national and local league table systems became accepted as a useful strategy for quality assurance (Postlethwaite 1999). Since the IEA studies are perhaps the most well known and highly resourced comparative studies in the arena of education, the influence of comparative research carried out from the 1970s can thus – with dubious honour – be seen to have had a marked impact worldwide.

Also connected to changing economic circumstances, European studies of post-compulsory education carried out by writers such as King *et al.* (1974, 1975; UNESCO 1977) reflected growing awareness of the increased speed of change, and of the need to prepare new generations for uncertain futures. E.J. King's (1979a) concern with 'uncertainty', indeed, anticipated later developments that are now reflected in contemporary conceptions of the 'risk society' (Beck 1992). Work carried out within the last two decades of the twentieth century is also notable for its attention to feminist theory and gender (see work by Stromquist 1997, 1998), and for recognition of the increased plurality of societies worldwide (Grant 1977; Fry and Kempner 1996). This included attention to the educational implications of multiculturalism and the needs of minorities, indigenous peoples and diverse language groups. Despite this, however, economic priorities, perhaps inevitably, continued to dominate many core policy and research agendas alike.

The last two decades have also seen much global convergence in terms of educational policies and priorities resulting from the combined influence of international development agencies such as UNESCO, UNDP and the World Bank. Edited collections published by Buchert (1998) and King and Buchert (1999) help to chart such trends, but these developments deserve closer attention in the light of the globalisation dilemmas being considered here. In Chapter 6 we therefore more thoroughly explore the role that international agencies have played in promoting the international transfer of, for instance, policy proposals relating to marketisation, accountability, de-centralisation, management training, skills development and assessment. In Chapter 6, we also examine the rise to prominence of the commitment of global agencies to basic education throughout the South, to poverty reduction strategies, to gender equality and inclusivity, and to the quality and relevance of educational provision. These are all issues of such contemporary importance that they will inevitably continue to dominate educational policy and research agendas worldwide for the foreseeable future.

More recently, however, widespread policy deliberations have also begun to focus upon newer issues, such as the impact and application of new information technologies, the concepts of lifelong learning and the learning society and – most pertinently here – the implications of intensified globalisation for the reform of education and training. In the context of these and related developments, we now explore what, in the light of our own analysis, we see as new and emergent priorities that could make a creative, stimulating and helpful contribution to the advancement of the field of comparative and international research as a whole.

Emergent and future priorities

Reflecting on concern with the relationship between globalisation, context and difference that runs throughout this volume, we first, and most fundamentally, argue that future comparative and international research agendas have much to gain from more concerted efforts to promote increased cultural and contextual sensitivity. At the broadest level this points to the need for more in-depth and critical analyses of the diverse implications of globalisation for education in different cultural contexts. Green (1997), for example, has shown how Western conceptions and assessments of globalisation currently dominate the existing literature – and the related policy discourse. His work also demonstrates how, in many Western nations, skills formation is rapidly assuming increased prominence in educational policy, to the detriment of the more human, aesthetic and liberal aspects of education – whereas values and social and cultural objectives remain more clearly visible in Asia. As indicated earlier, however, little in-depth, empirical work has been done on differing local and national conceptions of globalisation, and of related perceptions of the implications for education and training. The result is that Western perspectives and Western research in this relatively new arena are currently in danger of overly dominating policy considerations elsewhere – to the possible detriment of both improved success in policy implementation and further theoretical advancement. A growing awareness of such issues is visible in work by writers across a wide range of disciplines – including political science, economics, sociology and cultural studies – but, as we argue throughout this volume, the field of comparative and international education is particularly well placed to make a more substantial contribution to such research. We have already noted, for example, how, to date, few in-depth and critical studies relating to the implications of globalisation have been carried out within Sub-Saharan Africa (Tikly 2001). This is despite the fact that development co-operation agencies are already advancing new 'skills for development' initiatives, founded largely upon existing Western interpretations of the potential benefits of globalisation for the South as a whole (DFID 2000). Here is a crucial arena for future multidisciplinary, comparative and international research that holds significant applied and theoretical potential, to explore how beneficial such 'skills for development' really are. It may be, for example, that local craft skills, communities and cultures are being threatened by the economic forces of globalisation. A social 'mapping' of community views, as advocated by Paulston (1996), may thus be helpful in documenting differing perspectives – perhaps conducted through collaborative and participatory strategies of field research (Penny *et al.* 2000). Preliminary collaborative research carried out in Tanzania and Rwanda by one of the present writers, and colleagues (Dachi *et al.* 2002) certainly demonstrates the multi-level implications of such analyses – revealing how the perceived impact of globalisation differs between social groups at the local level. Tanzanian stakeholders from the educated urban élite thus perceive greater opportunities stemming from increased globalisation in Tanzania than do research informants from poorer, more isolated rural community contexts. The potential for further in-depth ethnographic and comparative studies, as advocated by Crossley and Vulliamy (1984, 1997a), thus emerges forcefully from this work. So too does the significance of studies undertaken by, or in collaboration with, local researchers familiar with the cultures and contexts in question.

At the international level the engagement with globalisation highlights the enduring significance of the comparativist's critique of the processes of international transfer (Crossley 1984; Phillips 1989; Finegold *et al.* 1992). Building upon Dale's (1999) work on the mechanisms of globalisation, empirically grounded studies of the new architecture of international development co-operation (see, for example, Mundy and Murphy 2001), and of the implications of bodies such as the World Trade Organisation (WTO) and the General Agreement on Trade in Services (GATS), therefore have much to contribute. As Robertson *et al.* (2002) argue, GATS interprets education as a private and commercial enterprise, and failure to critique the application of market principles in this arena ignores the political foundations and neo-colonial implications of such global enterprises.

Moreover, such analyses point to the differences identified between internationalism and globalisation, and to attendant concerns about democratic prospects worldwide. As Jones (1998:143) pertinently observes:

> The logic of globalisation contrasts markedly with that of internationalism. The latter, with its intrinsically democratic foundation, looks to a world ordered by structures supportive of that functionalism which is embedded in accountability. Globalisation, by contrast, implies few logical imperatives in favour of accountability, but rather looks to the pursuit of interest on the global level through the operation of unfettered capitalism.

Connecting with our consideration of priorities for future attention, Jones (1998:153) goes on to maintain that:

> Those interested in promoting or studying education in international perspective will find a more complex world order than ever before, with the logic of internationalism under threat from an increasingly differentiated and anarchic framework for the conduct of international relations ... Of particular importance is the need to think afresh about the nature and importance of democracy, democratic institutions and accountability.

Further attention to the changing nature and modalities of international agencies is given in Chapter 6; however, as Welch indicates (2001), concern with democracy also points to future priorities for comparative and international research on a variety of other theoretical, methodological and substantive levels. A recent special issue of *Compare*, the journal of the British Association for International and Comparative Education (BAICE), for example, suggests ways forward by looking at *Changing Contexts For Democracy And Citizenship*, and highlighting 'evidence of the challenges to education for democracy and citizenship that are posed by changes in the world order' (Davies 2002:4; see also Schweisfurth *et al.* 2002). Contributors to this special issue identify threats to democracy generated by the reproduction of a 'dominant culture, which is increasingly becoming influenced by the global economic market' (Jarvis 2002:5). While Jarvis is specifically concerned to maintain the democratic and radical foundations of adult education traditions, other contributors explore implications for feminist perspectives on citizenship and governance (Preece 2002); the democratisation and decentralisation of education in South Africa (Sayed 2002) and in Taiwan (Law 2002); and analyses of educational reform, culture and citizenship in Germany (Pritchard 2002; Arthur 2002) and Brazil (Bueno Fischer and Hannah 2002). Pertinently, the potential benefits of multi-level analyses are also usefully demonstrated by this collection of studies – emphasising the relationship between global, national and local trends and issues.

Linking to notions of diversity and difference that underpin much of our analysis, cultural issues, it is argued, deserve greatly increased attention in future comparative and international research. To some extent this reflects earlier emphasis pursued within the field, and relates to the importance of the context sensitivity arguments articulated above. It is also connected, for example, to growing awareness of the role of cultural identity in facilitating learning, acknowledgement of the place of values in education (Cummings *et al.* 1998), and – in an ever more mobile world – the increased demand for educators able to deal with the learning needs of multicultural groups of students. Perhaps even more pertinently for our own analysis, the emergence of a diversity of new comparative and international literatures – often stemming from different cultural perspectives – points to major new intellectual arenas for the future. Illustrating the potential of such developments is Hayhoe and Pan's work on Knowledge Across Cultures (2001), and Bray and Gui's seminal study (2001) of comparative education traditions across Greater China – the Mainland, Taiwan, Hong Kong and Macau. The latter is a study that draws upon many rich and original Chinese language sources to examine how comparative education has evolved differently across the four Chinese contexts, and how these differences compare with developments elsewhere. In doing so, this work draws renewed attention to the importance of historical analysis, and challenges much of the existing English language literature by demonstrating the cross-cultural limitations of the generic Western phases formulated to represent the history of the field as a whole. In a related study documenting the research career of Gu Mingyuan (2001) Professor of Comparative Education at Beijing Normal University, the post-1949 Chinese traditions reflected in Professor Gu's approach to comparative education thus contrast strongly with the more empirical 'scientific' paradigm that is used to represent the post-World War II period by writers such as Noah and Eckstein (1969, 1998). This further emphasises the future potential of work that acknowledges the past and ongoing diversity of the many comparative educations – work that, we argue, much enriches this multidisciplinary field.

Looking more directly at the cultural dimension of teaching and learning, research by writers such as E. Thomas (2000); Cummings *et al.* (2001) and Louisy (2001) highlights the need for future studies that more systematically explore the influences of culture upon the processes of teaching and learning. Alexander's (2000) in-depth study of Culture and Pedagogy in five nations (England, France, India, Russia and the United States) helps to point the way for further work in this respect, by exploring the ways in which children's educational experiences are shaped by multiple levels of contextual, cultural and historical influences. In this he is building on the work of earlier comparative scholars such as Hans (1959a and b; 1964) and Mallinson (1975) – and upon the work of more contemporary colleagues. While significant contributions have also been made with reference to *The Chinese Learner* (Watkins and Biggs 1996, 2001), these advances clearly establish the need for work in a wider range of cultural contexts, and with reference to situations where teaching and learning is carried out with and within cross-cultural groups (Trahar 2002). Louisy (2001) thus maintains that questions about 'whose knowledge' we use and 'for whose benefit' are central to the future of comparative and international education. Arguing for a stronger Caribbean perspective in the establishment of contemporary educational research agendas, she draws upon Creole languages, post-colonial theorising, cultural studies and local conceptions of knowledge. Work informed by such perspectives, Louisy argues, will more effectively contribute to an improved understanding of educational dilemmas within her home state of St Lucia. In considering the regional implications of globalisation, this work contributes more to the future development of the field by advocating the strengthening of local research capacity, and by calling for Caribbean nationals to play a more central and international role in comparative and international research within the social sciences, across the humanities and beyond. In concluding, Louisy also well demonstrates the creative potential of increased cross-cultural dialogue, and echoes the multi-cultural aspirations for the future of the field that are central to Hayhoe and Pan's (2001) edited collection referred to above. Indeed, the designation of 2001 as the 'Year of Dialogue among Civilizations' by the United Nations, helps to reinforce our own commitment to collaborative research, to the bridging of cultures and traditions (Crossley 2000) and to increased dialogue between all stakeholders in both educational research and educational development. These are, however, more methodological issues that we will return to in later chapters. Implications of these emergent trends are, moreover, closely related to ongoing concerns with the relationship between learning and identity and with familiar and ever important equity issues connected to class, race and gender.

Much of the above discussion draws attention to the centrality of power differentials, and the implications of political factors for advances in the future of comparative and international research. This can be seen in the analysis of global influences on educational policy, and in teaching and learning dilemmas related to aspects of culture and identity. Issues of power can also be seen to underpin many questions relating to the contemporary emergence of what has been called the 'knowledge economy'. As Foucault argues 'power is closely related to the ability to control knowledge and meaning' (cited in Ward 2002:290). Comparative and international studies of the impact and implications of the knowledge economy thus have much to offer – especially in the light of the enhanced position given to 'knowledge for development' in the re-framing of the World Bank as a knowledge bank. As Gmelin and King (2001:5) point out:

> ... another fashion seems to be sweeping through the agency world, a fascination with knowledge management and knowledge sharing. Again, there is a connection with the World Bank and its sponsorship of a series of 'knowledge projects'. And again, our concern is with the implications for the developing world of the new knowledge architecture being erected in the North.

While we pay detailed attention to international agency issues in Chapter 6, the implications of the relationship between power and knowledge generate a broader range of issues that warrant future consideration and further attention here. These include the role and impact of information and communications technology in pioneering new forms of teaching and learning, concepts and implications of the 'Network Society' (Castells 1996), the dilemmas of the 'digital divide' both within and between nations, and the impact of English as the dominant global language to the detriment of the local (Watson 1999d). To cite Marginson and Mollis (2001:601), there is an urgent need to recognise power relations within the scope of comparative and international education, and for new research on:

> ... the new geo-political educational structures of power in a globalizing world, to study international education including on-line education, and to consider new forms of governance and identity ... other than the national.

More disturbingly, many contemporary policy trends potentially heighten the role of education and knowledge in the intensified competition that is being experienced from the global to the individual level (see, for example, Carnoy 1999). This in itself warrants careful comparative analysis – but if it is combined with increasing global inequalities that can fuel cross-cultural conflict and misunderstandings, the dangers for all in our globally connected world could be further magnified. Re-connecting with the traditional humanitarian concerns of the field of comparative and international education thus emerges, for us, as a major priority for the future. In recognising this dimension of the field, Retamal and Aedo-Richmond (1998:1) draw attention to the deepening of global disparities and the way in which the political optimism generated following the fall of the Berlin Wall has been:

... challenged by the appearance of religious, ethnic and nationalistic conflicts witnessing profound inhumanity and viciousness. New and old
forms of ideological nihilism and political intolerance have generated
uncontrollable explosions of violence around the world.

This work focuses upon the significance of refugee education, first as a
humanitarian response, and secondly with reference to its implications for
political transition and national development.

More broadly, we see comparative and international research concerning
education's role in national reconstruction in distressing contexts such as
Palestine, Afghanistan or Rwanda, as a strategically important contribution to
efforts to understand the causes of conflict. In a similar way, this could
include future comparative work on the educational implications of national
reconciliation initiatives such as those pursued in South Africa, and broader
analyses designed to foster improved international understanding and
reduced global conflict. In many senses this relates closely to the cross-cultural understanding rationale for comparative and international education
articulated most strongly in the post-World War II era, and to the contemporary calls for increased dialogue between cultures that we considered earlier
in this chapter. Certainly, comparative and international research is well
placed to highlight the nature and extent of global disparities, the dilemmas
encountered by marginalised groups and the potential role for education in
dealing with such issues.

Pointing to the distinctive dilemmas faced by the world's small states, for
example, the March 2002 Commonwealth Heads of Government Meeting
(CHOGM) held in Australia reported that:

> Heads of Government reaffirmed their view that small states are particu-
> larly vulnerable to international developments and natural disasters and
> confront a range of structural challenges to sustainable development ...
> In that context, they endorsed the New Agenda for Commonwealth work
> on small states, which identified key priorities for the short and medium
> term. These included notably that the Commonwealth should provide
> appropriate assistance on trade issues, including working with the inter-
> national community to strengthen small states representations at the
> WTO, promote dialogue on the OECD Harmful Tax Initiative and take
> action to help mitigate the impact on small states of the events of 11
> September and their aftermath.
>
> (CHOGM 2002:4)

While this usefully articulates the contemporary problems faced by one marginalised group of nation-states, it also illustrates the importance of the
multidisciplinary perspective that enables comparative and international
research to develop a holistic analysis of development problems, and of the
relationship between education, society and globalisation. The humanitarian
dimension of the field also draws attention to education beyond mainstream

provision, be it in the form of non-formal provision, adult education, lifelong learning or community development initiatives as emphasised by many NGOs (Preston 1997).

In tune with our evolving critique of the field much of the foregoing analysis calls for increased reflexivity in the research process. This, in turn, requires the repeated questioning of many previously taken for granted assumptions by all participants. Given our parallel concern to seek ways of improving the contribution of the field to educational policy and practice, our own research suggests that a more culturally sensitive reconsideration of the concept and use of time, time as a resource, be built into future work on the process of educational reform. As argued elsewhere (Van der Eyken *et al.* 1995), the ticking of the 'Western clock' dominates the progress of much international development work – often to the detriment of the formation of effective partnerships, collaboration, ownership – or, indeed, meaningful dialogue. Unrealistic and culturally insensitive time factors are perhaps most often recognised as a problem by practitioners but, to date, this is an issue that has been given only lip service by policy makers and scant theoretical attention by the research community. What makes it especially significant in the comparative and international arena is the fact that the pace of change is currently intensifying, and different cultures engage with this somewhat invisible resource differently (Crossley 1993). By way of illustration, the following extract taken from an editorial from the Pakistan daily newspaper, *The News* (29 December 1999), usefully reveals differing interpretations and implications of time, both within and between nations:

> We in Pakistan fluctuate between several calendars. Most people still begin the day at first light and not at midnight. They fast according to the lunar calendar and celebrate the Eid, which is changeable, according to the cycles of the moon. The offices, which live by the Gregorian calendar, give two days holidays but hardly ever three to cater for the Eid falling after 30 days. The tiller of the soil counts his months from an ancient Hindu calendar which goes back to 1000 BC. That is why he still talks of Saun, Bhadon (the months of rain) and Jeth (the month of heat). Modernity has brought the ticking clock but the ordinary Pakistani still lives in the Agrarian, pre-modern mindset. In this mindset the season is important as it is connected with food but arbitrary divisions of it are not. Time, after all, is an unending flow and it becomes a tyrant only when we enter the modern age.
>
> (cited in Ward 2002:viii)

Differences such as these go a long way in explaining cultural resistance to innovation, contrasting responses to reform initiatives, and the barriers faced in translating partnership rhetoric into successful practice. This can be seen to apply not only in the international arena, but also in increasing our understanding of differences in the perceptions and actions of different levels of policy makers and practitioners. Implications for a more thorough, sustained and reflexive critique of the assumed benefits of international development targets represent a further related issue for priority attention. Indeed, as we document in the following chapter, such international targets, and time frames, are repeatedly revised (and renamed) in the light of apparently 'disappointing' experiences in meeting their expectations.

Sustainability thus emerges as a further connected theme that we suggest warrants increased attention in the future – and this we relate to many of the issues raised above. It is a dilemma faced by policy makers and practitioners in both the North and the South, and it is an issue that has both practical and theoretical implications. Perhaps more pointedly here, this is an example that demands increased attention to the importance of cultural and contextual sensitivities in both educational research and educational development. Studies of sustainable educational reform or sustainable national development – perhaps focused upon successful practice – could benefit greatly from more in-depth cross-cultural analyses, enhanced reflexivity and a more critical and culturally informed consideration of time as both a concept and a resource.

Furthermore, this brief exploration of the centrality of sustainability also well illustrates potential linkages between substantive research issues and research processes. As we have argued elsewhere, much existing comparative and international research suggests that participatory approaches to research, and collaborations between theorists, policy makers and practitioners hold considerable potential for the improved sustainability of innovatory practice in the future (Reimers and McGinn 1997; Crossley and Holmes 2001; Ginsburg and Gorostiaga 2001). This is characteristic of, for example, Gibbons et al.'s (1994) proposals for a 'transdisciplinary' mode of enquiry that sees research as a socio-cultural process. It is also reflected in Delanty's (1997) notion of social science as 'discursive practice' whereby collective problems are democratically identified and defined. Social researchers, Delanty proposes, must mediate between social science and society to enable research to recover its public role. These challenges to contemporary and future comparative and international educational research thus go beyond the choice of substantive issues, and are as much theoretical, methodological and organisational in nature.

To cite Reimers and McGinn:

> By recognising that education systems are not machines but are arenas for conflict, and that what education systems do reflects how people construct their roles regarding these systems, researchers can facilitate the development of knowledge and sustained organisational learning. The key guides are democratic dialogue, empowerment, time, persistence, and patience.
>
> (1997:190)

They conclude with a cautionary, and comparative, note, however, by adding: 'This is not a panacea, a quick fix, or a magic bullet that will lead to success everywhere' (Reimers and McGinn 1997:190).

Conclusions

In this chapter we have reflected in broad scope upon the changing issues and priorities that have commanded the attention of comparative and international research in education in recent decades. In doing so we have extended our historical analysis of the field, begun in Chapter 2, into the present. In the light of our emerging critique of the field, we have also identified a number of new issues and priorities that we suggest warrant increased attention in the future. This is not intended in any way to represent a complete and detailed review, or to suggest a comprehensive agenda for the future – but it is presented as one purposefully focused contribution to the contemporary advancement of the field. We have, therefore, concentrated upon identifying a select number of substantive issues that best demonstrate the wider significance of our related theoretical and methodological arguments. The chapter is thus designed to engage with contemporary developments in a way that emphasises, in particular, how a diversity of cultural and contextual factors demand increased recognition in the future development and re-orientation of the field of comparative and international research in education.

In undertaking the reviews presented both here and in the following chapter, we recognise that a number of currently dominant issues and priorities will, inevitably, continue to command much research attention in the future. These include, for example, a complex range of issues related to marketisation and the global spread of neo-liberal agendas, privatisation, decentralisation and assessment and accountability. They include the persistence of inequities stemming from issues of class, race and gender; skills development training and socio-economic transition; the quality and outcomes of education; and the international community's prioritisation of basic education reform and the role of education in poverty reduction strategies.

In looking to the future we also acknowledge the emergence of new globally significant priorities relating to issues such as the impact on education of new information technologies, AIDS and other health-related concerns, notions of lifelong learning, especially in societies where people are living longer, as well as the impact of globalisation itself. Our own analysis, however, points more directly to the need for greater critique in such analyses – and to the centrality of cultural and context sensitivity within both the educational research and educational development arenas. Our substantive research priorities for the future of the field thus emphasise issues of culture, identity, democracy, power and difference. We highlight the importance of enhanced cross-cultural dialogue; the social, educational and citizenship goals of education; the role of knowledge in development; the cultural dimension of teaching and learning; the new architecture of international development; reflexivity, and culturally informed critiques of the concept of time; the sustainability of educational reform; and the resurgence of the humanitarian dimension of comparative and international research in education.

At the heart of our rationale, however, are questions that relate as much to theory and methodology as they do to the emergence of new substantive issues. This brings us back to the potential of the different cultural contributions to the field of comparative and international research, to the advances that poststructuralist critiques have made across the social sciences and humanities in recent times, and to the importance of more substantial dialogue between all involved in educational research and development. In calling for a more effective bridging of cultures and traditions, we are therefore acknowledging the importance of the diversity of comparative educations – while, simultaneously, recognising the immense potential for the field that can be gained from the enhanced interchange of ideas, insights and understandings. This requires increased recognition of differing perspectives, mutual respect for alternative positions and a more genuine commitment to the sort of intellectual, professional and multi-level dialogue that is essential for truly multidisciplinary comparative and international research in education.

We return to the implications of this analysis for the future of the field in Chapters 7 and 8. This follows a more detailed consideration of issues, some of which have been foreshadowed here, that relate more directly to global agendas and international development cooperation.

Chapter 6

Educational research, global agendas and international development co-operation

Among the major influences that have shaped global education policy, and evolving comparative and international research agendas, has been the impact of powerful agencies such as UNESCO and the World Bank. In this chapter we document how multilateral and bilateral agencies have influenced international perspectives on education, and how global agendas have emerged and been reformulated in the half century since the end of World War II. Building upon a number of issues first raised in Chapter 5, we pay particular attention here to the less developed countries of the world, and to changing relationships between the rich countries of the North and the poorer ones of the South. In this respect, we consider efforts to move away from a development assistance paradigm characterised by the terms 'donors' and 'recipients' – with their overtones of neo-colonial superiority – towards models that attempt to promote new forms of co-operation and collaborative partnerships. [The terms 'North' and 'South' first became widely accepted in both academic and development discourse as a result of the Brandt Reports in the early 1980s (Brandt 1980; 1983)]. We also demonstrate how global solutions have increasingly come to be promoted as a means of dealing with apparently common problems across different societies – regardless of their appropriateness in such varied contexts. Indeed, despite increased theoretical recognition of the importance of policy dialogue between local and global stakeholders, in practice the power and financial dominance of the funding countries and agencies means that they can, and do, still lay down conditionalities for development assistance, and they can still promote dependency by shaping what they perceive to be in the best interests of others. As we argue throughout this chapter, and the book as a whole, such global disparities necessitate new ways of pursuing the long-term relationships between local, national and global agencies if we are genuinely to improve the quality and impact of comparative and international research, consultancy and development co-operation.

Aid for educational development

Overseas aid has been part of the international political scene for over 40 years, although the more euphemistic term, technical assistance, which came to refer to aid to the education, health and welfare sectors, emerged a little later. Some of the early books on aid (Pearson 1969; Hayter 1971; Mende 1973; Cassen 1986; Mosley 1987) hardly mentioned education, reflecting the low priority given to human resource development at the time. Mosley (1987:1) thus states that 'Aid is money transferred on concessional terms by the governments of rich countries to the governments of poor countries'. In the immediate post-war years, with the creation of the International Monetary Fund (IMF) and the International Bank for Reconstruction and Development (the World Bank), initial concerns were thus focused upon the economic reconstruction of Europe and Japan, rather than upon social issues or the development priorities of the rest of the world. The latter were still largely assumed to be the responsibility of the colonial powers, even though they had, in turn, been weakened by war.

Five factors were to change this and were to help locate education more firmly within the development process – though this is not well reflected in spending terms, and many agencies have been unable to disaggregate the sums spent on education as opposed to general economic development (Mende 1973; King and Carr-Hill 1992; Lewin 1992; Bennell and Furlong 1997). As Watkins (2000:239) points out: 'At least eight OECD countries allocate less than 1 per cent of their aid programmes to education, while only three – Denmark, Germany and Sweden – allocate 5 per cent or more.'

Nevertheless, factors that helped to heighten the role of education in both the conceptualisation and process of development were:

1   The creation of UNESCO in 1945 as a key United Nations agency with a responsibility for developing basic education and literacy (Jones 1988, 1990; IJED 1999).
2   The signing of the United Nations Declaration of Human Rights in December 1948, Article 26 of which identified education as a central and basic human right. This was to have a profound influence on the shape of educational development throughout the world in the subsequent decades, and can be seen to have influenced many of the then newly independent countries' constitutions and education plans.
3   The process of de-colonisation which began in the late 1940s with the granting of independence to India, Pakistan, Burma (Myanmar), Ceylon (Sri Lanka), and the Philippines and which accelerated during the 1950s and 1960s. Many of the newly independent governments saw the expansion of their fledgling education systems as essential for their social and economic development and sought assistance from their former colonial powers.
4   The designation of the 1960s, by the United Nations, as the first Development Decade. This, combined with the de-colonisation process, led to the creation of many bilateral aid agencies in Europe and North America. Amongst these were the United States Agency for International Development (USAID); Britain's Overseas Development Ministry, later the Department for International Development (DFID); the Canadian

International Development Agency (CIDA); Norway's aid agency
(NORAD); Sweden's International Development Agency (SIDA); and the
German Foundation for International Development (DSE). These and
other emergent agencies each formulated their own educational priorities
and agendas.

5   The publication of the World Bank's first Education Sector Working Paper
(World Bank 1971), which heralded the emergence of the World Bank as a
significant player in the educational development arena. Gradually the
Bank assumed a position of pre-eminence, not only in its role as chief funder for education, but also through its research and data bases which
have come to dominate the shaping of the policies of many bilateral agencies and individual nation states (King, K. 1991a and b, 1992; Jones 1992;
Samoff 1996a; Mundy 2002).

These five developments were to change the ways in which the rich countries
related to the developing world; were to stimulate the international transfer
of ideas and policies; were to generate new theoretical perspectives and
research in the field of comparative and international education; and were to
have a major influence on the educational agendas of nations worldwide. It is
to the nature of these developments that we now turn, with particular reference to the educational priorities and dilemmas that they have generated,
their implications for multilateral and bilateral aid agencies, for changing
modalities of development co-operation and for the nature and focus of
related comparative and international research.

UNESCO, literacy and international development priorities

Founded in 1945, with its headquarters in Paris, UNESCO has long been at the
forefront of campaigns for 'basic education', 'functional literacy', and 'universal
primary education'. Because of its early prominence as the only international
body specifically concerned with education, because of the enthusiasm and zeal
with which it set about its task, and because very little was known about the
state of illiteracy around the globe, its major report on *World Illiteracy* (UNESCO
1957) was to have a profound influence on educational thinking and policies
throughout the world. This report was especially significant for highlighting
the fact that the world map of illiteracy coincided with the world map of
poverty. This is a situation that remains as true today as it was in 1957.

Three principles enunciated in the report suggested that (i) the best means
of eradicating illiteracy is through primary education, a view that has re-
emerged and has underpinned all subsequent debates since the World
Conference on Education for All held at Jomtien in Thailand in 1990 (WCEFA
1990); (ii) the higher the levels of literacy prevailing in a country, the greater
the level of economic development is likely to be; and (iii) the greater the dif-
fusion of literacy throughout society the greater is the likelihood of industrial
and economic development.

At the time, there was little research evidence to support these assertions and, as Jones (1988) points out, they were never challenged. However, coming as they did from such an august international body, this was a very powerful message which profoundly shaped the thinking and actions of many governments in the years to come. Such thinking also coincided with a renewed interest in educational reform as a means of economic development. Bowman and Anderson (1963) and Anderson (1965) thus argued, from data gathered from a number of countries, that a 40 per cent rate of adult literacy, or the equivalent levels of primary schooling, was an essential threshold before economic development could begin. Several other writers tried to show that economic growth in the USA and Europe was closely linked to the growth of literacy rates (see, for example, Cipolla 1969; Oxenham 1980). Street (1984), however, pointed out that economic growth in Canada in the nineteenth century, and in India in the twentieth century, took place with far lower rates of literacy than 40 per cent. In fact India only claims to have reached a 50 per cent literacy rate during the last few years of the 1990s. Moreover, as noted in Chapter 3, there has never been an agreed definition of what literacy means (or in which language), though the annual publication of global literacy figures by UNESCO is still seen as an indicator of economic development. This is partly because, in an age of globalisation, an ability to read instructions or posters relating, for example, to health, or computer technology, is seen as essential if people are to move out of poverty.

Adopting a more critical perspective, Street (1999) maintains that such global agendas relating to literacy have distorted people's thinking because they have overlooked the fact that within any culture there are many different 'literacies,' each with its own code and validity. Street, therefore, argues that the simplistic approach adopted by many development agencies has been problematic because it has ignored how language is used culturally in daily discourse in different settings. This view is shared by two recent and empirically informed studies on the use of literacy in Nepal (Robinson-Pant 2000) and in Botswana (Commeyras and Chilisa 2001). Brock-Utne (2000) is even more scathing in her criticisms since she believes that donor agencies have been so concerned with supporting international languages that they have hampered educational development, destroyed local textbook production in indigenous languages and weakened local cultures. Indeed, her critique of the contemporary prioritising of primary education, at the expense of secondary and tertiary provision, leads her to argue that the international agencies are guilty of 'recolonising the African mind.' Writing from a post-colonial perspective, Hickling-Hudson (2002) extends the challenge further. She criticises the World Bank's statement (World Bank 1999:17) that 'advances in literacy and other learning may have done more to improve the human condition than any other public policy' as simplistic and dangerous because it overlooks how literacy operates, and has been used in different socio-historical and cultural contexts. Hickling-Hudson thus argues : 'The way literacy has been used has been to solidify the social hierarchy, empower elites, and ensure that people lower in the hierarchy accept the values, norms and beliefs of the elites, even when it is not in their best interests to do so.' (2002:568). This points to another crucial role that can be played in the future by comparative and international researchers in education, in working further alongside critical theorists and language and anthropology specialists to chart what is happening to indigenous languages and cultures worldwide. We shall reconsider such possibilities later.

Returning to our historical perspective, the powerful rhetoric of UNESCO's early arguments clearly had a major political impact because, for the first time, governments became convinced that educational investment and economic development were in some way interlinked. The result was that UNESCO poured billions of dollars into mass literacy programmes, such as the Experimental World Literacy Programme (Goldstone 1979). Unfortunately, in doing so it made many of the classic agency mistakes that are so well documented today. It failed to appraise the local cultural, administrative and political constraints facing many countries; it failed to involve local governments in underwriting the campaigns once a UNESCO team had left the scene; and, as a result, it failed to develop long-term sustainability. UNESCO's involvement in educational television projects in Colombia and the Ivory Coast, and its encouragement of the use of teachers as rural animateurs, or change agents, in countries as diverse as Cameroon, Indonesia, the Philippines and Thailand, also ended in failure because of its inability to ensure that such projects were sustainable.

It is lessons such as these that have influenced contemporary rethinking about how international agencies should work with one another, and above all, how they should work with national and local governments. On a more positive note, some of these setbacks have been overcome and UNESCO has regained some influence in the international education arena with the more recent publication of the Delors Report (UNESCO 1996) exploring new priorities and developments for the twenty-first century. While there are some interesting statistics and proposals in this work, there is, however, a decided lack of analysis of how better to address global educational and social problems (Watson 1999a). Several commentators have also queried whether a large multilateral agency such as UNESCO can ever do more than exhort governments since it lacks the finance, trained staff and professional know-how to make any significant inroads at the grassroots level (Jones 1999; Limage 1999; Mundy 1999).

Bilateral agency interventions and priorities

As European governments established their own bilateral aid agencies through which they could both help, and influence, the economic and educational developments in their former colonies, other OECD countries, including Japan, followed suit. This was often as much from a sense of moral altruism as it was for economic or political gain. As Mosley (1987) argues, aid rarely achieved political advantage, especially at the height of the Cold War. Each country, however, had its own distinctive agenda. The French, British and Dutch government agencies, for example, initially concentrated on supporting and developing secondary and tertiary education in their former colonies, helping to build schools, teacher training colleges and universities; providing teachers, teacher trainers, curriculum developers and equipment such as books, tape recorders, and language laboratories. It was seen as easier for them to deal with these areas, rather than with basic and primary education, because they had a colonial language in common, and the fledgling education systems with which they were dealing were modelled on those of the colonial powers.

The German government's support went mainly to technical and vocational education projects, for which they felt particularly well suited. Thus secondary technical schools were opened, staffed and equipped in Pakistan, South West Africa, now Namibia, Argentina and Tanzania amongst other countries. The Swedish and Norwegian agencies, free from any colonial ties, used as a guiding principle a belief that their aid should help the poorest in those countries where the government had placed social welfare high on its list of priorities (Nowak and Swinehart 1989; Smith, H. 2002). SIDA, for example, initially concentrated on basic primary education, non-formal and adult education and technical and vocational education, particularly in Tanzania and Kenya (Ishumi 1992). The Danish and Norwegians (DANIDA and NORAD) also prioritised primary education and community schooling. It is significant to note that it is the Scandinavian countries that have done best in reaching the Pearson Report's (1969) recommended target of allocating 1 per cent of GNP to overseas aid – a figure that was reduced to 0.7 per cent by the Brandt Report (Brandt 1980) and which has remained the official international target ever since. It is also significant that, historically, there was considerable rivalry between the bilateral donor agencies and that, until the 1990s, there was very little desire to engage in collaborative ventures. The change can be seen in new forms of co-operation, and by the fact that until well into the 1980s bilateral aid accounted for 60–70 per cent of the aid disbursed, while the multilateral agencies accounted for 30–40 per cent. These figures have now been reversed. For a brief period following the oil boom of the mid-1970s several OPEC (Organisation of Petroleum Exporting Countries), particularly Saudi Arabia and the United Arab Emirates, also joined the donor group, though their disbursement went almost exclusively to poor Islamic countries.

In many ways, it was this period of uncritical international transfer, often promoted by Northern agencies, that stimulated the emergence of much of the seminal research on dependency and neo-colonialism that was reviewed in Chapters 2, 3 and 4. In the light of the more recent post-colonial critiques, this line of analysis has advanced considerably, along with the intensification of globalisation. Thus, not only are many comparative and international scholars now arguing that Western values and formal educational structures have destroyed indigenous cultures (Teasdale 1998; Leach and Little 1999; Brock-Utne 2000), but they are also looking to the future and maintaining that all engaged in the development process must urgently acknowledge that there are more culturally sensitive ways of seeing and doing things. Our own arguments accord closely with this, and suggest that if international agencies are serious about developing improved partnerships with the poorer countries of the world, they need to do much more to heed the voices emerging from the South itself (Teasdale and Teasdale 1999; Holmes 2001). Again, we will return to such prospects in later chapters as we articulate the case for renewed change.

World Bank agendas and education

The World Bank's first educational loan was made in 1962 to help the Tunisian government build secondary schools, but it was not until the late 1960s that the Bank became actively involved in lending to education (see World Bank 1971, 1975). Since then the steady growth in its lending programme has ensured that it has become the world's largest single donor agency (Jones 1992). While the Bank became a pace-setter in thinking about educational development issues, according to Mundy (2002), its funding levelled off during the latter part of the 1980s and its thinking largely stagnated during the 1990s. Nevertheless, as Soudien (2002:440) reminds us: 'World Bank documents have, in the past couple of decades at least, been enormously important in influencing policy, shaping opinion and even providing benchmarks against which to assess progress in a number of social welfare fields'. By 1990 it had already financed 397 projects in over 100 countries to the tune of US$11,273 billion, accounting for over 20 per cent of all international assistance to education (Verspoor 1991). By 1999 this had risen markedly, and the Bank accounted for between 30 per cent and 40 per cent of global educational assistance with annual expenditure on educational programmes and projects amounting to over US$2 billion. By 2001, with a cumulative total of around 640 educational projects spread across 115 countries, the total figure that had been disbursed over the previous 35 years was calculated at US$28.8 billion (World Bank, Human Development Network 2002). This amounted to by far the largest proportion of international aid to education given by any multilateral agency. This places it, in both scale of operations and independence of action, in a league of its own (see Brown 1997). According to the World Bank, Human Development Network (2002), the Bank's current education portfolio is now US$11.5 billion spread across 172 projects in 88 countries. Inevitably this scale of operation has generated many critics. These challenge the way in which it conducts its affairs, the impact it has had on developing countries, and its inability to see issues other than from a global or North American perspective (Samoff 1993, 1996a; George and Sabeli 1994; Ilon 1996, 2002; Lauglo 1996; Watson 1996b; Chossudovsky 1997, 2000; Klees 2002; Soudien 2002). The Bank has also had more neutral commentators (see, for example, Mosley *et al.* 1995) and defenders who have both worked within the organisation and been able to view it critically from the outside (see, for example, Verspoor 1991; Heyneman 1999b). The latter recognise some of the organisation's faults, but argue that it operates with the best interests of the developing countries at heart. There are others who, like K. King (1991a, 1992), McGinn (1994), Watson (1995), Hickling-Hudson (2002) and Klees (2002), believe that the power and influence of the Bank ensure that it exerts an unhealthily strong influence on setting the agenda for educational policies throughout the South.

Perhaps this is inevitable given the scope of its influence, the size of its budget and the number of countries where it operates. Another danger is that its policies are mainly geared towards large countries and thus ignore, or misunderstand, the dilemmas faced by many small states with their own distinctive problems (see Crossley and Holmes 1999, 2001). Collectively, there is much to suggest that its own particular 'bank brand' of knowledge has ensured that a generic, sanitised version of global knowledge (Ilon 2002; Klees 2002) has become too dominant in the development arena.

This influence can be illustrated in many ways. Thus, for example, when the Bank began to change the focus of its assistance in the mid-1970s to rural and community development and non-formal education (World Bank 1975), bilateral donors like Britain's Overseas Development Ministry followed suit (HMSO 1975). So did the Scandinavian countries, since this emphasis was very close to their own domestic policies. When the British government produced a new policy paper on aid for the 1990s (ODA 1990) it too was greatly influenced by World Bank thinking and policy documents, a point that aroused considerable criticism from the British academic community at the time. Moreover, it is widely argued that when the Bank promoted technical and vocational education during the late 1970s and early 1980s, this had a deleterious effect on several countries whose education systems became distorted as a result (Psacharopoulos and Loxley 1985; Foster 1987; Ishumi 1992; Sifuna 1992; Watson 1993b; Bennell and Segerstrom 1998). By 1991, when the World Bank changed its views on the amounts it was prepared to put into technical education (World Bank 1991), many argued that the damage had been done. In any case the Bank's policies had changed yet again, this time towards a return to basic and primary education, the focus, as noted earlier, of UNESCO back in the late 1950s (Lockheed and Verspoor 1990; World Bank 1990). Because this shift of emphasis was also to mark the start of a new collaborative relationship between the World Bank and other donor agencies it will be examined in greater depth later in the chapter. First we consider what motivated this change of emphasis back to the primary sector, and what inspired the movement towards greater co-operation between the donors and the recipients of aid.

Changing development priorities and modalities

By the mid-1970s there was a faltering of overseas development assistance. This was partly because of the economic difficulties faced by many of the donor countries following the increase in oil prices in 1973 and 1974, partly because there was a decline in public support for overseas aid, and partly because, as Coombs (1985:287) argued:

> ... administrative and 'project' procedures tended to grow increasingly elaborate and rigid, impairing donor agencies' innovative capacity and their ability to respond promptly to changing needs and conditions.

There was also growing criticism of the whole concept of aid with many arguing that it was a form of economic imperialism (Hayter 1971); that it was leading to a new dependency (Cardoso 1972); that it merely served the self-interests of the donor governments (Mende 1973); and that it helped to maintain corrupt regimes, often military dictatorships, without alleviating poverty (Bauer 1981; Bauer and Yamey 1981). To be fair, many agencies were producing policy papers on rural development, healthcare, the environment, and community and non-formal education during the mid-1970s. However, the inability of all involved to translate these policies into practice because of a limited understanding of the issues involved, inadequate administrative structures or political differences, hampered progress (Watson 1982b; Robinson 1996a). Unfortunately, as Buchert (2002) shows, this is still an acute problem today. Nevertheless, the seeds of reform in the thinking of international development agencies were sown at this time.

Within the World Bank itself there was also considerable debate about why so many projects failed; what directions the Bank should be taking; whether there should be support for 'projects' with a limited time-span, or whether there should be broader assistance strategies for 'programmes' and sectors (such as health or education) or for sub-sectors such as primary education. According to Jones (1992) and Mundy (2002) some of these debates were very intense since there was genuine concern that, despite the huge sums generated through Bank loans, the problems in many developing countries remained intractable. An internal World Bank document, 'Review of Bank Operations in the Education Sector' (World Bank 1978), highlighted several serious deficiencies in the way the Bank operated: internal organisational weaknesses; poor planning and implementation of projects; unrealistic time frames; and poor communication with recipient country governments that led to misunderstandings. The two most fundamental weaknesses identified were seen as the fact that there was not enough emphasis on effective borrower participation in the identification and preparation of projects, and that there was too little concern about developing the borrower countries' own capacity for planning, managing and researching their own education systems. Concern was expressed not only for what came to be known as capacity building to ensure the sustainability of projects, but also for the need to root policies more firmly on empirical research.

Thereafter the Bank began to commission research that demonstrated the importance of basic education, management and planning skills, and the necessity for providing basic teaching resources such as chalk, textbooks, paper, even desks, if there was to be any improvement in the quality of what was offered (Verspoor 1989; Lockheed and Verspoor 1990). Revealingly, much of the subsequent research agenda was based on what was perceived to be essential for improving the efficiency of education systems modelled on the West. This took very little account of the local values, knowledge, skills and culture – factors that varied considerably from context to context.

There were other factors which contributed to this process of re-evaluation. Some of these centred around what was perceived as a growing socio-economic crisis facing Africa, when compared to the economic growth that was taking place in Asia. In 1981 the Berg Report (World Bank 1981) also argued that there were major problems with the ability of the management capacity of Sub-Saharan Africa to implement reforms. This identified weaknesses in priority setting and in the capacity for policy-making, along with a readiness to invest in higher education at the expense of basic education. It noted a lack of local analytical capacity that could effectively identify core problems. This Report also recognised a potential financial crisis facing Sub-Saharan Africa that, it argued, necessitated cost-cutting measures and economic restructuring. At that stage there was little recognition of the devastating impact that the economic Structural Adjustment Programmes, imposed by the IMF and the World Bank as conditions for assistance, were having on individual economies. Above all the Berg Report argued that 'the development of locally appropriate reforms, their implementation and evaluation, cannot be done without strengthened institutions and analytic capacities' (World Bank 1981:84–85).

Similar views were expressed in the Bank's Education Sector Policy Paper of 1980 (World Bank 1980). Recognition that higher education was taking a disproportionate amount of the education budget was highlighted by the work of Hinchcliffe (1988) and the Bank's own document on education in Sub-Saharan Africa (World Bank 1988). More than that, the Bank was beginning to consider that it would have to support recurrent expenditure at the primary level, that it would have to provide training in financial and educational management and that any educational reform would have to be seen in the larger economic and political context of any given country. This could have been pointed out by any reputable scholar involved in comparative and international research in education, but, in this case, it was a professional lesson well learnt the hard way. However, there were to be conditions laid down for any increase in development assistance. These were clearly articulated in the document, *Sub-Saharan Africa: From Crisis to Sustainable Growth* (World Bank 1989) where capacity building was seen as crucial for any aid increase. This theme was also pursued by the International Institute for Educational Planning (IIEP 1991, 1993) which offered to develop courses designed to improve indigenous planning and analytical capacities. Here was, at least, some acknowledgement that for any aid project or programme to be sustainable, there would need to be greater co-operation with local administrators and researchers to assess the feasibility of future proposals.

Much of the responsibility for the repeated disappointments noted above lay with the agencies concerned. It was they who changed direction over what was seen as the most suitable educational policy for sustainable economic development. It was they who repeatedly proposed shifting back and forth from formal schooling to non-formal initiatives; who advanced technical and vocational schooling whether or not the local economies could absorb the products of such institutions; and who promoted the hardware of educational technology in the absence of local capacity to maintain the equipment. These were all ideas that had been developed in the industrial West and which were exported to the developing world with scant regard to contextual differences.

Moreover, in this era, there was a tendency to bypass local officials in order to get a project off the ground, and there was a reluctance to do any substantial feasibility study since it was seen as far more important to provide 'success' stories for the electorate back in the donor's country. As K. King (1991a:259) wryly observed: 'Getting a project started and the money disbursed is more important than the procedures used to do so'. The rhetoric of partnership between donor and recipient, advocated in the Pearson Report (1969), was still little more than a hollow sham. Many donors operated in a confident, but cavalier, neo-colonial manner, as if they knew all the answers to what were often highly complex local problems. While not disagreeing with the above analysis, Verspoor (1993), an employee of the World Bank at the time, argued that there were four specific reasons why educational aid had been so ineffective. These were the insignificant sums involved in the educational aid programme; the operational practices already alluded to; the limitations of the research base, especially from the poorer countries; and weaknesses in staffing within the countries being supported.

While the worldwide economic recession persisted during much of the 1980s there was little that could be done to change things on the ground. By the end of the decade the climate of opinion in favour of a change of approach was, nevertheless, gaining ground. This became more urgent with the collapse of the Soviet Empire in Eastern Europe and with the implosion of the USSR itself, since more countries were looking for external assistance. Thus, while in the middle of the 1980s Coombs (1985:308) was able to write that 'the landscape of the Third World today is littered with the carcasses of pilot projects that failed to pilot anybody anywhere', the UNICEF executive director was a little more circumspect and encouraging when he wrote in his introduction to the 1989 *State of the World's Children* report (UNICEF 1989:3):

> To prevent poverty from being perpetuated from one generation to the next, the growing minds and bodies of children must be given priority protection. There could be no greater humanitarian cause. There could be no more productive investment. And there could be no greater priority for real development... What we need now is the political commitment, the managerial capacity and the financial resources.

Towards partnership: Jomtien and afterwards

The World Conference on Education for All held in Jomtien, Thailand, in 1990 marked what many saw as a new beginning in international development co-operation. For a start it was jointly co-ordinated by the World Bank and the three leading UN agencies concerned with education, welfare and development (UNESCO, UNDP and UNICEF). It also brought together government representatives from 155 different countries. Above all it tried to set goals and targets that would shape all of the work of the international community during the following decade. The six key goals identified related to:

- the expansion of early childhood care and development;
- universal access to, and completion of, primary education by 2000;
- reducing the rates of adult illiteracy, with special emphasis on female literacy by 2000;
- improved achievements in learning based on clearly defined levels of performance;
- expansion of basic education for youths and adults;
- improved dissemination of skills, knowledge and values for sustainable development.

As with all international conferences there was a mixture of compromise and idealism. Clearly some issues reflected priorities widely held in the rich countries while others more directly reflected concerns expressed within the South. There was , however, much agreement that there should be more concerted moves towards developing 'new partnerships' between the multilateral agencies and governments in the South; between bilateral agencies and national governments; and between the aid agencies and non-governmental organisations, whether national or international. In addition it was agreed that there would be closer co-operation and co-ordination between donor agencies. The actual words of Article 7 of the World Declaration on Education for All (WCEFA 1990) are as follows:

> National, regional and local educational authorities have a unique obligation to provide basic education for all, but they cannot be expected to supply every human, financial or organisational requirement for this task. New and revitalised partnerships at all levels will be necessary: partnerships among all sub-sectors and forms of education; ... partnerships between government and non-governmental organisations, the private sector, local communities, religious groups and families ... Genuine partnerships contribute to the planning, implementation, managing and evaluating of basic education programmes. When we speak of 'an expanded vision and a renewed commitment,' partnerships are at the heart of it.
>
> (reproduced in Little *et al.* 1994:234)

Progress towards meeting the Jomtien targets has, at best, been mixed (Little *et al.* 1994). For example the 'adult' element in the phrase Education for 'All' soon disappeared from the picture in favour of the more pressing needs of investment in primary education. As a result the number of illiterates has continued to rise, although the percentage declined globally from 42 per cent in 1980 to 29 per cent in 1995. According to UNESCO (1997) the number of illiterates had risen from 848 million (1980) to 872 million (1995), of whom 557 million (63.8 per cent) are women. What is even more striking is that the bulk of these are in India (288 million), China (167 million) and seven other countries. The numbers not enrolled in primary school have risen to 124 million of whom 60 per cent are girls, while 150 million drop out before attaining any level of basic literacy (DFID 2000; Watkins 2000). In Pakistan fewer than 50 per cent of the age group even start primary school and nearly half drop out before the end of Grade 2, while in Nepal over 60 per cent drop out before they reach Grade 4. Clearly, much remains to be done.

Progress towards the Jomtien goals was first reviewed at an Education for All Mid-term Review Conference in Amman, Jordan in 1996 and again at the World Education Forum in Dakar, Senegal in 2000. Following the United Nations' Millennium Summit in September 2000, the International Development Targets (IDTs) have also been reset, and renamed the Millennium Development Goals (MDGs). Gender equity in basic education is now to be achieved by 2005, universal primary education not until 2015, and the target for halving the numbers classified as poor has also been set as 2015. How far these targets are attainable is highly debatable (Bennell 1999; Watkins 2000), especially given the growing disparities in sums spent on education and the differences in wealth between the developed and the developing countries. While the percentage of GDP devoted to education is roughly equal between the developed and the developing countries (around 5–6 per cent), spending per pupil reveals a frightening gap, for while the average expenditure per primary and secondary pupil in the developed countries is US$4,636, in Sub-Saharan Africa it is US$165, and for all developing countries it is a mere US$45. This means that in many of the poorest countries, after payment of salaries for those in the education service, less than US$2 per student is left for writing materials, textbooks and other resources. By way of contrast, the British government is currently planning to spend over US$5 billion to connect every United Kingdom school to the Internet. This sum is equal to almost the entire educational budget for Sub-Saharan Africa! It is little wonder that, in spite of the progress made since Jomtien (UNESCO 1996), there are those who see many poor countries as being trapped in crisis (Watkins 2000).

Progress towards new partnerships has also been mixed (Bray 2001). On the one hand some bodies, such as the Commonwealth Secretariat and other Commonwealth agencies and organisations, have always emphasised collaboration and partnership. Many non-government organisations like Tear Fund, Christian Aid and the Catholic Relief Agency (CAFOD), which are concerned with both short-term relief as well as long-term development aid, have also long regarded themselves as in partnerships with local church communities and para-church organisations. Other NGOs which are involved in education and literacy programmes, such as Action Aid, Education for Development, the International Network for Development or the Summer Institute of Linguistics (United Kingdom) operate on a collaborative and partnership basis with local communities, often bypassing governments altogether. They view the grassroots approach to development as being far more effective than the top-down approach typically adopted by multilateral and bilateral aid agencies. On the other hand, there are some large multilateral organisations, including UNESCO, which by their very nature should be collaborative and participatory, that are still struggling to come to terms with what concepts such as accountability, donor co-ordination, partnership and national capacity actually mean in practice (Courtney 1999:26).

There are, however, signs of increased collaboration amongst the donor organisations concerned with educational development. The Association for the Development of Education in Africa (ADEA), which was originally founded as Donors to African Education, brings together national, international and private donor agencies to formulate policies and to analyse specific problems through working parties. The findings are then disseminated through various publications (see, for example, Buchert 1995), but as Kaluba and Williams (1999) assert, regardless of the closer collaboration exhibited in recent years, there is little evidence that the findings of the working groups have had much impact on either the policies or the practices of the donor agencies.

There is also growing evidence of greater co-operation amongst NGOs, although we need to be clear what constitutes an NGO. At the most basic level, of course, any organisation that is not a government agency is an NGO. The Commonwealth Foundation (1995:24) has defined an NGO as ' a specific type of organisation working in the field of "development", one which works with people to help improve their social and economic situations and prospects.' The World Bank's view is not too dissimilar. It describes NGOs as ' private organisations that pursue activities to relieve suffering, promote the interests of the poor, protect the environment or undertake community development' (World Bank 1989:1). Neither of these definitions really encapsulates the infinite variety of NGOs since they can range from national or international privately funded organisations, such as the Ford or Rockefeller Foundations or the Centre for British Teachers (CfBT), through large organisations such as Action Aid or OXFAM to small altruistic, voluntary and independent groups within countries of the South. Some are opposed by governments because they are perceived as being anti-government, which in some cases they are. Others are seen as complementary to government, even partners, because they have easy access to the poor and to local communities and are not viewed with as much suspicion as many government agents are. Bray's (2001) background study for UNESCO as part of the preparation for the Dakar, Education for All, meeting provides some encouraging reports of different types of partnership working effectively.

There are also success stories involving Northern academic researchers working in partnership with colleagues in the South, with networks such as NORRAG (as noted in Chapter 1) pioneering many initiatives. See, also, work by Crossley (1990, 2001) and the collaborative studies carried out by Juma *et al.* (2002) or those reported in Lewin and Stuart's (2002) collection of work. Such partnerships offer considerable scope for the future because, as argued elsewhere, the potential for outsiders to work with knowledgeable insiders has much to contribute to improved context sensitivity, to the application of post-colonial frameworks and to broad changes in the way comparative and international research is conducted. There is also emerging evidence of organisations such as DFID seeking to use the research they have commissioned from Northern academics to both critique and inform agency policy. This is an encouraging trend, though Hoppers (2001) points out that the DFID research agenda is still dominated by issues that are of greatest interest to governments of the North. More certainly needs to be done to take into consideration issues of concern that are prioritised within the South itself; and to ensure that the dissemination of findings is also improved throughout the South. One can, therefore, still question for whose benefit much development research is undertaken (see Holmes, K. 2001).

Returning to agency collaboration, there is evidence of closer links between Southern NGOs, as, for example, demonstrated by the Forum of African Development Organisations (FAVDO); self-help women's groups in India, Indonesia, the Philippines, Kenya and Tanzania; and the Bangladesh Rural Advancement Committee (BRAC), which is mainly concerned with empowering women through literacy and rural development programmes (Watkins 2000). There are also signs of closer collaboration between NGOs in the North and their counterparts in the South (Drabek 1987). The justification for this has, for example, been very clearly made by Action Aid (1993:8):

> Collaboration is more cost effective than direct operation; it expedites project start up time, facilitates Northern non-governmental work in countries and situations where their direct operations are prohibited; provides access to non-governmental skills and resources (such as innovative strategies, sensitivity to local conditions and culture, positive relations with the community, regional contacts with state agencies); ... enhances each organisation's legitimacy with different stakeholders...

They could also have added that such collaboration is more likely to lead to sustained development because of the closer involvement of local communities who have a direct stake in development projects.

While there may be improved collaboration on the part of many NGOs, the position with donor agencies is more problematic for, as Elliot (1987:65) observes, 'no amount of well intentioned dialogue can remove the asymmetry of power in a North-South partnership'. Moreover, it is more than likely that different donors are working to different financial timeframes and methods of accounting; that they have different objectives; or that different partners are reluctant to surrender their part of the ownership. The result is that often 'dependency and unequal relationships, the antithesis of the objectives of partnership and institutional development, are being enforced when they are least needed' (Elu and Banya 1999:196). More problematic is the fact that, however much both donors and local governments want to share ideas and be partners, some of the educational policies being pursued by the donor governments are exacerbating the difficulties. We shall look at examples of these dilemmas later, but, first, we need to further explore why this change of agenda came about.

The rhetoric of partnership and co-operation

Article 7 of the WCEFA (1990) argued that new and revitalised partnerships will be necessary at all levels if there is to be improvement both in aid flow and in implementation on the ground (see extracts reproduced in Little *et al.* 1994). These ideas were further developed by the President of the World Bank in his mid-1990s address on *New Directions and New Partnerships* (Wolfensohn 1995) and in the OECD's (1996) document, *Development Partnerships in the New Global Context*. As a result several of the bilateral donor agencies, particularly Sweden's (SIDA), Norway's (NORAD), the United Kingdom's (DFID) and Japan's (JICA), have refocused many of their policy documents to take into account conceptions of new partnerships. The Swedish government, on behalf of SIDA, published *Partnership with Africa* in the mid-1990s (Sweden 1997) but, in spite of many good intentions, well-informed commentators suggest that these ideas have proved very hard to implement in reality (Buchert 1998; Wohlgemuth 1999). The initiative for much action clearly still rests with the donor agency, as demonstrated by recent developments in countries such as Tanzania, Botswana and Namibia (Kann 1999). K. King (1999:13) has gone so far as to say:

> It seems entirely possible that these new trends … [towards closer co-operation and partnerships].. may remain more at the level of rhetoric than implementation, with the result that the older patterns of relationship between aid provider and recipient will continue.

The British Government's DFID White Paper on aid, *Eliminating World Poverty*, (DFID 1997:38) also stated:

> Where we have confidence in the policies and budgetary allocation process and the capacity for effective implementation of the partner government, we will consider moving away from supporting specific projects to providing resources more strategically in support of sector wide programmes or the economy as a whole.

Some will see an element of patronisation in the above statement, and this is visible in other related documents, such as the policy framework for education *Learning Opportunities For All* (DFID 1999). In this it is stated that the British government will seek 'new development relationships,' will 'support sustainable, well-managed education institutions, systems and partnerships,' and will 'seek to develop stronger partnerships with bilateral agencies in defining supportive ways of working and in the sharing of collective experience' (DFID 1999:38). Translating partnership principles into practice is, thus, a problematic and complex process.

The concepts of partnership and co-operation can certainly help to portray aid donors as being concerned with the best interests of the poorer countries of the world rather than with self-interest. Yet this is not especially new. Going no further back than the Pearson Report (1969) on *Partners in Development* and the Brandt Reports (1980, 1983), it can be seen that this is a familiar thread that has run through much past thinking – even though the reality has been one of continued dominance from the North (Riddell, R.C. 1997; Klees 2002). We will, therefore, argue in our own conclusions, that only if there is a more genuine form of partnership between the rich countries and donors of the North and their counterparts in the South, will there be a realistic chance for global disparities to be resolved. However, this is an issue that first benefits from further consideration of the reasons why the partnership concept has re-emerged with such vigour during the past decade.

Firstly, at the most basic, and cynical, level, the partnership rationale is in the contemporary self-interest of the rich and powerful nations. Stirrat and Henkel (1997:75) thus argue that talk of 'partnership' merely legitimises the inequalities of the aid relationship, while Crewe and Harrison (1998:73 and 90) maintain that the real (if hidden) concern of many agencies is to find ways of managing aid more efficiently, rather than to address unequal relationships between donors and recipients. Ilon (1996:413) is, likewise, critical when she argues that bodies like the World Bank, in particular, have moved away from promoting education for economic purposes per se (as, for example, technical and vocational education), to 'educational policies aimed at maintaining economic, political, social, health and environmental stability'. This, she suggests, is because 'such a shift reflects the emerging needs of a growing global economy for relatively stable environments'. More recently, Ilon (2002) has argued that the Bank, while professing to be concerned with the poor is, in effect, acting as an agent of global markets. This is a point that has not been lost on the anti-globalisation protesters. In essence the argument is that it is much easier for global corporations and businesses to invest in countries where there is social and political stability, and that the Bank prefers to work alongside individual governments so that it can help to shape their social, educational and welfare programmes on a partnership basis. From this perspective the Bank's work at the basic education and welfare level can be portrayed as a form of global welfare, deflecting criticisms that it is a villain in the development process – while allowing transnational corporations to operate unfettered and unregulated across the globe. Mundy (2002), similarly, argues that the Bank has little alternative, since it is now having to pick up the pieces following its disastrous policies on structural adjustment. Unfortunately, as many have argued, its policies on structural adjustment are not quite so benign as the Bank claims them to be, and there is much evidence to suggest that they have led to increased worldwide poverty and to a breakdown in social cohesion.

A second reason for new partnerships is economic. In an age of intensified globalisation and marketisation (Colclough 1997; Kwong 2000) there is a growing reluctance on the part of governments in both the North and the South to increase taxation to underwrite ever-expanding social welfare, health and education budgets. This is despite the protestations of many to the contrary. From this perspective, there is clearly a need for governments to seek partners to share the financial burden. These may be other governments, private sector bodies, or donor agencies. The process also helps to ensure that there is reduced duplication of effort and resources. Moreover, it is argued that it is possible that innovative partnerships will develop with non-governmental organisations who work at the grassroots level, and are therefore more likely to be in touch with the expressed needs and aspirations of poorer communities.

A third reason is the growing realisation that development cannot be imposed from the top-down, nor from the outside. Proponents of this perspective argue that development can best be generated from within a country, or a community, provided there is local ownership both of the identification of ideas and of the solutions to local problems. Only then, it is suggested, will any sustainable development be possible. This supports our own research capacity argument for local insiders to be more directly involved in research into local problems. It also acknowledges that if external researchers or policy makers seek to impose their views, both resentment and resistance may be generated. Strategies that prioritise local ownership are reflected in the experience of Japan's successful aid programmes in South-East Asian countries like Malaysia and Thailand. As the Japanese openly acknowledge:

> The idea that serious self-help efforts by developing countries are the most important elements in development's success is based on Japan's own post-war experience and on the experience of the Asian countries that Japan has supported in these development efforts.
>
> (Japan 1997:17)

The concepts of ownership and partnership are, moreover, very closely linked to each other, as K. King (1999:10) reminds us:

> The term partnership is an essential corollary and complement to ownership. Ownership has become a standard item in agency language. On its own it may not always signify any changes in the aid relationship except at the rhetorical level, but in the new partnership discourse recognition of national ownership of projects and programmes by the South is an important counterbalance to the admitted financial dominance of the North.

A fourth factor is the growing realisation that, whatever the supporters of Fukuyama (1992) might argue, the West has not triumphed universally. There is no one agreed and best global model of social and economic development. Indeed, the Brandt Report (1983) drew attention to the lessons that the North can learn from the South. More recently Forster (1999) has argued that if new models of development are to be generated they can no longer be imposed from the North. This acknowledges that the forces of globalisation are affecting the industrial world – albeit differently – as they are impacting upon the countries of the South. The social problems of crime, drug abuse, unemployment, environmental degradation and poverty are not confined to the South.

In an increasingly interdependent world, lessons learnt in all contexts can thus be usefully shared – but the insights gained are unlikely to lead to universal answers, since cultural and contextual differences need greater attention than has often been acknowledged to date. This suggests the need for closer co-operation combined with increased attention to context sensitivity – themes that we argue are also pertinent to the future of comparative and international research itself.

A final reason for the shift to new development modalities stems from changes in the global geopolitical context since the collapse of the Soviet Union. Not only are old Cold War rivalries no longer dominant, but new relationships are being forged. Indeed, following the tragic events of 11 September 2001, there has been a significant rapprochement between the USA and Russia; and an easing of tensions between China and the West has accompanied the latter's acceptance into the World Trade Organisation. There is also a new generation of leaders in the South, notably in Africa, who did not have to fight against a colonial regime, who have been democratically elected, and who are eager to advance an African Renaissance and a New Partnership for African Development (NEPAD) (Olukoshi 1997; Mbeki 1999; Gilmour and Soudien 2001).

However laudable the justifications for new approaches to aid relationships, and however fine sounding is the language of closer co-operation and partnerships, we have already seen how changing practice in any fundamental sense has been more problematic. There are also countervailing forces that can be seen to be generating increased dependency, not in the sense that it was first articulated by writers such as Frank (1967), Fanon (1968) or Cardoso (1972), but through what has been called 'market colonialism' (Chossudovsky 1997:37). We shall now turn to these somewhat paradoxical issues.

Countervailing pressures and policies

Much of the argument threading throughout this book has highlighted the need to recognise the impact of globalisation on educational policies and practice, and on the ways in which education is studied and analysed. While on one level, there would seem to be an inevitability about the intensification of globalisation, on another level we can see the policies of influential agencies encouraging international transfer with scant regard to the significance of contextual differences. Despite vastly changed circumstances, the dominant development paradigm is, in practice, still often very closely aligned to that of a neo-liberal version of the modernisation theories that we outlined in Chapter 2. This is generating its own momentum and reinforcing the hegemony of global marketisation. Here we revisit such issues and the movement towards increased partnership and collaboration with reference to the countervailing pressures and policies that deserve specific, and critical, attention in the future.

The economic impact of globalisation on education

While we have already shown that there are almost as many definitions of globalisation as there are academic disciplines, it is worth revisiting here how this impacts on international trends in education and how bodies like the International Monetary Fund (IMF) and World Bank are part of the process. Reflecting our earlier analysis, Carton (1999:60–61) argues that one of the most succinct definitions suggests that globalisation 'is a process of systemic elimination of institutional and technological obstacles to the movement and profitability of financial capital'. He thus sees it as financially driven. The result is that the global economy is dominated by fewer and fewer international banks and global corporations which are constantly merging and taking over smaller, competing, bodies in order to reduce the levels of competition and take a larger share of the market. It is the executive directors of these powerful banks and transnational corporations (TNCs) that can direct, or at the least influence, the policies of individual countries and national economies by integrating them into regional or global economies, and by making it increasingly impossible for them to regulate and control their own affairs. If globalisation means the interdependence and interlinking of financial markets, commercial banking, trade, the media and transportation via the Internet, satellites and other electronic means of communication (24 hours a day for 365 days a year), the lifestyles and ways of thinking of millions of people are being transformed. Needless to say the impact on education and the labour market is profoundly significant in a number of ways.

Not only do TNCs seek to open production plants wherever labour costs are low, thus depressing wages further, but they can equally close them down if they find that production costs, or the costs of transportation and raw materials, are cheaper elsewhere. Inevitably this can have a major impact on technical and vocational education and training. Either large companies can dictate the kinds of skill training that they require, thus having an impact on the curriculum, or they can suddenly depart from the local scene. This can again change training needs and create unemployment since it may be unlikely that the skills the labour force has acquired can be easily transferred. This can be particularly acute if there has been little, or no, technological transfer – a claim that is frequently levelled against the largest corporations. In such cases, research and development relating to new technologies remains firmly in the hands of the high-income countries. This has implications for communities as well as for how we view education. Soudien (2002), for example, argues that production units are becoming smaller and that employees can only market themselves and their skills if they set up networks. These inevitably require a particular kind of education and training.

Schluter and Lee (1993) have thus argued that as societies become enmeshed into the global community their sense of community identity breaks down. For while governments might encourage cable or satellite television and information technology, they also realise that they cannot control these or the impact that they have on local communities. When new technologies are introduced, especially if this is from the outside with little or no consultation, they can do much to destroy existing communities, lifestyles, and cultures, as has been shown by Leach and Little (1999). To some extent this has always been true, but modern technology has intensified the individualisation and fragmentation of society. This is particularly acute in the industrialised world but it is spreading to the urban Third World with alarming rapidity. The gap between those who have access to such technology and those who do not also becomes ever more acute. Eighty per cent of the world's population has no access to a telephone or other technological means of communication, while the 20 per cent that do have access to the Worldwide Web and the Internet are located in the urban areas of the world. The result is that, for some, the communications revolution means they have become citizens of the world with all that that implies for accessing knowledge; for others, enmeshed in poverty and subsistence level survival, it means that they are confined to their local communities. For some the education system is already 'wired' up to use these technologies; for others they are lucky to have access to the old 'technology' of chalk and paper. The differential effects of the communications revolution on education, in all its manifestations, is thus, as noted earlier, a new priority area for exploration by those concerned with persistent dilemmas of access, inequality and marginalisation, as well as with distinctly new issues such as the digital divide – and with the future profile of comparative and international research in education itself. Ilon (1998) also claims that globalisation is having a new impact on female enrolments in schools over and above any local cultural constraints. She demonstrates that as TNCs seek cheap labour, the demand for a modestly educated workforce rises. Since female labour is usually cheaper, more compliant and more willing to accept lower wages, the demand for more female education will also rise. There are, of course, many social and economic implications that arise from this.

As national economies become linked either into regional or global trading and manufacturing patterns, they have to adjust their economies to compete in global markets. Old trading partnerships can no longer be taken for granted. Inevitably poorer countries often suffer the most, and within those countries the poorest people suffer further. Countries that join larger groupings or regional trading blocs such as the European Community (EC), the North Atlantic Free Trade Association (NAFTA), or the Association of South-East Asian Nations (ASEAN), may be better able to withstand trading shocks than are isolationist countries like Myanmar or North Korea. But this does not necessarily mean that it will be any easier for the vulnerable, wherever they are located. Because of the need to compete in global markets, many employers will seek to keep their labour costs down and may, as a result, defy government attempts to introduce legislation on health and safety at work, gender equality, or minimum wages for fear that these will add to their costs and thus make them uncompetitive. They may also resist additional educational taxes if these will add to the costs. Thus governments have found themselves cutting back on school and social welfare expenditure as a result.

These factors can have an impact on formal schooling in at least three inter-linked ways: the generation of a globally tiered education system; the enlargement of the private sector; and the reform of the curriculum. Thus, often under government auspices, the wealthy classes and TNCs are seeking to expand private schooling in the belief that this will open up opportunities at a global or international level. The curriculum in such schools emphasises international languages, computer skills, information sciences, mathematics, analytical skills as well as the more traditional subjects. The International Schools Movement, the United World Colleges and a host of new colleges and universities that advertise in the international media would be examples of these developments. Here is another priority arena for future comparative research. The middle classes in many societies, who do not aspire to an inter-national role for their offspring, but who, nevertheless, believe that they have a role in servicing TNCs and other businesses within their own countries, are also pressing for higher academic standards in schools, for a more relevant curriculum and for better facilities. They too are willing to make additional contributions through fees or other practical means to ensure better schooling for their children. Finally, located at the bottom of the tiers are poor schools for the poor. As Ilon (1994:199) so succinctly puts it:

> Professions will be divided between those that are globally competitive but where mastery and competence are highly valued; and jobs where global competition means that people with limited and low level skills are competing on a world market of others with similar backgrounds. In order to attract businesses which need these types of workers, nations will still have to provide a minimum level of public education, but that education need not go much further than literacy, numeracy and the dis-cipline and tolerance that comes with being in a structured environment. Ironically, curriculum for the poor will also take on a global flavour as job skills become similar and basic needs and problems become globalised.

In the light of such changes the situation that is developing in many countries is

> ... where the future employees of global organisations attend elite, often private, schools, the second tier make financial sacrifices to support pub-licly run schools, while the remainder get what schooling they can, if it is available. If it is true that comparative advantage results from a shift in favour of knowledge, its creation, acquisition, manipulation and applica-tion, then only those countries where school systems address the issues arising from new technologies are likely to survive.
>
> (Watson 1998:17)

In addition, because TNCs are constantly having to re-brand themselves and update their products in order to compete, and stay one step ahead of their rivals in the global marketplace, they are always seeking new knowledge and new ways of doing things. In seeking to influence future customers, many have also become involved not only in lending their logo and brand name to sponsor a school or university, but they have also sponsored textbooks and even parts of the curriculum. Indirectly they are influencing what is learnt and taught (Heyneman 2001). As a result the social and liberal purposes of education are increasingly being subordinated to the economic needs of the global market, while more and more emphasis is placed on standardised knowledge and measurable outcomes. This becomes apparent from a study of the way TNC 'universities' or training institutions, such as those belonging to Motorola, Coca-Cola or Ford, standardise the knowledge and skills to be learnt regardless of the country or local culture. Thus what is taught in the USA is the same as that which is taught in China or Brazil. As Heyneman (1995:2) has argued:

> Standards of performance of an educational system do not differ system-
> atically between Ghana and Georgia (either the state or the country).
> Educational officials in Africa, Asia and Latin America ... hold the same
> standards and, as a result, they are demanding the same knowledge of
> innovation and system reforms as educational leaders within the OECD
> countries.

They have been encouraged in this by multilateral organisations such as the World Bank (World Bank 1994, 1995) and UNESCO (1996), which have pressed hard for greater private involvement and for the privatisation of education systems (see also Bray 1996a and b; Tooley 1999).

Another key aspect of globalisation which is having a dramatic effect not only on labour markets but also on education and social cohesion is that of migration. Different studies of migration patterns in the past and in recent times (see, for example, Castles and Miller 1993; Schuster 1994; Bunt-Kokhuis 1997; Skeldon 1997) all suggest that this is a phenomenon which will accelerate as global disparities widen and as political unrest, instability and wars force people from their homes to seek a better life elsewhere. The migration of such large numbers of people of different cultural, ethnic, religious and linguistic backgrounds has major implications for educational provision, language rights and curriculum content.

From the above, further priorities for future comparative and international research emerge. First, it is clear that future research must explore the differential implications of globalisation in varied contexts – most notably in the South, where, as we have previously observed, little work of this nature has been done to date (Mebrahtu et al., 2000; Tikly 2001). Second, given the power of neo-liberal and marketisation agendas, critically informed and comparative studies are required of the different facets of private education compared with the public sector. Third, much will be gained from studies relating to how different societies are dealing with the implications of large-scale immigration on their education systems.

The impact of structural adjustment programmes

We have already demonstrated how, for much of the last two decades of the twentieth century, international agencies have progressively set a global agenda that has recognised the scope of world poverty and the need to alleviate it, even if eradication might prove impossible (Watkins 1996). In March 2002 Britain's DFID, in conjunction with the Treasury, produced a document setting out the progress made and the work still to be done in tackling global poverty (DFID 2002). While Britain's Overseas Development Institute (ODI 1999) has noted that it is not always easy to define poverty, let alone measure it in different societies, it is important to ask who constructed this international conception of poverty, and thence the solutions to it, and who, or what, has been identified as the main cause of growing global poverty. According to George and Sabeli (1994:38), within the first five years of Robert McNamara becoming the President of the World Bank in 1968, he 'launched the concept of "absolute poverty"'. At the same time, he gave the Bank a missionary fervour towards the eradication of poverty which has helped to shape the organisation's subsequent policy (Ilon 1996). McNamara also believed that poverty could be quantified both by numbers as well as by income, and that success could be measured by redefining who is classified, and by monitoring changes in such data. He argued that poverty and starvation lead to wars, very much the argument of Olaf Palme, the former Swedish Prime Minister (Palme 1982), and that if only the former could be eliminated wars would cease. Not only was McNamara's analysis overly simplistic, but it clearly ignored the fact that the policies by which the Bank exerted leverage over recipient countries, could, notably in the form of structural adjustment policies (SAP), become a major cause of increased poverty – and contribute to the undermining of movements towards improved partnerships in development co-operation.

As we have shown, the investment recipe of both the Bank and the IMF insisted on specified changes to the economic structures of a country, including the downsizing of the government bureaucracy, the privatisation of key services such as public health and education, devaluation of the currency, and the development of export led markets, as a prerequisite for receiving aid loans and as a precursor to engagement with global capitalist markets. Moreover, according to George and Sabeli (1994:56) structural adjustment lending 'has marginalised people on a scale previously unheard of, while simultaneously undermining their political capacity to fight back'. They argue, for example, that the economy of Zimbabwe was completely undermined by Bank policies. This was seen to have been little short of catastrophic for the poorest in society because it had weakened the capacity to fund basic education, health and welfare programmes. In his book, *The Globalisation of Poverty*, Chossudovsky (1997:16), is even more damning when he argues that 'SAP sponsored by the IMF and the World Bank constitutes a new interventionist framework which has not only led to the impoverishment of millions but has enabled an international bureaucracy to supervise national economies through the deliberate manipulation of market forces' – and has helped advance the breakdown of entire countries such as Rwanda, Somalia and Yugoslavia. According to Chossudovsky, Bangladesh and India are under the direct influence of IMF and Bank officials and the results of such policies have been to depress wages, to lead to price increases, growing unemployment, increased poverty – and even death by suicide amongst handloom weavers in Andhra Pradesh (Chossudovsky 1997:133). As noted previously, the work of Mosley and colleagues (Mosley *et al.* 1995) into the effects of SAP and other conditionalities is less critical since they argue that much of the way in which negotiations are carried out is part of a 'bargaining game', and barely 60 per cent of agreed conditions are ever met – though they do recognise that the impact of such policies on public sector spending on health and education has been adverse. Needless to say, the extent to which multilateral agencies believe that they have the 'right' analysis of the global problems and also the 'correct' solutions to them, emerges as a key countervailing force and an important, if familiar, focus for future research. This economic analysis applies equally to the field of education as argued below.

The marginalisation of local knowledge

As already indicated, the impact of educational agency thinking and uncritical support for externally inspired agendas has generated considerable dissent throughout the South over the past few decades. If co-operation and partnerships are to improve matters, we, therefore, need to question whether the modality changes claimed in the post-Jomtien era are more than skin deep. Apart from UNESCO's commitment to basic education and literacy programmes, and SIDA's work in Guinea-Bissau (Carr-Hill 1982) and Tanzania (Ishumi 1992), prior to Jomtien, most donor agencies steered clear of any involvement in primary education. This was seen as a local responsibility, or at least the responsibility of non-governmental organisations, partly because of the different languages involved and partly because such bodies had better access to the grassroots communities. Many agencies also feared that, if they became involved, it could prove to be a costly, open-ended and long-term commitment. This would have more risks than fixed timescale projects that could be more easily publicised with electorates back home. However, encouraged by the World Bank, and having pledged themselves to supporting primary education in Jomtien, most donor agencies have, since 1990, changed their policies to focus on primary and basic education, gender issues, poverty alleviation, and sector-wide approaches (SWAps) to reform. In the light of this, to what extent have modalities changed in comparison with past eras?

At the end of the 1980s Watson (1988) traced 40 years of previous development research to coincide with the Fortieth Anniversary of the Declaration of Human Rights. His analysis included studies which justified the expansion of education generally; the importance of universal primary education; literacy; university expansion; educational planning, equity and regional disparities; the purposes of schooling, which embraced the curriculum, examinations, teachers; the education of women; and finance, including overseas aid. Some of this was touched upon in Chapter 2. The paper also looked at research done by, or commissioned by, the agencies, as well as by individual academics. Significantly, it emerged that it was mainly work undertaken under the auspices of the agencies themselves that had influenced their policies; very little independent academic research was considered, as indicated from the references at the end of agency publications. This remains true of the World Bank *Education Sector Strategy* (World Bank 1999; IJED 2002). Both Psacharopoulos (1990) and Theisen (1997) bemoan the fact that despite much work done by independent scholars, with a few exceptions, very little use is made of this by the international agencies. In the light of this, it is argued that an important avenue for future comparative and international research is to analyse the processes by which educational research reaches and influences policy makers. Some such work has been done by Samoff (1996b) and McGinn (1996), but there needs to be far more attention to this area if critical, independent research is to increase its chances of improved impact in the future.

Not only is the World Bank strong on ideology, as we have argued in previous sections, but its influence in shaping the policies of many governments has been very strong. The *Education Sector Strategy* paper (World Bank 1999) has had a profound impact on the way governments have redirected resources from higher education towards basic education; on the way that they are seeking alternative patterns of finance; and on what is regarded as the best means of improving school systems. As indicated earlier, many critics believe that too much of this thinking has been based on Western paradigms applied to the developing world, regardless of its cultural appropriateness or the suitability of the local infrastructure (Samoff 1993, 1996b; McGinn 1994; IJED 1996a; Watson 1996b; Riddell, A. 1999; Klees 2002). As Buchert's (1998) analysis of *Education Reform in the South in the 1990s* reveals, the concepts of decentralisation; improved school management through the training of head teachers and the involvement of local communities; the diversion of funds from higher education to primary and basic education; increased privatisation and the introduction of user fees; school improvement policies through better use of time, greater participation in whole school plans, and curriculum reform centred around outcomes-based learning; and reforms of teacher education, all emanated from Northern, mostly Anglo-Saxon models and ideologies. The 1995 *Priorities and Strategies for Education: A World Bank Review* (World Bank 1995) even recommended school choice as an instrument for reform, despite the fact that most children in the Third World are lucky to have any school nearby, let alone more than one to choose from! Moreover there seems to be little recognition of the effect on education provision of different linguistic and ethnic groups, though the Delors Report (UNESCO 1996) showed far greater sensitivity to these issues. The problem as Jones (1992) and Ilon (2002) remind us, is that the Bank views education and educational reforms through the eyes of a bank seeking efficiency and value for money.

Not only have the ideas generated from such international agencies been presented in a top-down manner as generic solutions to perceived global education problems, but within the target countries the same top-down approach to reform has been applied – despite the rhetoric of partnership, local participation and ownership (Odora Hoppers 2001). This has frequently seen the further destruction of local community initiatives such as those in Mozambique, Zambia and Zimbabwe (Hoppers 1999) and Mexico (Martin 1999).

The marginalisation of local knowledge and local initiatives is all the more apparent from the ways in which related consultancy and research have typically been commissioned. Preston and Arthur (1996), McGrath (1998, 2001a and b), and Lacey and Jacklin (2001) have all pointed out that the way that consultancy requirements have developed over the last two decades means that the commissioning agency often knows what it wants to find out before the work begins. It therefore sets the terms of reference so narrowly that any sense of integrity on the part of the consultant or researcher is compromised. Only rarely are local nationals involved, often in a junior and supporting role. The time constraints set by most agencies also ensure that any meaningful research over a period of time is simply not possible. This critical perspective is confirmed well by the work undertaken by Samoff (1993) on educational reform in Africa during the previous decade; and by his (1996b) analysis of the content, personnel and procedures used in 240 educational surveys in Africa between 1990 and 1994. Samoff's findings reveal that apart from some nominal representation by a few local researchers these African surveys were almost exclusively carried out by expatriate personnel. They, in turn, carry with them their own biases and preconceived ideas (Leach 1994). As Habte (1999) points out the rhetoric of partnership and local capacity building mean nothing unless there is a concerted effort to build up local universities and research institutions. This may be about to change. Having denigrated, or at least downgraded, the role of the university and higher education sector in development in favour of basic education during most of the 1990s, the World Bank and UNESCO have, more recently, come to recognise that higher education has a key role to play in providing the leadership and necessary personnel for all other sectors of education – the future teachers, researchers, scientists, computer specialists, agronomists, doctors and the like (UNESCO 1996; World Bank 1999, 1999/2000, 2001).

Sector-wide approaches to development

Perhaps the greatest form of influence, if not overt control, of whole education systems could come as a result of more recent commitment to the sector-wide approach (SWAPs) to education reform. Through SWAPs funding agencies claim to be better able to work in partnership with national governments, to help them to establish their own priorities and 'to develop the capacity within ministries of education to take responsibility for managing sub-sector and programme development' (Smith, H. 2002:1). Smith, for example, shows how one private NGO has been developing this approach in Cambodia and Rwanda. What he does not touch upon is the danger of NGOs being absorbed into the global thinking of the large agencies, thereby losing some of their ability to work at the grassroots level, and to critique dominant policies. This danger was recognised by the ADEA Biennial Meeting held in Dakar in 1997 (ADEA 1997). There are also dangers that, through SWAPs, external bodies can shape national thinking more fundamentally, and that they will only agree to finance capacity building if the local government's priorities are in accord with the external agency's own agendas for support. This emerges more clearly in Buchert's (2002) analysis of SWAPs in operation in Burkina Faso, Ghana and Mozambique where she points out that, while all three countries adhere to the concepts proposed by the funding agencies, they are at different levels of ability to implement changes. In doing so, Buchert argues there can be no blueprint that fits every context; local situations and limitations need to be respected. Her conclusion is, therefore, that:

> The level of rhetoric concerning mutual respect, transparency, trust, dialogue, cooperation, coordination and genuine partnerships cannot eliminate underlying differences and structural relationships between aid providers and aid recipients.
>
> (Buchert 2002:83)

The latest Bank thinking about the role of education in development appears in the *Education Sector Strategy* noted earlier (World Bank 1999). This represents the culmination of the work, and thinking, undertaken by the Bank over the previous decade and, as Mundy (2002) argues, it is a compromise document following on from several internal struggles in the Bank between educational professionals and development economists. This sets out four global strategic priorities: (i) reaching for international goals such as basic education for girls and for the poorest; (ii) early interventions – early child development and school health programmes; (iii) innovative forms of delivery, such as distance education, open learning and the use of new technologies, and (iv) selected areas of systems reform. These include acquiring reliable statistics on standards of achievement, the curriculum and assessment; decentralisation and improving school governance; and encouraging investment by private entrepreneurs in developing access to new modes of learning. While recognising that each country situation is unique and promising to produce specific country and regional papers on education, the Bank, nevertheless, still manages to produce a set of strategies which it sees as having a global impact. More disturbing, however, is the fact that it, again, largely ignores educational research undertaken by non-Bank staff; it is still predicated on human capital theory which sees education solely as a means of economic expansion; it ignores the potential impact of local analyses and knowledge; it fails to address the very real, and complex, problems of weak states operating in a global economy; and it fails to recognise that education, health, rural development, the environment and the economy are all interdependent and that education cannot, therefore, be treated as a sector isolated from society as a whole. The *Education Sector Strategy* is thus a disappointing document that wraps up much old thinking in the guise of new ideas. According to Ilon (2002), this is a biased document which ignores the causes of global poverty, and ignores the academic critiques that point to the Bank's role in extending poverty. It is also seen as dismissive of local views which might not accord with the Bank's way of seeing things, and assumes that all education systems are primarily there to be a part of the global economy.

The management of knowledge for development

Discussion of the World Bank's Education Knowledge Management System has further serious implications since it assumes that the only educational research knowledge of any worth is that which is held by the Bank. As Soudien (2002) points out, the state's role in regulating what knowledge is learnt in school is being undermined by globalisation and new ways of acquiring knowledge. The Bank, however, sees little that is problematic in this, assuming that education is provided solely for an individual to be able to join the labour market. Klees (2002) and Hickling-Hudson (2002) are especially critical, arguing that the *Education Sector Strategy* reveals no new thinking about education's role in society, that it repeats well worn clichés and appears to have benefited little from past experience. There is little mention of teachers, except in a derogatory fashion; there is no mention of education as a basic human right; there is no sense in which education is seen as a public good, nor any acknowledgement that the state has a public duty to see that its citizens are as well educated as possible. Above all, it can be argued that the Bank is still trying to perpetuate and justify an outmoded system with little recognition of the diversity of the world's countries or peoples, and certainly with no recognition of its own part in promoting global inequalities. Hickling-Hudson (2002:566) puts this into perspective when she writes:

> As Michel Chossudovsky (2000) puts it, 'the late 20th century will go down in World history as a period of global impoverishment marked by the collapse of productive systems in the developing World, the demise of national institutions and the disintegration of health and educational programs'. And this occurred in spite of the large post World War 2 expansion of education that the Bank itself has highlighted.

Before drawing this chapter to a conclusion, there is one further arena in which the Northern international community can be seen to be undermining efforts to promote partnerships and collaborative development modalities, and having a negative impact on education and social welfare in the less developed countries of the world.

Political conditionalities and the debt burden

Conditions for receiving development assistance have been a central part of overseas aid since its inception (Mosley 1987) but, as we have argued, they became more aggressively applied in the late 1980s and early 1990s. This was partly because the collapse of the Soviet Empire in Eastern Europe persuaded many world leaders that Western democratic values, and economic capitalism of the free market variety, had triumphed over communism. If financial and technical assistance was to be given to the former Central and East European nations, it was argued, they should be persuaded to begin to reform along Western lines. Thus the European Bank for Reconstruction and Development expressly linked aid to the former communist countries with their willingness to reform their political structures and move towards democratic pluralism and free market economies. The World Bank and the IMF also applied these rules. There were also other reasons. Frustrated by the corruption of some African and Asian leaders, the international community argued that the only way to exert pressure on them to reform was by placing conditions on the continuance of aid. There was also a strongly held belief that multi-party democracies, where opposition parties could challenge the government of the day, were more open to change and reform than dictatorships. There were several notes of caution expressed, as reflected in the following quotation taken from the British Overseas Development Institute (ODI 1992:4), an independent NGO:

> Established democracies with a legitimacy stemming from a tradition of consultation can initiate economic reform. However, while there are some encouraging signs, developing country experience in the 1980s does not give a firm assurance that greater democracy will result in better economic management, effective adjustment policies or faster economic growth. Ultimately democracy's case may stand better on its own.

Certainly there is no proven link between political accountability through democratic means and economic growth, as several Asian tiger economies have shown, nor does political and economic reform come from internal pressures alone. Nevertheless, despite protestations to the contrary, economic and political conditionalities persist as a means of easing the debt burden for many countries as DFID policy documents reveal, and as Mingat and Tan (2001) show with regard to assistance for the world's most highly indebted poor countries (HIPC). Moreover, one could legitimately ask what right Western governments and multilateral aid agencies have to insist on democratic governments, good governance, gender equality, respect for human rights and concern for the environment when many OECD countries do not practise these themselves. Many countries also resent specific demands being placed upon them, as tantamount to interfering in their domestic affairs.

Irrespective of the conditionalities laid down by donor governments and agencies it needs to be recognised that aid has been decreasing over the years while the debt burden has been increasing. Neither situation helps poor countries to tackle their education and social problems. Forster (1999) has talked of 'aid fatigue' and the downturn in overseas aid would appear to confirm this. With the few exceptions referred to earlier in this chapter most OECD donors have fallen well short of the 0.7 per cent or the 1 per cent of GNP urged by Brandt (1980) and Pearson (1969) for overseas aid. Between 1961 and 1999 aid fell as a percentage of GNP from 0.61 per cent to 0.24 per cent, the lowest figure since 1950 (UNDP 2000; World Bank 1999/2000). The volume of aid is now less than in 1987 and the United Kingdom's Treasury and DFID have stated that:

> At the moment aid flows are around their lowest for a decade; in Africa, they fell from $32 per capita in 1990 to $19 per capita in 1998. ODA has fallen while at the same time there is concern over whether aid works or not, and whether poor country governments can ensure that aid is actually effective in assisting poverty reduction.
>
> (DFID 2002:1)

There is thus a clear recognition that the 2015 targets set by Jomtien and subsequently revised at Dakar in 2000 as Millennium Development Goals are unlikely to be met, especially in Africa.

Work undertaken by Bennell and Furlong (1997) for the CfBT confirms this trend and it makes depressing reading. They point out that ODA to education is now less than before the WCEFA . In Africa it fell from 11.2 per cent of overall aid in 1990 to 4.8 per cent in 1996; in East Asia and the Pacific it fell from 11.6 per cent to 8.1 per cent; in Eastern Europe it fell from 4.1 per cent to a meagre 0.1 per cent. Only in South Asia was there a very slight increase from 16.6 per cent to 17 per cent. Not only has there been an overall decline but what is given is expected to cover far more areas: humanitarian relief (ODI 2002) and emergency relief, as well as general help for educational development. Even here the list of aspects to be covered grows ever longer – health education, concern for the environment, AIDS and drugs awareness programmes, as well as support for teachers' salaries and equipment such as books. The likelihood of achieving the Millennium Development Goals is remote. No wonder that some see donor agencies as seeking to offload the burden of their international targets on to NGOs and local governments.

These figures only make the issue of the international debt burden, which now stands at a staggering US$2 trillion, even more acute. In Africa alone the debt burden amounted to US$235 billion in 1999, the debt service average (i.e. the sums spent on repaying the interest on loans) amounted to US$17 billion, equivalent to 3.8 per cent of Africa's total GDP, or 16 per cent of annual export earnings, or the equivalent of 35 per cent of total expenditure on education (ADEA 2001). Seventeen African countries actually saw investment in, and enrolments in, the primary sector fall during the 1990s (DFID 2002). While 41 of the world's most highly indebted poor countries are in Africa, only three have met the strict conditions laid down for debt relief, and as of the beginning of 2002 only 15 per cent has been cut from HIPC debt despite the promises made at the G8 summit meeting held in Bonn in 1999. That has only been cut because of pressure brought by bodies such as the Jubilee Campaign, an alliance of disparate NGOs, church groups and other related interest groups that cut across international boundaries working in partnership.

Conclusions

This chapter has sought to discuss to what extent the relationship between Western governments, multilateral and bilateral development agencies, NGOs and poor countries of the South has changed from that of donors and recipients to one of development co-operation and productive partnership; how Northern development agencies are part of the process of globalisation; how they have helped to further the international transfer of educational policy and practice; how this has impacted on education in poor countries; and how the most powerful international agencies have come to dominate the development discourse with scant regard for local knowledge, local context and local research capacities. The way that international educational research and consultancy initiatives are often established and pursued can also be seen to help ensure continued Northern domination through new processes of neo-colonial control.

There is clearly much to suggest that the broad intellectual tensions identified at the outset of this book, between the intensification of globalisation and increased sensitivity to cultural and contextual differences, are being actively played out in the arena of international development co-operation. We, thus, have evidence of the increased influence of powerful international agencies at the global level, at the same time as contemporary policy discourse extols the virtues of new partnerships, co-operation and cross-cultural collaboration. This highlights many problematic issues relating to the uncritical international transfer of research and development priorities; acknowledges the increased significance of ongoing efforts to change development modalities; and draws attention, once again, to the importance of culture and context in the processes of both research and international development co-operation.

The following concluding chapters take these and other arguments forward to present the case for fundamental change, and to articulate ways in which the reconceptualisation of comparative and international research in education may be carried out to help the field make a more effective contribution in this and other arenas in the future.

Chapter 7

Reconceptualising comparative and international research in education

In this chapter the various themes and arguments developed throughout the book as a whole are brought together in articulating the case for a comprehensive reconceptualisation of the field of comparative and international education. The case builds upon the rationale outlined in Chapter 1, our review of the history and evolution of the field, the analyses of theoretical and methodological challenges, and our awareness of contemporary issues, priorities and research problems as discussed in Chapters 3 to 6.

The most influential challenges that we have identified stem from dramatic changes in geopolitical relations; the intensifying pace of globalisation; the pervasive influence of market forces and neo-liberal economics; the changing roles and impact of international agencies; rapid advances in information and communications technology; demand for strengthened linkages between educational research, policy and practice; growing tensions between the economic and cultural dimensions of national development and social reform; and varied poststructuralist challenges to dominant theoretical and methodological frameworks. These challenges, it is argued, all call for urgent and critical reflection, and for a repositioning of the field of comparative and international education to better address contemporary priorities and meet the emergent needs of the twenty-first century.

In addition, it is argued that without a clear repositioning, the field remains open to critique and challenge from others with an active interest or involvement in the international dimension of educational policy and practice, and in the implications of globalisation for both educational research and development. To some extent this is a paradoxical dilemma because such interests – if well connected to the experience, literature and traditions of comparativists – could in themselves be an important source of renewal and intellectual reinvigoration for the field itself. Such positive engagement, however, is more likely to develop if the distinctive comparative and international constituency can better demonstrate the continuing contemporary relevance of its work – and if others engaging in related activities can then more clearly see the enduring significance of both the traditions and contemporary advances being made within the field. For such reasons a 'bridging of cultures and traditions' (Crossley 2000) lies at the very heart of the reconceptualisation proposals articulated here. Moreover, it is emphasised that this is a bridging that implies a multi-dimensional process (between, for example, theoretical and applied arenas, policy and practice, micro and macro levels of analysis, historical and contemporary research, and studies of the North and the South), and genuine dialogue where all involved learn from the experience, practice and literatures of each other. From this perspective, those who see themselves working primarily within the field must actively look further outwards beyond conventional borders (Alexander 2001) and, where appropriate, into other intellectual, professional and cultural territories and worldviews. It is in this critical but forward-looking and creative spirit that our case for the reconceptualisation of the field of comparative and international education is advanced here.

In doing this we are concerned to value diversity and not to overlook the very real strengths that have characterised the field from its origins in the nineteenth century plans and aspirations of Jullien (Jullien 1817; Fraser 1964) and Sadler's 1900 benchmark lecture (see Higginson 1979). As we have argued earlier, Sadler inspired many generations of comparativists on both sides of the Atlantic and beyond, including his student Isaac L. Kandel (1933), with his then pioneering and interpretive social, historical and cultural studies of education. While academic territories (Becher 1989) can and do often limit creativity and intellectual advances, comparative education as a field can justifiably point to its long cherished, multidisciplinary foundations and traditions, as a notable strength on which to build in the future.

Previous efforts to synthesise challenges to the post-war empirical social sciences phase of comparative and international education were made by Altbach and Kelly (1986) in their compilation of relevant articles drawn from the *Comparative Education Review*. Reflecting upon what they then saw as the theoretical dominance of structural functionalism, combined with positivist methodological assumptions, Altbach and Kelly identified four main challenges that had emerged since previous 'state of the art' reviews of the field were published in 1977 (see *Comparative Education Review* 21, 1977; *Comparative Education* 13, 1977). These were seen as (i) challenges to the nation-state as the exclusive research framework; (ii) challenges to input–output models and reliance upon quantification; (iii) challenges to structural functionalism, and (iv) the emergence of new substantive concerns, most notably gender research, institutional studies and critiques, the content and processes of education and the legitimisation of educational knowledge. According to Kelly and Altbach (1988:14), 'prior to 1977 these issues scarcely entered the discourse of the field and were not promoted through its major journals or texts'.

While this fourfold framework remains useful today, and can be used to categorise more contemporary work that has been carried out, clearly much has changed in the intervening years. The emergent nature of some of these changes is reflected in the contributions to a number of more recent edited collections (see Alexander *et al.* 1999; Arnove and Torres 1999; Alexander *et al.* 2000). Our present discussion draws upon such work and our own related studies, but articulates an original, comprehensive and sustained analysis, within its historical and intellectual context, in advancing the case for a thorough reassessment and a fundamental reconceptualisation of the field overall. Since the nature and extent of the contemporary challenges have been discussed throughout the text, the present chapter focuses mainly upon their implications for the processes of reconceptualisation in practice, and upon possible ways forward for the field in the future.

Reconceptualising comparative and international education

At the broadest level we have argued that it is the research dimension and research potential of comparative and international education that has underpinned the contemporary resurgence of interest in the field. Moreover, it is research activity, and related research training, that has played the most strategic part in the reinvigoration of the institutional base. From the work reviewed here, it can be seen, for example, that the relatively new Comparative Education Research Centre (CERC) established at the University of Hong Kong in 1994 has played a pivotal role during the 1990s and subsequently in stimulating and documenting comparative studies throughout Greater China (Bray and Gui 2001) and South-East Asia.

Building upon these research strengths in a more explicit way offers much for the future in a world where it is increasingly difficult to understand education in any context without reference to global issues and international trends and comparisons. But, in the light of the analysis presented here, there are clearly many questions to raise relating to both the focus of such research and the ways in which it might be carried out. The implications of such questions for the nature of the reconceptualisation process are considered below.

Research and evidence-based policy

In addressing the contemporary critique levelled at social and educational research in general, comparative and international education can justifiably point to its traditional strengths as an applied, problem-oriented field (King, E.J. 1989). New and better ways, however, must be found to engage more directly, and critically, with the ongoing concerns and priorities faced by mainstream educational research – and with the worldwide call for cumulative and professionally oriented, evidence-based research and policy-making. As Goodson (1997) argued, in speaking at the British Educational Research Association's annual conference, it is time for educational researchers to reposition themselves closer to practice. Since many mainstream educational researchers and policy-makers have also taken renewed interest in international trends, the potential for new partnerships and for a distinctively strategic, and possibly cautionary, contribution from comparative and international education has increased. Noah (1986:161), for example, pointed out some time ago that while:

... comparative education is an applied field of study that finds particular justification in the service of evaluation, management, administration and policy-making. Like all fields, it is open to potential abuse by those who wish to use its results to support (or oppose) a specific program of change.

Secondary analyses and politically inspired interpretations of the influential IEA Studies, as we have seen, illustrate such dangers well in a global context where relative positions on international league tables often tempt decision-makers to consider the adoption of apparently successful pedagogic practice from foreign cultural contexts. Comparativists can thus make a uniquely valuable contribution when reports of foreign educational policy are considered by reminding decision-makers that they can be:

> ... fully and fruitfully used in discussion only if they are seen as a part of a much broader enterprise, with HMIs [inspectors] contributing their particular insights along with others: scholars, researchers and students whose job it is to take more sweeping views, not necessarily tied to this month's policy problem ... . the health of policy-making in an interdependent world must depend in part on the health of comparative education research in the broadest sense.
>
> (Beattie and Brock 1990:4)

The explicitly comparative IEA studies are particularly pertinent examples of the sort of large-scale, cumulative and evidence-based research that is advocated by contemporary stakeholders in education. This is partly because governments find it easier to seize upon eye-catching findings rather than to grapple with the complexity of many issues. Ironically, however, criticism (often relating to context insensitivity) of this highly influential, and still evolving model, has come more from within the field of comparative and international education than it has from without. Dialogue and discourse across professional and intellectual boundaries can thus be much improved. This critique is also valuable because it draws attention to the limitations of policy transfer and to further lessons that can be learned from the comparative perspective. It is in considering such issues that distinctive implications for theory, context and culture re-emerge with renewed force and relevance.

Theoretical implications of context and culture

It should, perhaps, not be too surprising that the IEA comparisons of school achievement should have gained widespread recognition in the broader arena of policy-making. The sequence of assessment studies produced, since their origins in the early 1960s, have focused upon issues relating to the quality of teaching and learning that have increasingly come to dominate the priorities and agendas of decision-makers worldwide. Data have been systematically quantified on a large scale, core school subjects such as Science and

Mathematics have received concerted attention and substantial resources have been invested in the research enterprise in countries drawn from a wide spectrum of developed and developing countries (Goldstein 1996; Postlethwaite 1999).

The critique noted above relates as much to the way in which findings have been used as it does to the methodological and theoretical limitations of the IEA studies themselves. Acknowledging this, Goldstein (1996) draws attention to the contextual relevance of IEA findings and the dilemmas encountered when attempts are made to focus upon comparisons of achievement across national systems of education. Such critiques draw more directly upon the core concepts of context and culture – concepts that remain central to the work of those specialists in the field of comparative and international research that have long questioned the methodological rationale of the IEA model. It is possible, however, to argue, as does Cumming (1996), that useful policy results can be more realistically derived from comparisons of differing groups within the same national education system data set – and that such findings can be related to differences in social and cultural factors. In the light of such issues Kellaghan (1996) draws upon many insights and perspectives central to the comparative canon in outlining key parameters for those involved in the disciplined application of IEA findings in the policy arena. In doing this, Kellaghan helps to add renewed legitimacy to the distinctive characteristics of comparative and international research in education, in a policy context central to the management and performance concerns of governmental agencies worldwide. This discussion also draws attention back to the importance of contextual and cultural factors in cross-national research and to the dilemmas, long recognised by comparativists, associated with international transfer in all dimensions of educational research and development.

Rapprochement between comparative and international research

A useful irony is embedded in the above analysis. Revealingly, the contextual critique emerges more strongly from the theoretically-oriented comparative tradition of the combined field of comparative and international education, than it does from the more explicitly applied and action-oriented expertise associated with international education. This, it is argued, is one of the most fundamental issues for consideration in the reconceptualisation of the combined field, for it simultaneously demonstrates the weaknesses of *both* established traditions, while identifying priorities for future attention in a way that is of considerable theoretical and methodological significance. As already indicated, in broad scope this relates to long-standing criticism of much international education for being too closely related to policy agendas of the day, and to the implementation of reform projects tied to development assistance agency assumptions and priorities (Buchert and King 1996; Samoff 1996a; Jones 1998). Counterpoising this perspective is the critique of the more explicitly comparative dimension of the field for being too preoccupied with abstract theoretical scholarship divorced from the real world of educational policy and practice (IJED 1996b; Watson 1998). While the polarisation of this analysis may oversimplify the issues involved, it is revealing, and the latter critique is reminiscent of the broader challenge to educational research that calls for cumulative, applied and professionally relevant research that is clearly, and unambiguously, communicated to policy-makers and practitioners. There are, however, no simple answers here, even if a closer relationship between theoretical scholarship and applied research warrants careful exploration.

Experience within the international education arena also points, somewhat ironically, to the very real limitations of undue reliance upon applied, policy-oriented studies (Crossley 2001). In many post-colonial countries greater degrees of austerity (Lewin 1987) have long accentuated accountability, evaluation, project relevance and generalisability in research but, despite this, the success rate of many intended reforms has, as we have demonstrated, been disappointing, particularly with regard to their sustainability beyond periods of external funding (King, K. 1991b; Buchert 1998). Moreover, it is argued here that it is the failure of many international development initiatives to give sufficient weight to the broad spectrum of theoretical insights, and to contextual and cultural issues, that lies at the heart of this dilemma. It is only rarely that those working within the professional culture of international development co-operation have, to date, been able to apply the literature, experience and perspectives characteristic of the more detached comparative social science constituency in any challenging and sustained way. Unfortunately, the irony is greater still, for, while the comparative dimension of our combined field accords particular premium to such issues, it is this constituency that is most open to the ongoing challenge to mainstream educational research for not adequately addressing the policy issues and practical concerns of the day. In this context, and as noted earlier, the 1997 amalgamation of professional and academic constituencies that led to the formation of the British Association for International and Comparative Education (BAICE), represents important structural and organisational bridge building. This was a positive and practical movement towards reconceptualisation in itself, and one that helps further to consolidate efforts made to unite comparative and international education societies in the 1980s, while providing a foundation for more fundamental interpersonal, sub-cultural and intellectual advances in the future.

Perhaps more intractably the task of rapprochement will be more complex than this somewhat over simplified portrayal and analysis implies, for there are often sound reasons for the persistence of intellectual and organisational divisions between research cultures and communities. There are also well-established traditions and political and territorial imperatives to negotiate (see, for example, Alexander 2001). As Furlong (1998:23) points out, educational research is 'constantly subject to fads and fashions, to competing, ill-defined and sometimes contradictory goals'. Moreover, to be realistic, we should recognise the limitations of research and not expect the impossible, or forget that:

> The connection between research and practice is not one in which research influences practice, as many researchers might hope, nor one in which practice influences research as many might hope, but rather one in which both research and practice are influenced by and are perhaps even victims of the same shifting social and political context.
>
> (Kennedy 1997:9–10)

Recognition of the impact of such changing socio-political trends, nevertheless, points to a more profound rationale for concerted efforts towards reconceptualisation and rapprochement in comparative and international education. This is especially so when old conceptual divisions between, for example, 'developed' and 'developing' countries are increasingly problematic, when global forces influence the educational arrangements of all nation states, and when issues relating to culture, identity and context are challenging rationalism and modernist assumptions and development priorities worldwide (see also Little 2000b). In such times the bridging of traditional divisions, the challenging of old certainties and the forging of new discourses is essential for the advancement of all fields of enquiry.

Widening the discourse in comparative and international education

Central to the thesis developed here is the argument that the increasingly rapid pace of socio-economic change demands vastly improved forms of communication and interchange between human groups, organisations and cultures worldwide. This, as we have already noted, includes professional cultures, international agencies, policy makers, practitioners, paradigmatic frameworks, ethnic groups, the general public, periods of time, and researchers across all disciplines and fields. Such cross-cultural bridging is essential if we are to better conceptualise and understand the dramatic changes that contemporary globalisation processes have set in train. Indeed, in tune with Huntington (1993) it is argued that the changes now being faced across the globe are as profound as any previously encountered. Globalisation, spurred on by 'appeals to unfettered capitalism',[1] is indeed progressing hand in hand with the poststructuralist challenges to the Enlightenment project, positivistic science and modernisation theory that we have discussed earlier. Tensions between ideas and developments that underpin globalisation on the one hand, and poststructuralism on the other, thus generate, what we now reiterate, are some of the most fundamental of all intellectual challenges of the present day. Dealing with such challenges will demand the bridging of much more than intellectual traditions and cultures. It will require fundamental social change and new discourses that recognise the limitations of deeply embedded ways of thinking about the world, for as

---

1   We owe thanks to Phillip Jones, University of Sydney, for this evocative phrase.

Giddens (1997:2) points out, globalisation 'describes the increasing inter-penetration between individual life and global futures, something which … is relatively new in history'. Giddens goes on to say that 'it is a wholly contradictory process' and that 'we are the first generation to enter a global age' (1997:2). Discourses that can help improve our conceptualisation of globalisation processes, while engaging with the diverse challenges raised by poststructuralist critiques of meta-narratives have the potential to go beyond the well-known limitations of deconstruction (Norris and Benjamin 1996), and to contribute to advances that may be both affirmative and more effectively tuned to the cultural differences and multi-polar geo-politics of the twenty-first century.

Within the field of comparative and international education the reconceptualisation thesis articulated here thus suggests that there is much to be gained from a fundamental challenge to the barriers that limit wider debate and interchange, especially between what Altbach and Kelly (1986) labelled the 'new realists' and the post-modern proponents of critical scholarship. This is not to imply that comparative and international education should be too disparaging of itself for, within the broader field of education, it is particularly well placed to advance genuinely multidisciplinary research across cultural boundaries – with an inherent concern for contextualisation and respect for differing social constructions of reality. Nevertheless, given the turbulence of the times in which we live there remains, as already expressed, much to be done – and it is to the potential of a number of the more significant possibilities that we now turn in more specific detail.

Links betwen research and scholarship

The broad epistemological issues raised above help to highlight the significance of strengthening linkages between the predominantly action-oriented, applied, international constituency of the field, and the more traditionally theoretical, comparative dimension. This also points to the importance of forging a more substantial dialectic between empirical research – from all paradigmatic foundations – and critical, in-depth, and theoretical scholarship. Unfortunately, intensified financial, managerial and micro-political imperatives have in recent years been notorious in increasing the pressures on researchers to compete rather than collaborate, and to seek new externally funded projects before sustained reflection upon the findings of 'completed' studies has been possible. Such missed opportunities and conflicts of interest can be costly in themselves, and undue haste, often generated by external pressures, does little to improve the range and quality of research dissemination repeatedly called for by concerned stakeholders. Efforts to bridge the research and scholarship divide also draws attention back to the limitations of prevailing research cultures that separate the study and conceptualisation of education in developing countries from other dimensions of comparative and international research – all the more so in a world where global forces have an increasingly influential impact in all socio-economic contexts. Despite encouraging organisational trends, barriers between the personnel, networks and literatures of researchers working on European and development studies, for example, remain pervasive and detrimental to the field as a whole. This is especially pertinent when faced with the questionable legitimacy of long-established socio-economic classifications, and the dramatic impact of major socio-economic transformations characteristics of the late twentieth century.

Strengthened cross-disciplinary studies

Discourses and studies that build upon the multidisciplinary traditions of the field are particularly apposite in times when cultural forces (Mazrui 1990) and political transformations (Bray and Lee 1997) are repeatedly demonstrating the limitations of linear, teleological assumptions about national and international development strategies. Holding significant potential for comparative and international education at this point in time are studies that combine the field's long engagement with language, literacy and culture (Masemann and Welch 1997; Brock-Utne 2001) with the advancement of the post-colonial critique (Hickling-Hudson 1998; Tikly 1999). This has the potential to stimulate new developments that more firmly recognise the contemporary significance of intellectual frameworks that deal with issues of identity, culture, race, gender and class. Compatible with multi-level analyses, post-colonial studies can be advanced, for example, through critical ethnography (Masemann 1982) and through further applications of the meta-level studies of critical theorists such as Bourdieu and Passeron (1977), Bourdieu (1998), Habermas (1978, 1990), Giroux (1997) and Apple (1999, 2000, 2001). As indicated in earlier chapters, post-colonial frameworks could also do much to challenge the Eurocentric profile of much post-modern theorising and the colonialist image of some ethnography, in a way that could better demonstrate their contemporary potential for applied, policy-oriented research. Indeed, as documented by Torres (1998), for many years comparativists have sustained interest in the work of Freire (1971, 1996) and its implications for development processes. The cultural critiques of Mazrui (1990, 1992), Thaman (1993), Hickling-Hudson (1998), Kumar (2001) and other non-Western analysts have also been acknowledged within the field – but the consistent application of such perspectives within the mainstream of international education discourse and development work remains limited or confined to the activities of non-governmental organisations (NGOs), detached theorists or polemical critics. On the other hand, there are some shifts in thinking and praxis inspired by the now worldwide influence of writers such as Freire, Chambers (1992) and others, that demonstrate ways in which more concerted post-colonial analyses may continue to advance theory while contributing in a productive way to the improvement of educational policy and practice in pluralist and multi-cultural communities. As with the post-modern critique and associated literature, however, the dangers of inaccessible theorising obscuring the applied potential of such cross-disciplinary and cross-cultural research deserve attention in their own right.

The mainstream challenge to what Becher (1989) has called 'academic tribes and territories', and reconsideration of the philosophical and historical traditions of Sadler's approach to comparative education also has much in common with the rationale and goals of contemporary socio-cultural studies of education (Wertsch 1995; Bruner 1996). Closer working relationships between social scientists from different fields thus have much to offer, as reflected by the justification for the recent establishment in the United Kingdom of an Academy of Learned Societies for the Social Sciences.

The above discussion also demonstrates the potential of stronger linkages between social science researchers and those working within the arts and humanities. Much of the inspiration for post-colonial theorising, for example, is derived from the literature of cultural studies – and Louisy (2001) an academic, and head of state, well illustrates this in her call for the rich cultural traditions of the Caribbean to play a more active role in shaping the future of comparative and international research. In urging Caribbean researchers to contribute more to the international debate she writes:

> Cultural analysts and comparative sociologists should study in more detail the distinctive social, cultural or even economic circumstances that nurture, for example, the creative imagination of Jamaican Robert Nestor Marley and the musical and social phenomenon of Reggae, Rastafarianism and dreadlocks, that has permeated so many other countries both in the developed and developing world
>
> (Louisy 2001:432).

In a different but similar vein, we have earlier noted how Kazamias (2001:439) applies concepts and insights from Greek mythology, develops a strong critique of positivistic approaches to social and educational research, and makes an impassioned case for 'reinventing the historical in comparative education'. For Kazamias, the displacement of history from the scope of much contemporary comparative education has contributed to its 'humanistic' impoverishment. This echoes a plea made by Watson (1998) in his 1997 Inaugural Presidential Address given to the British Association for International and Comparative Education (BAICE). Returning to these two examples usefully illustrates the case for the strengthening of linkages between the arts and the social sciences – and for stronger bridges to be built between current studies and disciplines, such as history, that may have played a more significant role for the field in the past. As Bourdieu's (1998) reflexive approach to sociology powerfully demonstrates, if we wish to understand each other better we also need to understand our own biographies, our own histories and, in doing so, where we are coming from. This, we argue, can apply as much to a field of study as it does to an individual agency. Contemporary researchers in comparative and international education can thus do much to remind policy makers of the importance of both philosophy and history.

Indeed, methodologically fruitful advances could also arise from more focused studies of the theory and practice of comparative methodology across faculties and disciplines. Øyen's (1990) work, for the International Sociological Association, is indicative of the methodological lessons that may be learned from other comparative fields, and this is appropriately related to Galtung's (1990) plea for pluralism in theory formation for social research. At a more specific level, the potential for innovative cross-disciplinary comparative and international research is demonstrated by studies of cognition and culture that are beginning to open up new insights into the nature and implications of legitimate 'ways of knowing' in differing cultural contexts (Oatley 1992). Masemann (1990) echoed such principles on a broader platform in her Presidential Address for the United States-based Comparative and International Education Society, and Noah (1986:161) reminds us that:

> A comparative approach enlarges the framework within which we can view the results obtained in a single country: by providing counter instances, it challenges us to refine our theories and test their validity against the reality of different societies; and, by providing parallel results, it can yield important confirmation of results obtained elsewhere.

Multiple frames of reference and units of analysis

Early challenges to the nation-state as the primary unit of analysis have been sustained and reinforced in more recent years by the ethnographic movement at the micro-level and by the rapidly changing socio-political events of the 1990s.

Returning to the macro-level, the impact of intensified globalisation is, nevertheless, of particular significance as we have argued earlier. While the nation-state continues usefully to frame much research within the field, understanding the relationship between the state and globalisation as a process is currently of increasing importance – and a global framework for analysis is especially pertinent for comparative studies. Dale (2001:493) thus suggests that 'it should be the central aim of comparative education to lay bare the nature of and the reasons for the different impacts globalisation has had in differing contexts worldwide'. To emphasise the significance and complexity of globalisation discourses he goes on to caution against simplistic alignments with the 'globalisation boom' (2001:494) and to argue for critical comparative analyses of globalisation's place in the 'knowledge economy' … from the distance afforded by a 'very long spoon'. Such arguments clearly have much to contribute to the widening of frames of reference and units of analysis advocated in this section.

Beyond this, much can also be gained from Bray and Thomas's (1995) plea for multi-level analysis, and from writers such as McLeish and Phillips (1998) who have focused upon frameworks relating to educational reconstruction in societies facing rapid socio-political transition (see also Mebrahtu et al. 2000). Others have seen potential in comparative studies of Pacific Rim contexts (Sullivan 1998), and of small states (Bray and Packer 1993; Crossley and

Holmes 1999). Thus Cowen (1996a:150) refers to 'transitology' and the need to give attention to forces beyond the nation-state, and to 'international and global structures associated with tendencies towards "post-modernity"' in his search for a 'new' comparative education. Paulston (1999), as we have seen, also endorses the opening up of the comparative and international discourse to the debate of post-modern ideas, by accepting Rust's (1991) challenge with his advocacy of social cartography as a framework for comparative studies in education.

Miller (1991) also captures the importance of recognising the 'other' in similar terms when he applies place theory to the dilemmas faced by small states at the periphery of international decision-making, and argues that:

> Marginal countries and marginal groups within these countries are in the most favourable position to take ... risk. They can convert disadvantage into opportunity and move to a more central place in the continued development of human civilisation.
>
> (Miller 1991:290)

From this perspective it can be seen that much can be gained from alternative units of analysis and from intellectual frameworks that apply poststructuralist notions of, for example, place theory and social cartography. Watson's (1998) plea for clear applications remains important, however, if the advantages of innovative theoretical frameworks and units of analysis are to be realised and communicated in a way that is accessible to those seeking assistance in the qualitative improvement of educational policy and practice. This returns the debate to the initial critique of mainstream educational research, and to the call for more substantial, cumulative, applied and relevant evidence-based policy and research.

Educational research, policy and practice

In many ways the present analysis began with the call for a strengthening of the relationship between educational research, and policy and practice. Much has already been said on this core theme to demonstrate how comparative and international experience can make a distinctive contribution to the broader debate. In particular, it is argued that the tendency for much traditional comparative research to focus upon detached theory, or, at best, comparisons of policy – and for much international work to eschew theory or implicitly adopt a modernist perspective, deserves concerted attention in the future. The poststructuralist debates articulated throughout this book, for example, help to demonstrate the potential and legitimacy of detailed qualitative research carried out within the field, of the opportunities presented by critical ethnography and of the centrality of cultural context in reputable studies designed to contribute to improved policy and practice (see, for example, Masemann 1982, 1990; Crossley and Vulliamy 1997a; Louisy 2001). In this international arena the strengths of collaborative studies carried out by combinations of insiders and outsiders are enhanced (Crossley 1990; Dyer and Choksi 1997). This is well demonstrated by the policy relevance of Broadfoot *et al.*'s (1993; 2000) studies of perceptions of teaching in England and France, and Stuart *et al.*'s (1997) efforts to improve classroom practice through action research in Lesotho. Strengthening partnerships between insiders and outsiders, researchers and practitioners and policy formulators and analysts could thus play an integral part in the reconceptualisation of the field as a whole.

In arguing this case it is acknowledged that comparative and international education has, once again, a credible track record. Wilson (1994:450), a former President of the Comparative and International Education Society (CIES), for example, has long noted the emergence of the 'academic-practitioner' within the field:

> … who has been equipped with a viable academic understanding of comparative education and who has used that orientation to further the *meliorative* function common to both international and comparative education in his or her subsequent international activities.

Once again, such foundations provide an excellent platform for future development.

However, while the case for the practitioner researcher is strong, Jarvis (1999) calls for broader scope within the field of education, and E.J. King (1997:85) warns comparativists that 'part of our conceptual reorientation lies in escaping from a purely pedagogical preoccupation: our "constituency" today includes not just other academics but a limitless array of participants'. Research strategies such as Participatory Rural Appraisal (Chambers 1992) are thus finding increased favour in international development work focused upon non-formal education and other community empowerment activities (NORAD 1995; DFID 1997). Such issues are explored at greater length by Crossley and Holmes (2001) with reference to contemporary trends in collaborative and participatory approaches to educational research, and to the potential of educational research partnerships, and international development co-operation.

In the international development arena, work of this nature highlights the importance of activities that contribute to the process goals of research capacity building, and the empowerment of local personnel. Achieving this in practice is, however, more complex than much of the partnership rhetoric would suggest – but it is here that a reconceptualised approach to comparative and international education has much to offer. At the forefront of such work is the influence of many non-governmental organisations (NGOs) such as the Swiss Commission for Research Partnerships with Developing Countries (KFPE). This organisation's *Guidelines for Research in Partnership with Developing Countries*, for example, identified 11 principles for successful research partnerships. Such guidelines point to innovative modes of operation for comparative and international researchers that require new levels of

'... mutual respect, honesty and openness. The partners must be able to communicate effectively and must be able to commit themselves to a long-term involvement' (KFPE, 1998:8).

Thus, in the development arena, research capacity building through partnerships between local and external personnel, could well prove to be one of the most effective ways of increasing context sensitivity and of bridging the gap between educational policy and practice. K. King (1991b) certainly views such activities as the equivalent of a new model of development co-operation that can help reduce the knowledge gap between the North and the South and enable more symmetrical North–South partnerships. The attention of research must also encompass a much wider spectrum of teaching and learning sites and issues if it is to deal effectively with the uncertainties, technologies and imperatives of the future.

Moreover, as more educational researchers engage with comparative and international studies, many additional insights and benefits, both intellectual and professional may accrue. This is evident in the policy work by Ball (1998c:117) in which he highlights the political motives for many cross-national studies where 'proposals and justifications for reform in one country provide resources for advocates and politicians interested in promoting change in others'. While Ball goes on to argue that, 'This is not so much a matter of policy exchange but the reinforcement of shared assumptive worlds', he also calls for 'more research and more theoretical development in the field of international policy' (p.117). Clearly, this identifies an important vein for future comparative studies but it also re-emphasises the dangers of uncritical international transfer, and of inadvertently reinforcing policy studies where a detailed knowledge of educational context and practice is often limited, and when the strengthening of evidenced-based policy is given a high premium by decision-makers and other key stakeholders.

Finally, it is argued that fundamental reconceptualisation must undoubtedly take greater cognisance of the advances in the field beyond the English language literature or dominant European discourses. As already argued, increased recognition of differing social constructions of reality, different cultural conceptions of development priorities (Cheng 1997) and innovative work on teaching and learning in contrasting socio-cultural contexts (Little 1988; Watkins and Biggs 1996, 2001; Tobin 1999) can all help to improve our impact upon specific policy and practice, while strengthening genuinely global theoretical insights and understandings.

In this respect the reconceptualisation process can be most effectively advanced by greater support for the promotion of comparative and international research from a wider range of cultural perspectives, and by the more active dissemination of research carried out in this way. Illustrative of this is the attention given by Bray and Gui (2001) to the various comparative education traditions in Greater China. Also of significance is the example provided by the translation and publication of the collected works of Gu Mingyuan (2001) titled *Education in China and Abroad: Perspectives from a Lifetime in Comparative Education.*

Returning to our bridging theme, and in the light of the United Nations designated 'Year of Dialogue Among Civilisations' (2001), comparative and international education is especially well placed to pioneer new dialogue across cultures and between civilisations. Hayhoe and Pan's (2001) study is therefore most helpful for demonstrating how the field can help in giving 'voice' to three major Eastern civilisations – Chinese, Arabic and Indian – in a way that generates a unique dialogue with the West on education, cultural differences and globalisation. Indeed, it can be argued that it is the changing nature of the dialogue between civilisations that has had the most profound implications of all for the reconceptualisation process advanced here.

As Hawkins (1998:1) points out:

> To accomplish a truly democratic education, it is necessary to promote dialogues among and across different perspectives and academic communities around the world.

Conclusions

In the light of our evolving critique of the nature and evolution of comparative and international education, the discussion in this chapter articulates ways in which the fundamental reconceptualisation of this multidisciplinary field can be advanced. At the outset of a new century it is argued that increasingly rapid socio-economic changes make such reconceptualisation essential. Tensions stimulated by the pace of globalisation, and the simultaneous impact of poststructuralist critiques of social research, generate some of the most fundamental intellectual challenges of the present day. These tensions underpin the case for reconceptualisation in our field, although it is further enhanced by the contemporary emergence of a sustained challenge to the nature and worth of mainstream educational research – and to its relevance and accessibility to those engaged in the improvement of policy and practice worldwide.

Looking to the future it is argued that the diverse and multidisciplinary traditions of comparative and international education make it especially well placed to deal with the increasingly complex, global and cross-cultural issues that will characterise the twenty-first century. It is, for example, a field that has long recognised the significance of global forces in educational research and development, and one that has consistently examined the dilemmas associated with the transfer of educational policy and practice from one cultural context to another. While some of the traditional strengths of the field provide a foundation for renewed growth, the case for fundamental critique and reconstruction, nevertheless, demands priority attention – if its potential to contribute to the improvement of policy and practice, or to advance theory in the educational and social sciences, is to be fully and effectively realised.

This process must necessarily involve a reconsideration of long accepted assumptions and sub-cultures within the field, and a reconceptualisation that engenders new priorities, discourses and modes of operation that are more closely in tune with the exigencies of the contemporary world. Of primary importance in this respect is the need for fundamental reconceptualisation and rapprochement relating to the comparative and international dimensions of the field. The significance of this is explicated with reference to the need for new or revitalised forms of discourse; for greater integration between empirical research and theoretical scholarship; for the advancement of cross-disciplinary studies; for the application and development of new frames of reference and units of analysis and – perhaps above all – for a strengthening of the relationship between educational research, policy and practice.

A research orientation for the field, if systematically but creatively constructed, is especially pertinent in a world marked by increasingly powerful global trends, and cross-cultural tensions founded upon issues of culture, identity and difference. Such turbulent times will also generate their own research issues and priorities which will, in turn, influence the nature of the work conducted. With regard to contemporary issues and priorities, the analysis conducted here suggests that these will inevitably be influenced by a combination of international, national and local agendas and include studies of:

- the nature and impact of globalisation;
- the further advancement and critique of the neo-liberal performance model of education;
- increased focus on culture, identity and learning in differing contexts;
- policy implications of the cross-cultural transfer of educational innovations;
- large-scale cross-national studies building upon or challenging the IEA model, and increasingly funded by international agencies;
- the extension (and critique) of mainstream/national studies into the international arena;
- the changing nature and role of international agencies and the implications for education;
- the impact, potential and dilemmas of information and communication technologies;
- studies of power, gender and marginalised groups, such as refugees, the disadvantaged, or small states;
- the relationship between education and poverty across all levels of society.

They will also include studies of new ways of teaching and learning, both within and across national boundaries; the implications of increasingly elderly populations in some societies and the devastating impact of HIV/AIDS in others; the growth of private tutoring at one level and of global corporation involvement in educational services at another.

Perhaps, more fundamentally, while closer linkages with other disciplinary arenas and with mainstream educational research communities, debates and agendas may have much to offer comparative and international education, the dangers of the uncritical transfer of dominant research paradigms, theories and agendas also arise. This draws attention back to the field's distinctive strengths and expertise that relate to the importance of the two core concepts of context and culture. Indeed, for these reasons, it is argued that a reconceptualised field of comparative and international education will be especially well placed for the future study of issues relating to globalisation, culture and identity, and of the continued emergence and impact of international educational agendas. To some extent this further challenges the nation-state as the primary unit of analysis without, as demonstrated by Green (1997), denying its continued relevance. A case is therefore made for the reconceptualised field to be more explicitly associated with the socio-cultural study of education in context. This reaffirms the principle that context matters, but repositions the field to engage in the study of education in all its varied and new forms, with regard to contextual factors operating at all levels, ranging from the personal, through the organisational, to the global.

Returning to theoretical and methodological themes and to the debate relating to policy and practice, it is clear that there is much for all engaged in the educational arena to learn about the inter-relationship between theoretical scholarship and applied research from, and within, the field of comparative and international education. Firstly, the dangers of an either/or conceptualisation, tempting researchers to abandon culturally sensitive theoretical studies in the face of the contemporary applied critique, are well demonstrated by the cautionary experience of much policy-oriented research carried out in developing countries. However, tensions long existing between the comparative and international traditions also help to reinforce criticism of too much research becoming too divorced from the needs of policy and practice. The argument here is therefore for greater recognition of the interdependence between improved theory, policy and practice, and of the potential of related bridge building between the various research discourses and professional cultures involved.

As demonstrated above, the field of comparative and international education can add much to broad social science debates in this respect, and it can, and should, do this confidently in the light of its own distinctive experience and traditions. This will, in itself, contribute to the process of strengthening its own institutional base through the professional networks and research capacity building initiatives that it is equally well placed to support. This is not to imply that there is one definitive path to follow for, in sympathy with E.J. King (1989:37), it is argued that any such proposals could 'divide comparative education's scholars from each other while distracting attention from urgent tasks, from new opportunities, and indeed from the need to continue our growth'. A strengthened institutional base may, therefore, be best seen as a core component of a thoroughly reconceptualised field, that welcomes the incorporation of multiple research discourses, recognises the potential of many different comparative educations, and simultaneously supports further advancement through disciplined comparative and international initiatives conducted in collaboration with a diversity of others, including mainstream educational researchers and their frameworks and organisations. Such a combined strategy for development and repositioning may well help the field to accommodate the systematic and rational impulse for renewed growth, with the inevitable strategic and political imperatives of all fields of study – in a way that is compatible with the respect for identity and difference that is so characteristic of the global era.

Chapter 8

Context and culture in educational research and development

In this concluding chapter we reflect upon the analysis presented so far, draw a broader level of conclusions, and look forward to the widening of intellectual, professional and cross-cultural engagement with the issues raised in the future. Underpinning the work as a whole is recognition of the widespread revitalisation of interest in comparative and international research in education, the renewed growth of the field worldwide, and the research orientation that has become increasingly evident. The diversity and multidisciplinary nature of the field, stemming from its early foundations, continues as a source of much creativity, as do long recognised tensions between theoretical and applied traditions and aspirations.

The field of comparative and international education has, however, also undergone significant change during recent decades. It is, for example, not appropriately or accurately characterised, as it sometimes is, as an encyclopaedic and largely descriptive form of study – concerned to improve the collection and dissemination of knowledge about different educational systems. Such studies may have played a part in its history, but, as our work demonstrates, they represent only one dimension of the much broader intellectual landscape that comprises the challenging and diverse field of today. Nor is the range of current activity as closely related to programmes of initial teacher education as it once was – or to positivistic notions of research as characterised in the Western literature during the resurgence of the empirical social sciences in the 1960s and 1970s. Indeed, most university teaching in the field is now closely aligned to a wide range of creative and ongoing research initiatives, and to related research training programmes.

On the other hand, comparative and international research in education is currently facing more fundamental challenges today than ever before. These challenges have been considered in detail throughout this volume. Some are externally generated while others relate more to internal debates and developments within the field itself. Significantly, they include the implications of changing geopolitical relations, the intensification of globalisation, advances in information and communications technologies, and paradigmatic developments across the social sciences and humanities. Moreover, the growth of interest in comparative and international research has both expanded the audience for such work, and broadened the constituency of the field of enquiry. Decision-makers, at all levels, are, as we have seen, increasingly looking to comparativists for practical applications of their work, and for guidance that may help to improve the efficiency or effectiveness of educational policy and practice. Indeed, this applies in many arenas, and it is therefore not uncommon to see new comparative initiatives and research centres emerging in a diversity of fields today. Indicative of this, for example, the International Social Science Council recently launched a comparative research programme focused on poverty – and, in 2002, the University of the South Pacific established a new Regional Comparative Employment and Labour Studies Unit with support from the European Union. On a broader level, Giddens (2002) recognises the comparative and international ascendancy, and urges analysts of public policy to look outside their own systems in the search for critical insights relating to future policy and practice.

Attention to the applied and policy-oriented potential of comparative studies, however, brings with it further challenges, as noted by Cowen's (1999:73) previously cited observation that the field is now 'going through a dangerous moment', in a global climate displaying the re-emergence of simplistic assumptions about the transferability of policy and practice. Much of this, as we have shown, is driven by economic objectives, competitive motives and political advocacy. The dangers of intensified and ever faster uncritical international transfer thus loom large on the contemporary research agenda – further enhancing the need for critical, disciplined and independent comparative investigation. Moreover, to be done effectively, this needs time: time for in-depth research, time for reflection. Policy makers, however, typically wish to make decisions quickly – and herein lies an ongoing tension. On the other hand, costly development mistakes will continue to be made if speed of action continues to inhibit high-quality, reflective work. In earlier chapters we have thus drawn attention to the dilemmas generated by the speed of technology transfer, to the implications of the increased power of international agencies over educational agendas worldwide, and to the need to recognise and document the differential impact of globalisation on education and society worldwide.

It is in this complex and rapidly changing global climate that, we argue, a more fundamental reassessment and reconceptualisation of the field of comparative and international education is essential. To return to Miller's (1991:i) pertinent reflections (as cited at the outset of the book) – and to reflect upon his insights more directly for this field:

> The world is never static. Even in periods when everything appears to remain the same, streams of change, however small, exist. But in some periods myriad streams of change all flow into a giant river of transformation. Change becomes apparent when the different currents 'encounter' each other and the obstacles in their paths ... All the streams of change that have been flowing quietly and even slowly during the century are now overflowing their banks.

This somewhat poetic commentary reflects the central thesis of our book well. Recent and contemporary changes are indeed visible, but the challenges continue to rise, and the banks of the field of comparative and international education can now be seen to be overflowing. Deeper and more fundamental change is therefore necessary if comparative and international research in education is fully to realise its considerable potential to contribute to the advancement of both educational research and educational development in the future. Drawing from our own analysis, we here conclude by arguing that this requires fundamental, simultaneous and consistent reconceptualisation on four related fronts: the theoretical, methodological, substantive and organisational dimensions of the field. Moreover, as indicated in Chapters 2 and 3, this has related implications for the ways in which we see, and engage with comparative and international research problems – and, indeed, how we construct the history of the field itself.

In the following sections, we briefly reflect on these implications in turn, acknowledging that, because the issues and categories are so closely interrelated, it is often difficult, and inappropriate, to separate one from the other. This final analysis emerges from the more detailed considerations and proposals presented earlier. These intentionally brief concluding comments thus draw upon earlier discussions where appropriate, but focus more directly upon articulating and clarifying the broader scope of our overall contribution.

Theoretical and methodological implications

As captured in the title of Chapter 4 'Globalisation, context and difference', we argue that tensions generated by the simultaneous intensification of globalisation and increased attention to the significance of cultural and contextual differences lie at the heart of many of the most fundamental problems of our age. If comparative and international research is actively to recognise this, it is to ways of respecting a greater diversity of cultural and contextual perspectives that we believe the field must look most carefully in the future. In this regard the dangers of dominant discourses emerge more strongly than ever – and the importance of future work that prioritises differing world views and cross-cultural dialogue is heightened.

There is already much evidence in the existing literature to suggest that, for example, improvements to the quality of education cannot be imposed, and that 'universally applicable' models of educational reform are highly problematic. Successful educational innovation, many now argue, is more closely related to mediated action, negotiation and collaboration between different stakeholders. See, for example, the socio-cultural and psychological perspectives articulated by writers such as Wertsch (1995) and Bruner (1996) on one level, and the case for greater cross-cultural dialogue in the wider arena of international development co-operation as advanced by Ward (2002). The poststructuralist critiques that we have engaged with thus advance increasingly pertinent theoretical and methodological approaches to educational research and development that challenge learning theory, the contemporary hegemony of neo-liberal, marketisation policies and the increased power of international agencies.

In the light of such arguments, and our detailed reconceptualisation proposals as articulated in Chapter 7, we therefore highlight here the need for increased attention to differing cultural perspectives on policy priorities; the potential of collaborative research involving insiders and outsiders; the strengthening of research and evaluation capacity within the South; the prioritisation of context-sensitive research and evaluation methodologies; and the generation of independent and critically informed analyses of education and development.

Louisy's (2001) challenge to Caribbean researchers to engage more firmly in comparative studies from their own cultural perspective is particularly apposite in this context. Her respect for cultural sensitivity also reflects the influence of what has been called the 'literary turn' in the Social Sciences (see also Brock-Utne 2001), and the emergence of narrative research as a way of exploring the impact of cultural differences and identity on learning. For those wishing to pursue innovative studies of this nature, work by Jessop and Penny (1999) and O'Sullivan (2002), and recent doctoral research by Cross (2002) usefully illustrates the narrative potential within a comparative and international framework.

As with our review of problems and difficulties encountered in this field of study, in concluding here it is pertinent to emphasise the increased significance of theoretical and philosophical issues that has consistently emerged from our critical reflections. In doing this, however, we argue that greater attention to such issues also, somewhat paradoxically, holds much potential for the improvement of educational policy and practice. It is therefore again to improved dialogue and to a strengthening of the relationship between theory and practice that we look for advances in the future. As much of our analysis suggests, well-grounded theorising can make a most significant contribution to our collective understandings of problems, and to our assessment of appropriate ways forward in improving educational policy and practice.

To some extent this is well reflected in Apple's (2001:421) commitment to theoretical perspectives and the critique of neo-liberal projects – but, to cite his own words, in a way:

> ... that examines their ... class, *and* race *and* gender effects at the level of who benefits from their specific institutionalisations and from their contradictory functions within real terrains of social power.

Theoretical work on globalisation, as we have shown, also most clearly demonstrates the limitations of the traditional nation-state framework for analysis. Ilon's conceptualisation of three global (and hierarchical) tiers of education, for instance, has major implications for our understandings of new transnational class formations – and for the implications of this for future work on inequalities relating to class, race and gender. This certainly demonstrates the potential of new comparative and international perspectives – and the limitations of the more familiar and orthodox focus upon national level analyses.

Theoretical and methodological reconceptualisations also point down-wards as well as upwards in scale – as Bray and Thomas's (1995) diagrammatic representation for multi-level analysis so well illustrates. In prioritising only selected themes here, however, our own concluding comments highlight the significance of studies that explore the relationship between the global, the national and, most importantly, the local levels. It is at the local level where, we suggest, differing perspectives, priorities and problems are more likely to surface – given the greater likelihood of common values and world views being held by global and national élites.

With methodological implications more firmly in mind, the latter argument further reinforces our own commitment to participatory and qualitative forms of research that engage with a diversity of stakeholders and cultures at the grass roots level. This can be interpreted in ways that focus upon the classroom and professional cultures of pupils and teachers or, in a broader way, to post-colonial analyses of the indigenous languages and cultures of marginalised groups in society. This has further potential to contribute to the democratisation of research processes, and highlights the increased centrality of reflexivity – at all levels – in our vision for the future of disciplined and context-sensitive comparative and international research in education.

Returning to our ongoing critique of the demarcation of historical phases for the field, increased reflexivity does much to reveal the benefits to be gained from a more cross-cultural reconceptualisation of the history of comparative and international education. This helps to demonstrate the diversity of comparative educations that our analysis recognises as, perhaps, one of the greatest strengths of the field. Such critiques also help to re-value the role of legitimate historical analysis in comparative and international education, as we ourselves, and writers such as Sweeting (2001) and Kazamias (2001), advocate. Bray and Gui (2001) demonstrate, however, that there are many different histories of comparative and international education that are still to be written. This is, in itself, an exciting prospect for the future.

Substantive and organisational implications

The articulation of our reconceptualisation thesis has equally diverse implications in substantive and organisational terms. It is not appropriate to revisit the detail of our earlier considerations here, but, in concluding, we can, again, usefully reflect upon their broader, collective significance. A diversity of substantive issues will clearly continue to command attention and emphasise the perspectives of different stakeholders in the future. Many of these issues will also continue to reflect current internationally recognised priorities, such as ongoing improvements to the quality of education, lifelong learning, advances in information and communications technologies, or the role of education in poverty alleviation worldwide. Consistent with our theoretical and methodological reflections, however, our earlier analysis suggests that many new research priorities will be derived from increased sensitivity to the impact of culture and context upon both educational research and educational development. A field that reconstructs itself along lines suggested here, will certainly prioritise new substantive issues for attention that are related to aspects of culture, difference and identity formation. Comparative studies of values education (Cummings *et al.* 2001) have, for example, recently pointed to the increasingly individualistic aspirations of élites worldwide – even within cultures and systems that have traditionally emphasised collectivity. While we have shown that the latter decades of the twentieth century were dominated by economic priorities – the impact of economic globalisation has, somewhat paradoxically, heightened awareness of cultural dilemmas that the field of comparative and international education is especially well placed to examine. Already, innovative cross-cultural research is beginning to show how intensified globalisation has different effects in different contexts – adding further legitimacy for new themes in comparative and international research. Future research on the growing 'digital divide' within and between nations could illustrate this well, but case studies of globally inspired initiatives such as the African Virtual University (Juma 2002) are also pertinent.

The implications of reconceptualisation extend to the organisational arena in other related ways, reflecting the changes in geopolitical relations that we have noted throughout. Recognising worldwide advocacy for partnerships in all walks of life, the June 2002 G8 Meeting of world leaders, for example, emphasised its support for the New Partnership for African Development (NEPAD). Reflecting South African President Mbeki's (1999) rationale for the African Renaissance, the NEPAD initiative is itself based upon enhanced African self-determination and on active and critical engagement with the global economy. Similarly, in the arena of comparative and international education, it is argued that the revitalisation of the field will benefit greatly from the strengthening of partnerships between Northern and Southern agencies and personnel; from increased cross-cultural collaboration; from greater openness and permeability of disciplinary and professional boundaries; from new on-line and other international networks that may generate innovative forms of enquiry; and from greater collective efforts to advance the work of collegial and collaborative bodies such as NORRAG or the WCCES.

New journals that are being founded in both the North and the South are already contributing to the organisational revitalisation of the field. Taking advantage of computerised technologies, for example, a new on-line *European Educational Research Journal* was begun in 2002, aiming to foster clearer communication between researchers, policy-makers and teachers. Another such initiative is the on-line journal *Current Issues in Comparative Education* (CICE) run largely by graduate students from Teachers College, Columbia University, New York. This example also draws attention to the importance of the field finding new ways, such as this, to involve and induct future generations of researchers into the field. It is they who have many innovative ideas to contribute and on whom the future health of the field depends.

In a related vein, many of the changes that we have outlined have significant implications for university teaching related to the broad area of comparative and international education. As we have noted elsewhere, in many cases this teaching has also been directly influenced by the emergent research orientation. Today teaching in the field is therefore less closely associated with initial teacher education than it once was, and it is more likely to feature in programmes of continuing professional development or research training (Bergh 1998). This has implications for the organisation, focus and content of university programmes that deserve greater attention in their own right. Building upon Comparative and International Education Society (CIES) and WCCES deliberations about teaching within the field, a framework for analysis has thus been proposed in a related study to the present volume. In this, Tikly and Crossley (2001:561) examine 'whether or not it is appropriate to integrate comparative and international teaching more firmly into other courses and programs of study'. Recognising a diversity of possible responses, however, the overall aim of this work is to add to the ongoing debate about teaching, while exploring different ways of contributing to the future organisational strength of the field of comparative and international education. As with the present work, we hope this contribution will encourage others to engage with the issues, and advance the various debates, and related developments, further.

Looking to the future

In concluding, it is argued that the current resurgence of interest in comparative and international education generates many exciting possibilities for the future. Our own intellectual journey in this volume suggests that the diversity of forms that are increasingly being encountered is perhaps best visualised as a creative, and multi-disciplinary, constellation of fields. While there is also much that lends coherence to the global field, there are, indeed, many comparative educations. This generates both strengths and weaknesses. Our core thesis further suggests that a thorough reconceptualisation of the field has distinctive theoretical, methodological, substantive and organisational implications. Central to this essential reconceptualisation process, we argue, is a need to bridge this diversity of cultures and traditions more effectively, in a way that capitalises more appropriately upon their combined potential. This recognises the creative strengths of differing perspectives, but acknowledges how improved dialogue across traditional boundaries – be they cultural, regional, disciplinary, paradigmatic, professional or other – has much to offer advances in comparative and international research in education for the future.

The analysis presented here inevitably reflects our own specific interests, backgrounds and experience, although, in the spirit of the book's original rationale, we have tried to capture and reflect upon the diversity and complexity of the field as a whole. In doing so the reconceptualisation that we envisage reveals both similarities and major differences between past and present work – and an imperative to look back, while anticipating new directions for the future. This is reflected in the re-valuing of philosophical, historical and cultural modes of enquiry that emerges consistently from our analysis. Thus, for example, while intensified globalisation has been largely financially and economically driven, we have argued that many of the contemporary human dilemmas that have been generated have, essentially, political and cultural foundations and implications.

To some extent this further underpins the resurgence, again in new and creative formations, of the humanitarian dimension of comparative and international research in education. As McCarthy (1998:160) points out in considering the place of culture in the future of education, 'the complexities of this world must not be masked, but addressed and confronted, in the multicultural world that rages into the twenty-first century'. Highlighting the relationship between education, cultural identity and the fragility of current international relations reveals much comparative and international evidence to suggest that, 'cultural pluralism within nations and cultural dialogue across nations is more urgent than ever before' (Willan 2002:19).

Moreover, our review of changes in research approaches adopted within the field reveals how improved understanding of many contemporary educational problems is increasingly emerging from insights derived from innovative, constructivist, interpretive and critical research paradigms. Certainly, we can see how the field of comparative and international education has done much to demonstrate the dangers of overly positivistic assumptions, and the uncritical international transfer of educational policy and practice from one context to another. We do, however, suggest that this critique also applies more to the contemporary transfer of educational theory and research methodologies than is often recognised. The advancement of theoretical and 'scientific' knowledge is undoubtedly of great importance, but the comparative and international field is particularly well placed to highlight the complexities and dilemmas involved in knowledge transfer. In this regard, our own position acknowledges the insights that can be derived from the poststructuralist critique, and from the potential of the interpretivist– hermeneutic paradigm. We therefore agree with Stenhouse's (1979:5) helpful observation that comparative research 'deals in insight rather than law as a basis for understanding', and that such research is therefore best used to help 'tutor our judgement' on matters of policy and practice elsewhere.

There is therefore much to be gained from a re-reading of earlier work within this complex field – but in the critical light of more contemporary philosophical, epistemological and cross-cultural advances. The development of an innovative on-line library of classic, but out of print, comparative education texts by the Comparative Education Research Centre at the University of Hong Kong and Teachers College, Columbia University, New York, is thus one timely and pertinent bridge between past and present scholarship.

Our overall analysis, however, is distinctly forward looking and one that fundamentally challenges the linear phases representation of the field that is so prominent in much of the traditional Western literature. We therefore argue for a clearer future vision of the diverse field of comparative and international research in education, within which different paradigms and cultural perspectives can creatively co-exist. In proposing this, our reconceptualisation therefore calls for much improved dialogue between the various stakeholders and constituencies – in the spirit of the bridging of cultures and traditions rationale articulated earlier. This we believe has considerable potential for both theoretical advancement and for the improvement of educational policy and practice worldwide.

This points, again, to the need for more holistic understandings of education in its diverse contexts, to the role of increased reflexivity and critical reflection in the research process, and to the related and still rarely addressed need for increased attention to the new ethical dimensions necessitated by the advancement of cross-cultural research. Bond (1999), for example, draws attention to the difficulties faced in constructing contemporary pan-European statements of professional ethics, in a way that has considerable potential for comparative and international researchers in other fields – including education.

The differences between past and future research that we envisage within the field of comparative and international education are therefore both deep and comprehensive. Our reconceptualisation thesis recognises the past achievements and the contemporary potential of the field, but it poses fundamental challenges that have substantial implications for the theoretical, methodological, substantive and organisational dimensions of comparative and international research in education. In examining these issues we have also suggested various ways forward, and have begun to explore how those engaged in such work may make further creative contributions in the future.

Finally, the arguments pursued here highlight the contemporary significance of context and culture throughout our analysis. Concern with context is perhaps the most enduring characteristic of disciplined comparative and international research in education. It is also central – but in many different ways – to the proposed reconceptualisation of the field. Increased sensitivity to context underpins the importance of new comparative work from a diversity of cultural perspectives. It is also central to post-colonial theorising; to the critique of globalisation; to the rationale for differing and multiple units of analysis; to the re-valuing of comparisons over time; to improved reflexivity; and to many proposed strategies to bridge the gap between research and educational policy and practice. In looking to the future, therefore, it is argued that context matters more than ever as we search – with justifiably renewed enthusiasm – for new directions in the field of comparative and international research in education.

References

Action Aid (1993) *Task Report on Working with Local Institutions*, Bangalore: New India Press.

Adams, D. (1971) *Education in National Development*, London: Routledge and Kegan Paul.

Adams, D. and Bjork, R.M. (1969) *Education in Developing Areas*, New York: McKay and Sons.

ADEA (Association for the Development of Education in Africa) (1997) *Partnerships for Capacity Building and Quality Improvements in Education, Papers from the ADEA 1997 Biennial Meeting*, Dakar, Senegal, October 1997, Paris: ADEA/IIEP.

ADEA (Association for the Development of Education in Africa) (2001) *ADEA Newsletter*, 13, 2.

Aikman, S. (1995) 'Language, literacy and bilingual education: an Amazon people's strategy for cultural maintenance', *International Journal of Educational Development* 15, 4:411–422.

Aikman, S. (1997) 'Interculturality and intercultural education: a challenge for democracy', *International Review of Education* 43, 5–6:463–479.

Alexander, R. (1995) *Versions of Primary Education*, London: Routledge.

Alexander, R. (1999) 'Culture in pedagogy, pedagogy across cultures', in R. Alexander, P. Broadfoot and D. Phillips (eds) *Learning from Comparing: New Directions in Comparative Educational Research, Volume 1, Contexts, Classrooms and Outcomes*, Oxford: Symposium Books.

Alexander, R. (2000) *Culture and Pedagogy: International Comparisons in Primary Education*, Oxford: Blackwell.

Alexander, R. (2001) 'Border crossings: towards a comparative pedagogy', *Comparative Education* 37(4):507–523.

Alexander, R., Broadfoot, P. and Phillips, D. (eds) (1999) *Learning from Comparing: New Directions in Comparative Educational Research, Volume 1, Contexts, Classrooms and Outcomes*, Oxford: Symposium Books.

Alexander, R., Osborn, M. and Phillips, D. (eds) (2000) *Learning from Comparing. New Directions in Comparative Educational Research, Volume 2, Policy, Professionals and Development*, Oxford: Symposium Books.

Altbach, P.G. (1971) 'Education and neo-colonialism', *Teachers College Record* 72:543–558.

Altbach, P.G. (1975) 'Literary colonialism: books in the third world', *Harvard Educational Review* 45, 2:226–236.

Altbach, P.G. (1977) 'Servitude of the mind? Education, dependency and neo-colonialism', *Teachers College Record* 79, 2:187–204.

Altbach, P.G., Arnove, R.F. and Kelly, G.P. (eds) (1982) *Comparative Education*, New York: Macmillan.

Altbach, P.G. and Kelly, G.P. (1978) *Education and Colonialism*, New York: Longmans.

Altbach, P.G. and Kelly, G.P. (eds) (1986) *New Approaches to Comparative Education*, Chicago: The University of Chicago Press.

Altbach, P.G. and Tan, J. (1995) *Programs and Centres in Comparative and International Education: a Global Inventory*, Buffalo: State University of New York.

Althusser, L. (1990) 'Theory, theoretical practice and theoretical formation', in L. Althusser (ed.) *Philosophy and the Spontaneous Philosophy of the Scientists and other Essays*, London: Verso.

Anderson, C.A. (1961) 'Methodology in comparative education', *International Review of Education* 7, 1:1–23.

Anderson, C.A. (1965) 'Literacy and schooling on the development threshold: some historical cases', in C.A. Anderson and M.J. Bowman (eds) *Education and Economic Development*, Chicago: Aldine.

Apple, M. (1978) 'Ideology, reproduction and educational reform', *Comparative Education Review* 22, 3:367–387.

Apple, M. (1993) *Official Knowledge: Democratic Education in a Conservative Age*, London: Routledge.

Apple, M. (1999) *Power, Meaning and Identity*, New York: Peter Lang.

Apple, M. (2000) *Official Knowledge*, London: Routledge.

Apple, M. (2001) 'Comparing neo-liberal projects and inequality in education', *Comparative Education* 37, 4:409–423.

Arnove, R.F. (1980) 'Comparative education and world systems analysis', *Comparative Education Review* 24, 1:48–62.

Arnove, R.F. (1982) 'Comparative education and world systems analysis', in P.G. Altbach, R.F. Arnove and G.P. Kelly (eds) *Comparative Education*, New York: Macmillan.

Arnove, R.F., Altbach, P.G. and Kelly, G.P. (eds) (1992) *Emergent Issues in Education: Comparative Perspectives*, Buffalo: State University of New York Press.

Arnove, R.F. and Torres, C.A. (eds) (1999) *Comparative Education. The Dialectic of the Global and the Local*, Lanham: Rowman & Littlefield.

Arthur, L. (2002) 'Precarious relationships: perceptions of culture and citizenship among teachers of German', *Compare* 32, 1:83–93.

Ashcroft, A., Griffiths, G. and Tiffin, M. (eds) (1995) *The Post-colonial Studies Reader*, London: Routledge.

Bacchus, M.K. (1990) *Utilization, Misuse and Development of Human Resources in the Early West Indian Colonies*, Waterloo, Canada: Wilfred Laurier University Press.

Ball, S. (ed.) (1998a) *Comparative Perspectives in Education Policy*. Special Number of *Comparative Education* 34, 2.

Ball, S. (1998b) 'Big policies/small world: an introduction to international perspectives in education policy', *Comparative Education* 34, 2:119–130.

Ball, S. (1998c) 'Introduction: international perspectives on education policy', *Comparative Education* 34, 2:117.

Bauer, T.R. (1981) *Equality, the Third World and Economic Delusion,* London: Weidenfeld and Nicolson.

Bauer, T.R. and Yamey, B. (1981) 'The political economy of foreign aid', *Lloyds Bank Review* No.142, October, 1–13.

Beattie, N. and Brock, C. (1990) 'Editorial', *Compare* 20, 1:3–4.

Becher, T. (1989) *Academic Tribes and Territories: Intellectual Enquiry and the Cultures of Disciplines,* Milton Keynes: Society for Research into Higher Education/Open University Press.

Beck, U. (1992) *Risk Society,* London: Sage.

Beeby, C.E. (1966) *The Quality of Education in Developing Countries* Cambridge, Massachusetts: Harvard University Press.

Bennell, P.S. (1999) *Education for All: How Attainable is the DAC Target in Sub-Saharan Africa?* Report for CfBT Education Services, Reading: CfBT.

Bennell, P.S. and Furlong, D. (1997) *Has Jomtien Made Any Difference? Trends In Donor Funding For Education and Basic Education Since The Late 1980s,* Brighton: University of Sussex, Institute of Development Studies.

Bennell, P.S. and Segerstrom, J. (1998) 'Vocational education and training in developing countries: has the World Bank got it right?' *International Journal of Educational Development* 18, 3:271–287.

Bereday, G.Z.F. (1964) *Comparative Method in Education,* New York: Rinehart and Winston.

Bereday, G.Z.F. (1967) 'Reflections on comparative methodology in education', *Comparative Education* 3, 3:169–187.

Bergh, A-M. (with Classen, C., Horn, I., Thobeka, M., van Niekerk, P.) (1998) *Teaching Comparative and International Education.* Report of a workshop held at the tenth World Congress of Comparative Education Societies in Cape Town, South Africa 14–15 July 1998.

Bond, T. (1999) 'European developments. One size fits all? The quest for a European ethic for counselling and psythotherapy', *European Journal of Psychotherapy, Counselling and Health,* 12, 3:375–388.

Bourdieu, P. (1998) *Acts of Resistance,* Cambridge: Polity Press.

Bourdieu, P. and Passeron, J. C. (1977) *Reproduction in Education, Society and Culture,* London: Sage.

Bowles, S. and Gintis, H. (1976) *Schooling in Capitalist Society: Educational Reform and the Contradictions of Economic Life,* London: Routledge and Kegan Paul.

Bowman, M.J. and Anderson, C.A. (1963) 'Concerning the role of education in development', in C. Goertz (ed.) *Old Societies and New States,* New York: Free Press.

Brandt, W. (1980) *North-South: A Programme for Survival,* London: Pan Books.

Brandt, W. (1983) *Common Crisis: North-South: Co-operation for World Recovery,* London: Pan Books.

Bray, M. (1981) *Universal Primary Education in Nigeria: A Study of Kano State,* London: Routledge and Kegan Paul.

Bray, M. (1996a) *Privatization of Secondary Education: Issues and Policy Implications,* Edc/5/11, Paris: UNESCO Publishing.

Bray, M. (1996b) *Counting the Full Cost: Parental and Community Financing of Education in East Asia,* Washington, DC: World Bank.

Bray, M. (1998) 'Comparative education research in the Asian region: implications for the field as a whole', *Comparative Education Society of Hong Kong Bulletin* 1 (May):6–10.

Bray, M. (1999) 'Methodology and focus in comparative education', in M. Bray and R. Koo (eds) *Education and Society in Hong Kong and Macau: Comparative Perspectives on Continuity and Change*, Hong Kong: University of Hong Kong, Comparative Education Research Centre.

Bray, M. (2001) *Community Partnerships In Education: Dimensions, Variations And Implications*, Background Document prepared for the World Education Forum, Dakar, Senegal, 26–28 April 2000. Paris: UNESCO Publishing.

Bray, M. (2003) 'Tradition, change, and the role of the World Council of Comparative Education Societies', *International Review of Education* 49, 1, in press.

Bray, M. and Gui, Q. (2001) 'Comparative education in greater China: contexts, characteristics, contrasts and contributions', *Comparative Education* 37, 4:451–473

Bray, M. and Lee, W.O. (eds) (1997) Education and Political Transition: Implications of Hong Kong's Change of Sovereignty. Special Issue of *Comparative Education* 33, 2.

Bray, M. and Lee, W.O. (eds) (2001) *Education and Political Transition: Themes and Experiences in East Asia*, Second Edition, Hong Kong: University of Hong Kong, Comparative Education Research Centre.

Bray, M. and Packer, S. (1993) *Education in Small States: Concepts, Challenges and Strategies*, Oxford: Pergamon Press.

Bray, M. and Thomas, R.M. (1995) 'Levels of comparison in educational studies: different insights from different literatures and the value of multi-level analyses', *Harvard Educational Review* 65, 4:472–490.

Brickman, W.W. (1960) 'A historical introduction to comparative education', *Comparative Education Review* 3, 3:1–24.

Brickman, W.W. (1966) 'The prehistory of comparative education to the end of the eighteenth century', *Comparative Education Review* 10, 1:30–47.

Brickman, W.W. (1988) 'History, concepts and methods' in T. N. Postlethwaite (ed.) *The Encyclopædia of Comparative Education and National Systems of Education*, Oxford: Pergamon Press.

Broadfoot, P. (1996) *Education, Assessment and Society*, Buckingham: Open University Press.

Broadfoot, P. (1999a) 'Stones from other hills may serve to polish the jade of this one: towards a neo-comparative "learnology" of education' *Compare* 29, 3:217–231.

Broadfoot, P. (1999b) 'Not so much a context, more a way of life? Comparative Education in the 1990s' in R. Alexander, P. Broadfoot, D. Phillips (eds) *Learning from Comparing. New Directions in Comparative Educational Research. Volume 1. Contexts, Classrooms and Outcomes*, Oxford: Symposium Books.

Broadfoot, P., Osborn, M., Gilly, M. and Bûcher, A. (1993) *Perceptions of Teaching. Primary School Teachers in England and France*, London: Cassell.

Broadfoot, P., Osborn, M., Planel, C. and Sharpe, K. (2000) *Promoting Quality in Learning. Does England Have the Answer?* London: Cassell.

Broadfoot, P. and Pollard, A. (1999) *The Assessment Society*, London: Cassell.

Brock, C. and Cammish, N.K. (1994) 'Constraints on female participation in education in developing countries', in G. Strowbridge and W. Tulasiewicz (eds) *Education and the Law: International Perspectives*, London: Routledge.

Brock, C. and Cammish, N.K. (1998) *Factors Affecting Female Participation in Education in Seven Developing Countries* (2nd edn), London: Department for International Development.

Brock-Utne, B. (2000) *Whose Education for All? The Recolonization of the African Mind*, New York: Falmer Press.

Brock-Utne, B. (ed.) (2001) *Globalisation, Language and Education*, Special Issue of *International Review of Education* 47, 3–4.

Brown, M.M. (1997) 'Keeping up with the next century: change at the World Bank', *Royal Society of Arts Journal* July, 65–69.

Bruner, J. (1996) *The Culture of Education*, Cambridge, Massachusetts: Harvard University Press.

Buchert, L (1995) *Recent Trends in Education Aid. Towards a Classification of Policies*, Paris: UNESCO Publishing, International Institute for Educational Planning.

Buchert, L. (ed.) (1998) *Education Reform in the South in the 1990s*, Paris: UNESCO Publishing.

Buchert, L. (2002) 'Towards new partnerships in sector-wide approaches: comparative experiences from Burkina Faso, Ghana and Mozambique', *International Journal of Educational Development* 22, 1:69–84.

Buchert, L. and King, K. (1995) *Learning from Experience: Policy and Practice in Aid to Higher Education*, The Hague: Centre for the Study of Education in Developing Countries (CESO).

Buchert, L. and King, K. (eds) (1996) *Consultancy and Research in International Education*, Bonn: German Foundation for International Development.

Bueno Fischer, M.C. and Hannah, J. (2002) '(Re)-constructing citizenship: the Programa Integrar of Brazilian Metalworkers' Union', *Compare* 32, 1:95–106.

Bunt-Kokhuis, S.G.M. van de (1997) *Academic Pilgrims: Determinants of International Faculty Mobility*, Tilburg: Tilburg University Press.

Burns, R. and Welch, A.R. (eds) (1992) *Contemporary Perspectives in Comparative Education*, New York: Garland.

Cardoso, F. (1972) 'Dependency and development in Latin America', *New Left Review* 74, July/August:83–95.

Carnoy, M. (1974) *Education as Cultural Imperialism*, New York: Longman.

Carnoy, M. (1999) *Globalisation and Educational Reform. What Planners Need to Know*, Paris: International Institute for Educational Planning.

Carr-Hill, R. (1982) *Education in Guinea-Bissau 1978–81: The Impact Of Swedish Assistance*, Stockholm: SIDA, Education Division Document No.5.

Carr-Hill, R., Carron, G. and Peart, E. (2001) 'Classifying out of school education', in K. Watson (ed.) *Doing Comparative Education Research: Issues and Problems*, Oxford: Symposium Books.

Carton, M.(1999) 'Aid, international co-operation and globalisation: trends in the field of education', in K. King and L. Buchert (eds) *Changing International Aid to Education*, Paris: UNESCO Publishing.

Cassen, R. and Associates (1986) *Does Aid Work?* Oxford: Clarendon Press.

Castells, M. (1996) *The Rise of the Network Society*, Cambridge: Blackwell.

Castles, S. and Miller, M.J. (1993) *The Age of Migration*, Basingstoke: Macmillan.

Chambers, R. (1992) 'Rural appraisal: rapid, relaxed and participatory', IDS Discussion Paper, Brighton: University of Sussex.

Chambers, R. (1994) 'Participatory rural appraisal (PRA): challenges, potentials and paradigm', *World Development* 22, 9:1437–1454.

Chambers, R. (1995) 'Paradigm shifts and the practice of participatory research and development', in N. Nelson and S. Wright (eds) *Power and Participatory Development: Theory and Practice*, London: Intermediate Technology Publications.

Chapman, D.W., Barcikowski, E., Sowah, M., Gyamera, E. and Woode, G. (2002) 'Do communities know best? Testing a premise of educational decentralization: community members' perceptions of their local schools in Ghana', *International Journal of Educational Development* 22, 2:181–189.

Chapman, D.W. and Mahlck, L.O. (eds) (1993) *From Data to Action: Information Systems in Educational Planning*, Oxford: Pergamon Press/UNESCO IIEP.

Cheng, K.M. (1997) 'Qualitative research and educational policy-making: approaching the reality of developing countries' in M. Crossley and G. Vulliamy (eds) *Qualitative Educational Research in Developing Countries*, New York: Garland

CHOGM (2002) *Coolum Communique*, http://www.chogm2002.org/pub/statements/communique.html

Chossudovsky, M. (1997) *The Globalisation of Poverty: Impacts of the IMF and World Bank Reforms*, Penang: Third World Network.

Chossudovsky, M. (2000) *Global Poverty in the Late 20th Century*, http/ www/algonet.se/ d581/features/chossu/global/poverty.html

Cipolla, C. (1969) *Literacy and Development in the West*, London: Penguin Books.

Colclough, C. (ed.) (1997) *Marketizing Education and Health in Developing Countries*, Oxford: Clarendon Press.

Coleman, J.S. (1965) *Education and Political Development*, Princeton, N.J.: Princeton University Press.

Commeyras, M. and Chilisa, B. (2001) 'Assessing Botswana's first national survey on literacy with Wagner's proposed schema for surveying literacy in the Third World', *International Journal of Educational Development* 21, 5:433–446.

Commonwealth Foundation (1995) *Non Governmental Organisations: Guidelines for Good Policy and Practice*, London: Commonwealth Foundation.

Comparative Education (1977) Special Number on *Comparative Education – its Present State and Future Prospects*, 13, 2.

Comparative Education Review (1977) Special Issue, *State of the Art Review*, 21, 2.

Coombs, P. (1985) *The World Crisis in Education: A View from the Eighties*, Oxford: Oxford University Press.

Coulby, D., Cowen, R. and Jones, C. (eds) (2000) *Education in Times of Transition. World Yearbook of Education 2000*, London: Kogan Page.

Courtney, W. (1999) 'Education and development co-operation: a UNESCO perspective' in K. King and L. Buchert (eds) *Changing International Aid to Education*, Paris: UNESCO Publishing.

Cowen, R. (1980) 'Comparative education in Europe: a note', *Comparative Education Review* 24, 1:98–108.

Cowen, R. (ed.) (1996a) *Comparative Education and Post-modernity*, Special Number of *Comparative Education* 32, 2.

Cowen, R. (1996b) 'Last past the post: comparative education, modernity and perhaps post-modernity', *Comparative Education* 32, 2:151–170.

Cowen, R. (1999) 'Late modernity and the rules of chaos: an initial note on transitologies and rims', in R. Alexander, P. Broadfoot and D. Phillips (eds) *Learning from Comparing: New Directions in Comparative Educational Research, Volume 1, Contexts, Classrooms and Outcomes*, Oxford: Symposium Books.

Crewe, E. and Harrison, E. (1998) *Whose Development? An Ethnography of Aid*, London: Zed Books.

Croft, A. (2002) 'Singing under a tree: does oral culture help lower primary teachers be learner-centred?', *International Journal of Educational Development* 22, 3–4:321–337.

Cross, B. (2002) *Children's Stories and Negotiated Identities: Bakhtin and Complexity in Upper Primary Classrooms in Jamaica and Scotland*. Unpublished PhD thesis, University of Edinburgh.

Crossley, M. (1984) 'Strategies for curriculum change and the question of international transfer', *Journal of Curriculum Studies* 16, 1:75–88.

Crossley, M. (1990) 'Collaborative research, ethnography and comparative and international education in the South Pacific', *International Journal of Educational Development* 10, 1:37–46.

Crossley, M. (1993) 'Comparative and international studies and education in the South Pacific, *Comparative Education* 29, 3:227–232.

Crossley, M. (1999) 'Reconceptualising comparative and international education', *Compare* 29, 3:249–267.

Crossley, M. (2000) 'Bridging cultures and traditions in the reconceptualisation of comparative and international education', *Comparative Education* 36, 3:319–332.

Crossley, M. (2001) 'Cross-cultural issues, small states and research: capacity building in Belize', *International Journal of Educational Development* 21, 3:217–230.

Crossley, M. and Broadfoot, P. (1992) 'Comparative and international research in education: scope, problems, potential', *British Educational Research Journal* 18, 2:99–112.

Crossley, M. and Holmes, K. (1999) *Educational Development in the Small States of the Commonwealth; Retrospect and Prospect*, London: Commonwealth Secretariat.

Crossley, M. and Holmes, K. (2001) 'Challenges for educational research: international development, partnerships and capacity building in small states', *Oxford Review of Education* 27(3) 395–409.

Crossley, M. and Jarvis, P. (eds) (2000a) '*Comparative Education for the Twenty-First Century*', Special Millennium Number of *Comparative Education* 36, 2.

Crossley, M. and Jarvis, P. (2000b) 'Continuity, challenge and change in comparative and international education', *Comparative Education* 36, 3:261–265.

Crossley, M. with Jarvis, P. (2001a) *Comparative Education for the Twenty-First Century: An International Response*, Special Number of *Comparative Education* 37, 4.

Crossley, M. with Jarvis, P. (2001b), 'Context matters', *Comparative Education* 37, 4:405–408.

Crossley, M. and Vulliamy, G. (1984) 'Case-study research methods and comparative education', *Comparative Education* 20, 2:193–207.

Crossley, M. and Vulliamy, G. (eds) (1997a) *Qualitative Educational Research in Developing Countries*, New York: Garland.

Crossley, M. and Vulliamy, G. (1997b) 'Qualitative research in developing countries: issues and experience' in M. Crossley and G. Vulliamy (eds) *Qualitative Educational Research in Developing Countries*, New York: Garland.

Crotty, M. (1998) *The Foundations of Social Research. Meaning and Perspective in the Research Process*, London: Sage.

Cumming, A. (1996) 'IEA's studies of language education: their scope and contributions' in Special Issue of *Assessment in Education* on the IEA Studies 3, 2:143–160.

Cummings W.K., Gopinathan, S. and Tomoda, Y. (eds) (1998) *The Revival of Values Education in Asia and the West*, Oxford: Pergamon Press.

Cummings, W.K. and McGinn, N.F. (eds) (1997) *International Handbook of Education and Development. Preparing Schools, Students and Nations for the Twenty-first Century*, Oxford: Pergamon Press.

Cummings, W.K., Tatto, M.T., and Hawkins, J. (eds) (2001) *Values Education for Dynamic Societies: Individualism or Collectivism*, Hong Kong, University of Hong Kong, Comparative Education Research Centre.

Dachi, H., Crossley, M. and Garrett, R.M. with Tikly, L., Mukabaranga, B. and Lowe, J. (2002) *Globalisation and Skills for Development. Tanzania Country Report*, Report to DFID, Bristol: University of Bristol, Graduate School of Education.

Dadey, A. and Harber, C. (1991) *Training and Professional Support for Headship in Africa*, London: Commonwealth Secretariat.

Dale, R. (1999) 'Specifying globalisation effects on national policy: a focus on the mechanisms', *Journal of Educational Policy* 14, 1:1–17.

Dale, R. (2000a) 'Globalisation: a new world for comparative education', in J. Schriewer (ed.) *Discourse Formulation in Comparative Education*, Peter Lang: Frankfurt am Main.

Dale, R. (2000b) 'Globalization and education: demonstrating a "common world education culture" or locating a "globally structured agenda for education"', *Educational Theory* 50:427–48.

Dale, R. (2001) 'Constructing a long spoon for comparative education: charting the career of the "New Zealand model"', *Comparative Education* 37, 4:493–500.

Dalin, P. with Ayono, T., Biazen, A., Dibaba, B., Jahan, M., Miles, M.B., and Rojas, C. (1994) *How Schools Improve. An International Report*, London, Cassell.

Daloz, J-P., and Chabal, P. (1999) *Africa Works: Disorder as Political Instrument*, Oxford and Bloomington: International African Institute in association with James Currey.

Davies, L. (ed.) (2002) *Changing Contexts for Democracy and Citizenship*, Special Issue of *Compare* 32, 1.

Delanty, G. (1997) *Social Science: Beyond Constructivism and Realism*, Milton Keynes: Open University Press.

Department for International Development (1997) *Eliminating World Poverty: a Challenge for the 21st Century*, London: HMSO.

Department For International Development (1999) *Learning Opportunities for All*, London: DFID.

Department For International Development (2000) *Eliminating World Poverty: Making Globalisation Work for the World's Poor*, London: DFID

Department For International Development (2002) *The Case for Aid for the Poorest Countries*, London: DFID Press Office.

Department of Education and Science (1975) *Education Systems in Six Countries*, London: HMSO.

Derrida, J. (1981) *Positions*, Chicago: University of Chicago Press.

Dimmock, C. (2000) *Designing the Learning-Centred School. A Cross-Cultural Perspective*, London and New York: Falmer.

Dore, R. (1974) *The Meiji Restoration in Japan*, London: Routledge and Kegan Paul.

Dore, R. (1976) *The Diploma Disease*, London: George Allen and Unwin.

Dore, R. (1997a) *The Diploma Disease. Education, Qualification and Development*, Second Edition, London: University of London, Institute of Education.

Dore, R. (1997b) 'The argument of the diploma disease: a summary', Special Issue of *Assessment in Education, The Diploma Disease Twenty Years On*, 4, 1:23–32.

Dove, L. (1980) 'The teacher and the rural community in developing countries', *Compare* 27, 1:3–29.

Drabek, A. (1987) *World Development Alternatives: The Challenge For Non Governmental Organisations*, Vol. 15 (Supplement) ix–xv, Washington, DC: World Bank.

Dunstan, J. (1978) *Paths to Excellence and the Soviet School*, Windsor: National Foundation for Educational Research.

Dyer, C. and Choksi, A. (1997) 'North–south collaboration in educational research: reflections on Indian experience', in M. Crossley and G. Vulliamy (eds) *Qualitative Educational Research in Developing Countries*, New York: Garland.

Dyer, C. and King, K. (1993) *The British Resource in International Training and Education. An Inventory*, Edinburgh: University of Edinburgh.

Elliot, R. (1987) *Final Report. Non-Governmental Organisations and Africa: A Strategy Workshop*, Geneva: United Nations.

Elsner, D. (2000) 'Reflections on mega-trends in education from a Polish perspective', in T. Mebrahtu, M. Crossley and D. Johnson (eds) *Globalisation, Educational Transformation and Societies in Transition*, Oxford: Symposium Books.

Elu, J. and Banya, K. (1999) 'Non-governmental organisations as partners in Africa: a cultural analysis of North–South relations', in K. King and L. Buchert (eds) *Changing International Aid to Education*, Paris: UNESCO Publishing.

Epstein, E.H. (1992) Editorial, *Comparative Education Review* 36, 4:409–416.

Epstein, E.H. (1994) 'Comparative and international education: overview and historical development' in T. Husen and T.N. Postlethwaite (eds) *The International Encyclopaedia of Education*, Second Edition, Oxford: Pergamon Press.

Fanon, F. (1968) *The Wretched of the Earth*, New York: Grove Press.

Fägerlind, I. and Saha, L.J (1989) *Education and National Development. A Comparative Perspective*, Second Edition, Oxford: Pergamon Press.

Farrell, J.P. (1979) 'The necessity of comparisons in the study of education: the salience of science and the problems of comparability', *Comparative Education Review* 23, 1:3–16.

Farrell, J.P. (1997) 'A retrospective on educational planning in comparative education', *Comparative Education Review* 41, 3:277–313.

Finegold, D., McFarland, L. and Richardson, W. (eds) (1992) *Something Borrowed, Something Blue? A Study of the Thatcher Government's Appropriation of American Education and Training Policy. Oxford Studies in Comparative Education*, 2, 2.

Forster, J. (1999) 'The new boundaries of international development co-operation', in K. King and L. Buchert (eds) *Changing International Aid to Education*, Paris: UNESCO Publishing.

Foster, P.J. (1987) 'Technical/vocational education in the less developed countries', *International Journal of Educational Development* 7, 2:137–139.

Foster, P. (1988) 'Area studies in comparative education' in T.N. Postlethwaite (ed.) *The Encyclopaedia of Comparative Education and National Systems of Education*, Oxford: Pergamon Press.

Foster, P. (1998) 'Foreword', in H.J. Noah and M.A. Eckstein *Doing Comparative Education: Three Decades of Collaboration*, Hong Kong: University of Hong Kong, Comparative Education Research Centre.

Foucault, M. (1972) *The Archaeology of Knowledge and the Discourse on Language*, New York: Tavistock Publications.

Foucault, M. (1977) *Discipline and Punish – the Birth of the Prison*, Harmondsworth, Penguin Books.

Frank, A.G. (1967) *Capitalism and Underdevelopment in Latin America*, New York: Monthly Review Press.

Fraser, S.E. (1964) *Jullien's Plan for Comparative Education 1816–1817*, New York: Bureau of Publications, Teachers' College Columbia.

Fraser, S. and Brickman, W.W. (1968) *A History of International and Comparative Education: Nineteenth Century Documents*, Glenview: Scott Foresman.

Freire, P. (1971) *Pedagogy of the Oppressed*, London: Penguin Books.

Freire, P. (1982) 'Creating alternative research methods: learning to do it by doing it', in B. Hall, A. Gillette and R. Tandon (eds) *Creating Knowledge: A Monopoly? Participatory Research in Development*, New Delhi: Society for Participatory Research in Asia.

Freire, P. (1996) *Letters to Cristina. Reflections on My Life and Work*, New York: Routledge.

Fry, G. and Kempner, K. (1996) 'A sub-national perspective for comparative research: education and development in north-east Brazil and north-east Thailand', *Comparative Education* 32, 3:333–360.

Fukuyama, F. (1992) *The End of History and the Last Man*, Harmondsworth: Penguin Books.

Furlong, J. (1998) *Educational Research: Meeting the Challenge, an Inaugural Lecture*, Bristol: University of Bristol.

Galtung, J. (1990) 'Theory formation in social research: a plea for pluralism', in E. Øyen (ed.) *Comparative Methodology*, London: Sage.

George, S. and Sabeli, F. (1994) *Faith and Credit: The World Bank's Secular Empire*, Harmondsworth: Penguin Books.

Gibbons, M., Limoges, C., Nowotny, H., Schwartzman, S., Scott, P., and Trow, M. (1994) *The New Production of Knowledge: the Dynamics of Science and Research in Contemporary Societies*, London, Sage.

Giddens, A. (1990) *The Consequences of Modernity*, Cambridge: Polity Press.

Giddens, A. (1997) 'Excerpts from a keynote address at the UNRISD Conference on globalisation and citizenship', *UNRISD News* 15:1–3.

Giddens, A. (1998) *The Third Way: The Renewal of Social Democracy*, Cambridge: Polity Press.

Giddens, A. (1999) 'Globalisation', Lecture 1 of the 1999 BBC Reith Lectures, BBC News Online Network, Homepage: 1–6.

Giddens, A. (2002) *Where Now for New Labour?* Cambridge: Polity Press.

Gilmour, J.D. and Soudien, C.A. (eds) (2001) *South African Educational Reforms*, Special Issue of *International Journal Of Educational Development* 21, 1:3–5

Ginsburgh, M.B. and Gorostiaga, J.M. (eds) (2001) *The Relationships Between Theorists/Researchers and Policy Makers/Practitioners*, Special Issue of *Comparative Education Review* 45, 2.

Giroux, H. (1997) *Pedagogy and the Politics of Hope: Theory, Culture and Schooling*, Oxford: Westview Press.

Gmelin, W. and King, K. (2001) 'Foreword', in W. Gmelin, K. King and S. McGrath, (eds), *Development Knowledge, National Research and International Cooperation*, Edinburgh: University of Edinburgh, Centre for African Studies, German Foundation for International Development, NORRAG.

Goldstein, H. (1996) 'Introduction', in Special Issue of *Assessment in Education* on *The IEA Studies* 3, 2:125–128.

Goldstone, M.F. (1979) 'The Experimental World Literacy Programme – its assessment', *Compare* 9, 1:45–57.

Goodson, I. (1997) 'The educational researcher as a public intellectual', the Lawrence Stenhouse Lecture, British Educational Research Association.

Grant, N. (1969) *Society, Schools and Progress in Eastern Europe*, Oxford: Pergamon Press.

Grant, N. (1977) 'Educational policy and cultural pluralism: A task for comparative education', *Comparative Education* 13, 2:139–150.

Green, A. (1997) *Education, Globalisation and the Nation State*, London: Macmillan.

Griffin, R. (ed.) (2002) *Education in Transition. International Perspectives on the Politics and Processes of Change*, Oxford: Symposium Books.

Gu, M. (2001) *Education in China and Abroad. Perspectives from a Lifetime in Comparative Education*, Hong Kong: University of Hong Kong, Comparative Education Research Centre.

Habermas, J. (1978) *Knowledge and Human Interests*, London: Heinemann.

Habermas, J. (1990) *Moral Consciousness and Communicative Action*, Cambridge: Polity Press.

Habte, A. (1999) 'The future of international aid to education', in K. King and L. Buchert (eds) *Changing International Aid to Education: Global Patterns and National Contexts*, Paris: UNESCO Publishing/NORRAG.

Hall, S. (1996) '"When was the post-colonial?"Thinking at the limit', in I. Chamber and L. Curtis (eds) *The Post-colonial Question: Common Skies, Divided Horizons*, London: Routledge.

Hallak, J. (1990) *Investing in the Future: Setting Educational Priorities in the Developing World*, Paris: UNESCO/International Institute for Educational Planning.

Halls, W.D. (1976) *Education, Culture and Politics in Modern France*, Oxford: Pergamon Press.

Halls, W.D. (1977) 'Comparative studies in education: a personal view', *Comparative Education* 13, 2:81–86.

Halls, W.D. (ed.) (1990) *Comparative Education: Contemporary Issues and Trends*, London: Jessica Kingsley.

Hammersley, M. (1995) *The Politics of Social Research*, London: Routledge.

Hans, N. (1959a) 'The historical approach to comparative education', *International Review of Education* 5, 3:299–309.

Hans, N. (1959b) 'English pioneers of comparative education', *British Journal of Educational Studies* 1, 1:56–59.

Hans, N. (1964) *Comparative Education*, London: Routledge and Kegan Paul.

Hanson, J.W. and Brembeck, C.S. (1966) *Education and the Development of Nations*, New York: McGraw Hill.

Harber, C and Dadey, A. (1993) 'The job of headteacher in Africa: research and reality', *International Journal of Educational Development* 13, 2:147–160.

Harber, C. and Davies, L. (1997) *School Management and Effectiveness in Developing Countries*, London: Cassell.

Harbison, F. and Myers, C.A. (1964) *Education, Manpower and Economic Growth*, New York: McGraw Hill.

Hargreaves, D. (1996) 'Teaching as a research based profession; possibilities and prospects', The Teacher Training Agency Annual Lecture 1996, London: TTA.

Hausmann, G. (1967) 'A century of comparative education, 1785–1885', *Comparative Education Review* 11, 1:1–21.

Hawkins, J.N. (1998) 'Comparative Education Review editorship changes hands after ten years', *Comparative and International Education Society Newsletter* 118 (May): 1–4.

Hawkins, J.N. and Rust, V.D. (2001) 'Shifting perspectives in comparative research: a view from the USA', *Comparative Education* 37, 4:501–506.

Hayden, M. and Thompson, J. (2001) *International Education: Principles and Practice*, London: Kogan Page.

Hayhoe, R. (2001) 'Introduction' in M. Gu *Education in China and Abroad: Perspectives from a Lifetime in Comparative Education*, Hong Kong: University of Hong Kong, Comparative Education Research Centre.

Hayhoe, R. and Pan, J. (eds) (2001) *Knowledge Across Cultures: A Contribution to Dialogue Among Civilisations*, Hong Kong: University of Hong Kong Comparative Education Research Centre.

Hayter, T. (1971) *Aid as Imperialism*, Harmondsworth: Penguin Books.

Hearnden, A. (1974) *Education in the Two Germanies*, Oxford: Basil Blackwell.

Hearnden, A. (1976) *Education, Culture and Politics in West Germany*, Oxford: Pergamon Press.

Held, D, McGrew, A, Goldblatt, D. and Perraton, J. (1999) *Global Transformations. Politics, Economics and Culture*, Cambridge: Polity Press.

Heyman, R. (1979) 'Comparative education from an ethnomethodological perspective', *Comparative Education* 15, 2:241–249.

Heyneman, S.P. (1995) 'International education co-operation in the next century', *CIES Newsletter* 1–2.

Heyneman, S.P. (1999a) 'The sad story of UNESCO's educational statistics', *International Journal of Educational Development* 19, 1:53–63.

Heyneman, S.P. (1999b) 'Development of aid in education: a personal view', *International Journal of Educational Development* 19, 3:183–190.

Heyneman, S.P. (2001) 'The growing international commercial market for educational goods and services', *International Journal of Educational Development* 21, 4:345–359.

Hickling-Hudson, A. (1998) 'When Marxist post-modern theories won't work: the potential of post-colonial theory for educational analysis', *Discourse* 19(3):327–339.

Hickling-Hudson, A. (2002) 'Re-visioning from the inside: getting under the skin of the World Bank's Education Sector Strategy', *International Journal of Educational Development* 22, 6: in press.

Higginson, H.K. (ed.) (1979) *Selections from Michael Sadler: Studies in World Citizenship*, Liverpool: Dejall & Meyorre.

Higginson, J.H. (1995) 'Michael Sadler's Groundwork as Research Director', *Compare* 25, 2:109–114.

Higginson, J.H. (2001) 'The development of a discipline; some reflections on the development of comparative education as seen through the pages of the journal Compare' in K. Watson (ed.) *Doing Comparative Education Research: Issues and Problems*, Oxford: Symposium Books.

Hillage, J. (1998) *Excellence in Research on Schools*, Research Report No. 74, London: Department for Education and Employment.

Hinchcliffe, K. (1988) *Education in Sub-Saharan Africa*, Washington, DC: World Bank.

Hirst, P. and Thompson, G. (1996) *Globalisation in Question: The International Economy and the Possibilities of Governance*, Cambridge: Polity Press.

HMSO (1975) *More Aid to the Poorest*, London: HMSO.

Hobsbawm, E. J. (1994) *The Age of Extremes: The Short Twentieth Century, 1914–1991*, London: Abacus.

Holmes, B. (1965) *Problems in Education*, London: Routledge and Kegan Paul.

Holmes, B. (1979) *Ivory Towers, The Glass Bead Game and Open Societies: The Social Functions of Comparative Education*, London: University of London Institute of Education.

Holmes, B. (1981) *Comparative Education: Some Considerations of Method*, London: George Allen and Unwin.

Holmes, B. and Robinsohn, S.B. (1983) *Relevant Data in Comparative Education*, Paris: UNESCO Publishing.

Holmes, K. (2001) *Whose Knowledge for Educational Development? Research Capacity in Small States with Special Reference to St. Lucia.* Unpublished doctoral dissertation, Bristol: University of Bristol Graduate School of Education.

Hoogvelt, A. (1997) *Globalisation and the Postcolonial World: the New Political Economy of Development*, Basingstoke: Macmillan.

Hoppers, W. (1999) 'Teachers' resource centres in Southern African education: an investigation into decentralization and educational change', in L. Buchert (ed.) *Education Reform in the South in the 1990s*, Paris: UNESCO Publishing.

Hoppers, W. (2001) 'About how to reach the truth in development co-operation: ODA/DFID's education papers', *International Journal of Educational Development* 21, 5:463–470.

Howard, M. and Louis, W.R. (1998) *The Oxford History of the Twentieth Century*, Oxford: Oxford University Press.

Hunter, G. (1969) *Modernising Peasant Societies*, Oxford: Oxford University Press.

Huntington, S. (1993) 'The clash of civilisations?', *Foreign Affairs* 72:22–49.

Ilon, L. (1994) 'Structural adjustment and education: adapting to a growing global market', *International Journal of Educational Development* 14, 2:95–108.

Ilon, L. (1996) 'The changing role of the World Bank: education policy as global welfare', *Policy and Politics* 24:413–424.

Ilon, L. (1997) 'Confronting the bully: regional educational trends in a global economy', *Compare* 27, 2:153–166.

Ilon, L. (1998) 'The effects of international economic trends on gender equity and schooling', *International Review of Education* 44, 4:335–356.

Ilon, L. (2002) 'Agent of global markets or agent of the poor? The World Bank's education sector strategy paper', *International Journal of Educational Development* 22, 5:475–482.

Inkeles, A. and Smith, D.H. (1974) *Becoming Modern*, Cambridge, Massachusetts: Harvard University Press.

International Institute for Educational Planning (1991) 'Strengthening national capacities: one of the Institute's permanent concerns', *IIEP Newsletter* IV, 2, April–June:1–3.

International Institute for Educational Planning (1993) 'Institutional capacity: a subject neglected by educational planners', *IIEP Newsletter* XI, January–March:1–3.

International Journal of Educational Development (IJED) (1985) Special Issue: *Research, Co-operation and Evaluation of Educational Programmes in the Third World*, 5, 3.

International Journal of Educational Development (IJED) (1996a) Special Issue: *The World Bank's Education Sector Review: Priorities And Strategies For Education*, 16, 3.

International Journal of Educational Development (IJED) (1996b) Special Issue: *Globalisation and Learning*, 16, 4.

International Journal of Educational Development (IJED) (1999) Special Issue: *Whose Knowledge And Whose Languages: Alternative Perspectives*, 19, 4–5.

International Journal of Educational Development (IJED) (2002) Special Issue: *The World Bank's Education Sector Strategy*, 22, 5.

Ishumi, A. (1992) 'External aid: a lever for social progress in developing countries? A case study of SIDA supported educational projects in Tanzania, 1970–1990s', *International Journal of Educational Development* 12, 4:265–276.

Japan, Ministry of Foreign Affairs (1997) *Japan's Official Development Assistance: Summary, 1997*, Tokyo: Association for the Promotion of International Cooperation.

Jarvis, P. (1999) *The Practitioner Researcher*, San Francisco: Josey-Bass.

Jarvis, P. (2000) 'Globalisation, the learning society and comparative education', *Comparative Education* 36, 3:343–355.

Jarvis, P. (2002) 'Globalisation, citizenship and the education of adults in contemporary European society', *Compare* 32, 1:5–19.

Jessop, T.S. and Penny, A.J. (1999) 'A story behind a story: developing strategies for making sense of teacher narratives', *International Journal of Social Research Methodology* 2, 3:213–230.

Jones, P.E. (1971) *Comparative Education: Purpose and Method*, University of Queensland Press.

Jones, P.W. (1988) *International Policies for Third World Education: UNESCO, Literacy and Development*, London: Routledge.

Jones, P.W. (1990) 'UNESCO and the politics of global literacy', *Comparative Education Review* 34, 1:41–60.

Jones, P.W. (1992) *World Bank Financing of Education. Lending, Learning and Development*, London: Routledge.

Jones, P.W. (1994a) 'United Nations' agencies', in *Encyclopædia of Educational Research* (Sixth Edition), New York: Macmillan.

Jones, P.W. (1994b) 'Research perspectives in the World Bank' in G. Walford (ed.) *Researching the Powerful in Education*, London: University College London Press.

Jones, P.W. (1997) 'On World Bank education financing. Policies and strategies for education', *Comparative Education* 33, 1:117–129.

Jones, P.W.(1998) 'Globalisation and internationalism: democratic prospects for world education', *Comparative Education* 34, 2:143–155.

Jones, P.W. (1999) 'Globalisation and the UNESCO mandate: multilateral prospects for educational development', *International Journal of Educational Development* 19, 1:17–25.

Jonietz, P. and Harris, D. (eds) (1991) *International Schools and International Education*, World Yearbook of Education, London: Kogan Page.

Jullien, M-A. (1817) *Esquisse d'un Ouvrage sur L'Éducation Comparée*, Paris: De Fain. Reprinted by the Bureau International d'Éducation, Genève, 1962.

Juma, M. (2002) *African Virtual University, The Case of Kenyatta University, Kenya*, London: Commonwealth Secretariat.

Juma, M., Waudo, J., Mwirotsi, M., Kamau, A., Herriot, A. and Crossley, M. (2002) 'The development and operation of head teacher support groups in Kenya: a mechanism to create pockets of excellence, improve the provision of quality education and target positive changes in the community', *International Journal of Educational Development* 22, 5: 509–526.

Kaluba, H. and Williams, P. (1999) 'Aid co-ordination through the other end of the telescope', in K. King and L. Buchert (eds) *Changing International Aid to Education*, Paris: UNESCO Publishing.

Kandel, I.L. (1933) *Studies in Comparative Education*, Boston: Houghton & Mifflin.

Kandel, I.L. (1959)'The methodology of comparative education', *International Review of Education* 5, 3:270–278.

Kann, U. (1999) 'Aid co-ordination in theory and practice: a case study of Botswana and Namibia', in K. King and L. Buchert (eds) *Changing International Aid to Education*, Paris: UNESCO Publishing.

Kay, W.K. (1981) 'Problems with the problem approach', *Canadian and International Education* 10, 1:5–19.

Kay, W.K. and Watson J.K.P. (1982) 'Comparative education: the need for dangerous ambition', *Educational Research* 24, 2:129–139.

Kazamias, A.M. (2001) 'Re-inventing the historical in comparative education: reflections on a protean episteme by a contemporary player', *Comparative Education* 37(4):439–449

Kazamias, A.M. and Massialas, B.G. (1965) *Tradition and Change in Education*, Englewood Cliffs, NJ: Prentice Hall.

Kellaghan, T. (1996) 'IEA studies and educational policy', *Assessment in Education* 3, 2:143–160.

Kelly, G.P. (1978) 'Colonial schools in Vietnam: policy and practice', in P.G. Altbach and G.P. Kelly (eds) *Education and Colonialism*, New York: Longmans.

Kelly, G.P. (1984) 'Women's access to education in the third world: myths and realities', in S. Acker (ed.) *World Yearbook of Education 1984: Women in Education*, New York: Kogan Page.

Kelly, G.P. (1992) 'Debates and trends in comparative education', in R.F. Arnove, P.G. Altbach and G.P. Kelly (eds) *Emergent Issues in Education: Comparative Perspectives*, Buffalo: State University of New York Press.

Kelly, G.P. (2000) *French Colonial Education. Essays on Vietnam and West Africa*, New York: AMS Press Inc. (edited by D.H. Kelly).

Kelly, G.P. and Altbach, P.G. (1988) 'Alternative approaches in comparative education' in T.N. Postlethwaite (ed.) *The Encyclopædia of Comparative Education and National Systems of Education*, Oxford: Pergamon Press.

Kelly, G.P., Altbach, P.G. and Arnove, R.F. (1982) 'Trends in comparative education: a critical analysis', in P.G. Altbach, R.F. Arnove and G.P. Kelly (eds) *Comparative Education*, New York: Macmillan.

Kelly, G.P. and Nihlen, A.S. (1982) 'Schooling and the reproduction of patriarchy', in M. Apple (ed.) *Cultural and Economic Reproduction in Education*, London: Routledge and Kegan Paul.

Kempner, K. (1998) 'Post-modernizing education in the periphery and in the core', *International Review of Education* 44, 5/6:441–460.

Kennedy, M.K. (1997) 'The connection between research and practice', *Educational Researcher*, 26, 8:4–12.

KFPE (1998) *Guidelines for Research in Partnership with Developing Countries: Eleven Principles*, Berne: KFPE http://www.kfpe.unibe.ch/guidelines_e.html

King, E.J. (1964) 'The Purpose of Comparative Education', *Comparative Education* 1, 3:147–159.

King, E.J. (1968) *Comparative Studies in Educational Decision Making*, London: Methuen.

King, E.J. (1976) *Education, Culture and Politics in the USA*, Oxford: Pergamon Press.

King, E.J. (1979a) *Education for Uncertainty*, London: Sage.

King, E.J. (1979b) *Other Schools and Ours*, Fifth Edition, London: Holt, Rinehart and Winston.

King, E.J. (1989) 'Comparative investigation of education: an evolutionary process' *Prospects* XIX, 3:369–379.

King, E.J. (1997) 'A turning-point in comparative education: retrospect and prospect' in C. Kodran, B. von Kopp, U. Lauterbach, U. Schäfer, G. Schmidt (eds) *Essays in Honour of Wolfgang Mitter*, Böhlan: Verlag.

King, E.J., Moor, C.H. and Mundy, J.A. (1974) *Post-Compulsory Education I: A New Analysis in Western Europe*, London: Sage.

King, E.J., Moor, C.H. and Mundy, J.A. (1975) *Post-Compulsory Education in Western Europe II: The Way Ahead*, London: Sage.

King, E.M. and Hill, M.A. (eds) (1993) *Women's Education in Developing Countries. Barriers, Benefits and Policies*, Baltimore: Johns Hopkins University Press for the World Bank.

King, K. (1991a) *Aid and Education in the Developing World*, London: Longman.

King, K. (1991b) *Capacity Building for Educational Research, Planning and Analysis: Summary Implications for Donors of a New Aid Strategy*, Edinburgh: University of Edinburgh.

King, K. (1992) 'The external agenda of aid in internal educational reform', *International Journal of Educational Development* 12, 4:257–263.

King, K. (1999) 'Introduction: the new challenges to international development co-operation in education', in K. King and L. Buchert (eds) *Changing International Aid to Education*, Paris: UNESCO Publishing.

King, K. and Buchert, L. (eds) (1999) *Changing International Aid to Education. Global Patterns and National Contexts*. Paris: UNESCO Publishing/NORRAG.

King, K. and Carr-Hill, R. (1992) *The Challenge of Educational Aid to Africa*, Paper presented for the Organisation of African Unity Donors Meeting, Dakar, Senegal, November, 1992. Mimeo.

Klees, S.J. (2002) 'World Bank education policy: new rhetoric, old ideology', *International Journal of Educational Development* 22, 5: 451–474.

Kumar, K. (2001) *Prejudice and Pride. School Histories of the Freedom Struggle in India and Pakistan*, New Delhi: Viking.

Kutnick, P. Jules, V. and Layne, A. (1997) *Gender and School Achievement in the Caribbean*, London: Department for International Development.

Kwong, J. (2000) 'Editorial introduction: marketization and privatization in education', *International Journal of Educational Development* 20, 2:87–92.

Lacey, C. and Jacklin, A. (2001) 'The evaluation of education development projects and bureaucratic cultures: prospects for the education sector within the context created by the White Paper on International Development', in K. Watson (ed.) *Doing Comparative Education Research: Issues and Problems*, Oxford: Symposium Books.

Latham, R. (1958) *The Travels of Marco Polo*, London: The Folio Society.

Lauder, M. and Hughes, D. (1999) *Trading in Futures. Why Markets in Education Don't Work*, Buckingham: Open University Press.

Lauglo, J. (1996) 'Banking on education and the uses of research: a critique of World Bank priorities and strategies for education', *International Journal of Educational Development* 16, 3:221–233.

Lauwerys, J. (1959) 'The philosophical approach to comparative education', *International Review of Education* 5, 3:281–298

Law, W-W. (2002) 'Education reform in Taiwan: a search for a "national" identity through democratisation and Taiwanisation', *Compare* 32, 1:61–81.

Lawton, D. (1992) *Education and Politics. Conflict or Consensus?* London: The Falmer Press.

Leach, F. E. (1994) 'Expatriates as agents of cross-cultural transmission', *Compare* 24, 3:217–232.

Leach, F.E. and Little, A.W. (eds) (1999) *Education, Cultures, and Economics*, London: The Falmer Press.

Lee, W.O. (1991) *Social Change and Educational Problems in Japan, Singapore and Hong Kong*, London: Macmillan.

Levesque, D. (2001) *Whose Money? Whose Education System? Improving Aid Effectiveness by Examining Paradigm, Policy and Implementation, Perception Gaps in Pakistan's Donor Funded Primary Education Development Programme 1991–2000*. Unpublished PhD thesis, the University of Reading.

Levin, H.M. and Lockheed, M.E. (eds) (1993) *Effective Schools in Developing Countries*, London: The Falmer Press.

Lewin, K.M. (1987) *Education in Austerity: Options for Planners*, Paris: UNESCO Publishing.

Lewin, K.M. (1992) *Dialogue for Development: A Policy Review of British Educational Aid Towards 2000*, London: Overseas Development Administration.

Lewin, K.M. and Stuart, J. (2002) 'Editorial postscript', *International Journal of Educational Development* 22, 3–4:411–421.

Lievesley, D. (2001) *International Information Systems: A Continuing Challenge*, Paper presented at the UKFIET Oxford International Conference on Education and Development, 19–21 September.

Limage, L.J. (1999) 'Literacy practices and literacy policies: where has UNESCO been and where might it be going?' *International Journal of Educational Development* 19, 1:75–89.

Little, A.W. (1988) *Learning from Developing Countries*, London: University of London, Institute of Education.

Little, A.W. (1996) 'Globalisation and educational research: whose context counts?' *International Journal of Educational Development* 16, 4:427–438.

Little, A.W. (1999) *Labouring to Learn. Towards a Political Economy of Plantations, People and Education in Sri Lanka*, New York and London: Macmillan and St Martin's Press.

Little, A.W. (ed.) (2000a) *Globalisation, Qualifications and Livelihoods*, Special Issue of *Assessment in Education* 7, 3.

Little, A.W. (2000b) 'Development studies and comparative education: context, content, comparison and contributors', *Comparative Education* 36, 3:279–296.

Little, A.W., Hoppers, C.A. and Gardner, R. (eds) (1994) *Beyond Jomtien. Implementing Primary Education for All*, London: Macmillan.

Lockheed, M. and Verspoor, A. (1990) *Improving the Quality of Primary Education in Developing Countries*, Washington, DC: World Bank.

Louisy, P. (2001) 'Globalisation and comparative education: a Caribbean perspective', *Comparative Education* 37 (4):425–438.

Lyotard, J-F. (1984) *The Postmodern Condition: A Report on Knowledge*, Manchester: University of Manchester Press.

Magnusson, M. (ed.) (1990) *Chambers Biographical Dictionary*, Edinburgh: Chambers.

Mallinson, V. (1975) *An Introduction to the Study of Comparative Education*, Fourth Edition, London: Heinemann.

Mangan, J.A. (1993) *The Imperial Curriculum: Racial Images and Education in the British Colonial Experience*, London: Routledge.

Marginson, S. and Mollis, M. (2001) '"The door opens and the tiger leaps": theories and reflexivities of comparative education for a global millennium', *Comparative Education Review* 45, 4:581–615.

Märja, T. and Jõgi, L. (2000) 'Estonia in the grip of change: the role of education for adults in the transition period', in T. Mebrahtu, M. Crossley and D. Johnson (eds) *Globalisation, Educational Transformation and Societies in Transition*, Oxford: Symposium Books.

Marshall, J. and Peters, M. (eds) (1999) *Education Policy*, Cheltenham: Edward Elgar Publishing Inc.

Martin, C.J. (1999) 'More for less. The Mexican cult of educational efficiency and its consequences at school level', in L. Buchert (ed.) *Education Reform in the South in the 1990s*, Paris: UNESCO Publishing.

Masemann, V.L. (1982) 'Critical ethnography in the study of comparative education', *Comparative Education Review* 26, 1:1–15.

Masemann, V.L. (1990) 'Ways of knowing', *Comparative Education Review* 34, 3:463–473.

Masemann, V.L. and Welch, A. (eds) (1997) 'Tradition, modernity and post-modernity in comparative education, Special Double Issue of *International Review of Education* 43, 5 & 6.

May, S. (1994) *Making Multicultural Education Work*, Clevedon: Multilingual Matters Ltd.

Mazrui, A.A. (1990) *Cultural Forces in World Politics*, London: James Currey.

Mazrui, A.A. (1992) 'Towards diagnosing and treating cultural dependency: the case of the African university', *International Journal of Educational Development* 12, 2:95–111.

Mbeki, T. (1999) *Speech to Launch the African Renaissance Institute*, Pretoria: African Renaissance Institute.

McCarthy, C. (1998) *The Uses of Culture. Education and the Limits of Ethnic Affiliation*, New York and London: Routledge.

McGinn, N.F. (1994) 'The impact of supranational organisations on public education', *International Journal of Educational Development* 4, 3:289–298.

McGinn, N.F. (ed.)(1996) *Crossing Lines: Research and Policy Networks for Developing Country Education*, Westport, Connecticut: Praeger.

McGinn, N.F. (1997) 'Supranational organisations and their impact on nation-states and the modern school' in W.K. Cummings and N.F. McGinn (eds) *International Handbook of Education and Development: Preparing Schools, Students and Nations for the Twenty-First Century*, Oxford: Pergamon Press.

McGrath, S. (1998) 'Education, development and assistance: the challenge of the new millennium', in K. King and L. Buchert (eds) *Changing International Aid to Education*, Paris: UNESCO Publishing.

McGrath, S. (2001a) 'Confessions of a long distance runner: reflections from an international and comparative education research project', in K.Watson (ed.) *Doing Comparative Education Research: Issues and Problems*, Oxford: Symposium Books.

McGrath, S. (2001b) 'Research in a cold climate: towards a political economy of British international and comparative education', *International Journal of Educational Development* 21, 5:391–400.

McLeish, E. A. and Phillips, D. (eds) (1998) *Processes of Transition in Education Systems*, Oxford: Symposium Books.

Mebrahtu, T., Crossley, M. and Johnson, D.(eds) (2000) *Globalisation, Educational Reconstruction and Societies in Transition*, Oxford: Symposium Books.

Mende, T. (1973) *From Aid to Recolonization*, London: Harrap.

Meyer, J.W., Kamens, D. and Benavot, A. (1992) *School Knowledge for the Masses: World Models and National Primary Curricular Categories in the Twentieth Century*, London: The Falmer Press.

Miller, E. (1991) *Men at Risk*, Kingston: Jamaica Publishing House.

Mingat, A. and Tan, J.P. (2001) 'The HIPC initiative: what will it do for education?' *ADEA Newsletter* 13, 2:3–6.

Mitter, W. (1997) 'Challenges to comparative education: between retrospect and expectation', *International Review of Education* 43, 4:401–412.

Mok, J. K-H. and Chan D.K-K. (eds) (2002) *Globalization and Education. The Quest for Quality Education in Hong Kong*, Hong Kong: Hong Kong University Press.

Morrow, R.A. and Torres, C.A. (1995) *Social Theory and Education. A Critique of Theories of Social and Cultural Reproduction*, Albany: State University of New York Press.

Mosley, P. (1987) *Overseas Aid: Its Defence And Reform*, Brighton: Wheatsheaf.

Mosley, P., Harrigan, J. and Toye, J. (1995) *Aid and Power: The World Bank and Policy-Based Lending*, Vol. 1, second edition, London: Routledge.

Muckle, J. and Morgan, W.J. (2001) *Post-School Education and the Transition from State Socialism*, London: Bramcote Press.

Mundy, K. (1999) 'Educational multi-lateralism in a changing world order: UNESCO and the limits of the possible', *International Journal of Educational Development* 19, 1:27–52.

Mundy, K. (2002) 'Retrospect and prospect: education in a reforming World Bank', *International Journal of Educational Development* 22, 5:483–508.

Mundy, K. and Murphy, L. (2001) 'Transnational advocacy, global civil society? Emerging evidence from the field of education', *Comparative Education Review* 45, 1:85–126.

Mwiria, K. and Wamahiu, S. (eds) (1995) *Issues in Educational Research in Africa*, Nairobi: East African Educational Publishers.

National Commission on Excellence (1983) *A Nation at Risk: the Imperative for Educational Reform*, Washington DC: United States Government Printing Office.

Noah (1986) 'The use and abuse of comparative education', in P. G. Altbach and G. P. Kelly (eds) *New Approaches to Comparative Education*, Chicago: University of Chicago Press.

Noah, H.J. and Eckstein, M.A. (1969) *Toward a Science of Comparative Education*, New York: Macmillan.

Noah, H.J. and Eckstein, M.A. (1998) *Doing Comparative Education: Three Decades of Collaboration*, Hong Kong: University of Hong Kong, Comparative Education Research Centre.

NORAD (1995) *NORAD's Support to the Education Sector. Basic Principles*, Oslo: NORAD.

Norris, C. and Benjamin, A. (1996) *What is Deconstruction?* Boston: Academy Editions.

Nowak, M. and Swinehart, T. (eds) (1989) *Human Rights in Developing Countries, 1989 Yearbook*, Kehl: N.P. Engel.

O'Neill, A. (2002) *Trust*, BBC Reith Lectures 2002, BBC News Online Network, *http://www.bbc.co.uk*

Oatley, K. (1992) *Best Laid Schemes: the Psychology of Emotions*, Cambridge: Cambridge University Press.

Odora Hoppers, C.A. (2001) 'Poverty, power and partnership in educational development: a post-victimology perspective', *Compare*, 31, 1:21–38.

Ohmae, K. (1995) *The End of the Nation State*, New York: Free Press.

Okoro, D.C.U. (1979) 'Progress towards UPE in Africa', in Commonwealth Secretariat (ed.) *Universal Primary Education in Asia and the Pacific*. Report of a Regional Seminar, Bangladesh, London: Commonwealth Secretariat.

Olukoshi, A.O. (1997) 'The quest for a new paradigm for Swedish development cooperation in Africa', in Kifle, H., Olukoshi, A.O. and Wohlgemuth, W. (eds) *A New Partnership for African Development: Issues and Parameters*, Uppsala: Nordic African Institute.

Organisation for Economic Co-operation and Development (1995) *Education at a Glance: OECD Indicators*, Paris: OECD.

Organisation for Economic Co-operation and Development (1996) *Development Partnerships in the new Global Context in OECD: Shaping the 21st Century. The Contribution of Development Co-operation*, Paris: OECD.

Organisation for Economic Co-operation and Development (1998a) *Education at a Glance: OECD Indicators*, Paris: OECD.

Organisation for Economic Co-operation and Development (1998b) *Education Policy Analysis 1998*, Paris: OECD.

Osborn, M. (2001) 'Life in school: pupil perspectives and pupil experiences of schooling and learning in three European countries', in K. Watson (ed.) *Doing Comparative Education Research: Issues and Problems*, Oxford: Symposium Books.

O'Sullivan, M.C. (2002) 'Reform implementation and the realities within which teachers work: a Namibian case study', *Compare* 32, 2: 219–237.

Overseas Development Administration (1990) *Into the Nineties: An Education Policy for British Aid*, London: ODA.

Overseas Development Institute (1992) *Aid and Political Reform*, Briefing Paper, London: ODI.

Overseas Development Institute (1999) *The Meaning and Measurement of Poverty*, ODI Poverty Briefing, 3, London: ODI.

Overseas Development Institute (2002) *International Humanitarian Action: A Review of Policy Trends*, ODI Briefing Paper, London: ODI.

Oxenham, J. (1980) *Literacy: Writing, Reading and Social Organisation*, London: Routledge and Kegan Paul.

Øyen, E. (ed.) (1990) *Comparative Methodology. Theory and Practice in International Social Research*, London: Sage.

Palme, O. (1982) *Common Security: A Programme for Disarmament*, London: Pan Books.

Parkhurst, J.O. (2001) 'Myths of Success: the Use and Misuse of Ugandan HIV Data'. Paper presented at the UKFIET Oxford International Conference on Education and Development, 19–21 September.

Paulston, R.G. (1976) *Conflicting Theories of Social and Educational Change*, Pittsburg: University of Pittsburg Center for International Studies.

Paulston, R.G. (1994) 'Comparative and international education: paradigms and theories', in T. Husen and T.N. Postlethwaite (eds) *The International Encyclopaedia of Education*, Vol. 2, Oxford: Pergamon Press.

Paulston, R.G. (ed.) (1996) *Social Cartography. Mapping Ways of Seeing Social and Educational Change*, New York: Garland.

Paulston, R.G. (1999) 'Mapping comparative education after postmodernity', *Comparative Educational Review* 43, 4:438–463.

Pearson, L.B. (1969) *Partners in Development, Report of the Commission on International Development*, New York: Praeger.

Penny, A.J., Mehru, A.A., Farah, I., Ostberg, S. and Smith, R.L. (2000) 'A study of cross-natural collaborative research: reflecting on experience in Pakistan', *International Journal of Educational Development* 20, 6:443–455.

Peschar, J. and Wal, M. Van der (2000) *Education Contested: Changing Relations Between State, Market and Civil Society in Modern European Education*, Lisse: Swets and Zeitlinger.

Peters, M. (2001) *Post-structuralism, Marxism and Neoliberalism. Between Theory and Politics*, Lanham: Rowman and Littlefield.

Peterson, A.D.C. (1977) 'Applied comparative education: the International Baccalaureate', *Comparative Education* 13, 2:77–80.

Phillips, D. (ed.) (1989) *Cross National Attraction in Education*, Special Number of *Comparative Education* 25, 3.

Phillips, D. (1994) 'Periodisation in historical approaches to comparative education: some considerations from the examples of Germany and England and Wales', *British Journal of Educational Studies* XXXXII, 3:261–272.

Phillips, D. (1999) 'On comparing', in R. Alexander, P. Broadfoot and D. Phillips (eds) *Learning from Comparing: New Directions in Comparative Educational Research, Volume One, Context, Classrooms and Outcomes*, Oxford: Symposium Books.

Phillips, D. (2000) 'Learning from elsewhere in education: some perennial problems revisited with reference to British interests in Germany', *Comparative Education*, 36, 3:297–307.

Phillips, D. and Economou, A. (1999) 'Conducting research into European Union education and training policy; some theoretical and methodological considerations' *Compare* 29, 3:303–316.

Pollard, A., Broadfoot, P., Croll, P., Osborn, M. and Abbott, D. (1994) *Changing English Primary Schools? The Impact of the Eduction Reform Act at Key Stage One*, London: Cassell.

Postlethwaite, T.N. (1988) 'Preface' in T.N. Postlethwaite (ed.) *The Encyclopaedia of Comparative Education and National Systems of Education*, Oxford: Pergamon Press.

Postlethwaite, T.N. (1999) *International Studies of Educational Achievement: Methodological Issues*, Hong Kong: University of Hong Kong Comparative Education Research Centre.

Preece, J. (2002) 'Feminist perspectives on the learning of citizenship and governance', *Compare* 32, 1:21–33.

Preston, R. (1997) 'Critical approaches to lifelong education', *International Review of Education* 45, 5–6:561–574.

Preston, R. and Arthur, L. (1996) *Quality in Overseas Consultancy: Understanding the Issues*, University of Warwick: The British Council.

Preston, R. and Arthur, L. (1997) 'Knowledge societies and planetry cultures: international consultancy in human development', *International Journal of Educational Development* 17, 1:3–12.

Price, R.F. (1977) *Marx and Education in Russia and China*, London: Croom Helm.

Pritchard, R.M.O. (2002) 'Was East German education a victim of West German "colonisation" after unification?' *Compare* 32, 1:47–59.

Psacharopoulos, G. (1990) 'Comparative Education: from theory to practice or are you A:\neo* or B:\ist?, *Comparative Education Review* 34, 3:369–380

Psacharopoulos, G. and Loxley, W. (1985) *Diversified Secondary Education and Development: Evidence from Colombia and Tanzania*, Baltimore: The Johns Hopkins University.

Puryear, J.M. (1995) 'International education statistics and research: status and problems', *International Journal of Educational Development* 15, 1: 79–91.

Radice, H. (1999) 'Taking globalisation seriously', *The Socialist Register 1999*, London: The Merlin Press.

Raivola, R. (1985) 'What is comparison?: methodological and philosophical considerations', *Comparative Education Review* 29, 2: 261–273.

Ramirez, F.O. and Boli-Bennett, J. (1982) 'Global patterns of educational institutionalization', in P.G. Altbach, R.F. Arnove, and G.P. Kelly (eds) *Comparative Education*, New York: Macmillan.

Reimers, F. and McGinn (1997) *Informed Dialogue. Using Research to Shape Education Policy Around the World*, Westport: Praeger.

Retamal, G. and Aedo-Richmond, R. (1998) *Education as a Humanitarian Response*, London, Cassell.

Reynolds, D., Creemers, B. P. M., Nesselrodt, P. S., Schaffer, E. C., Stringfield, S. and Teddlie, C. (1994) *Advances in School Effectiveness Research*, Oxford: Pergamon.

Reynolds, D. and Farrell, S. (1996) *Worlds Apart? A Review of International Surveys of Educational Achievement Including England*, London: HMSO

Riddell, A. (1999) 'Evaluations of educational reform programmes in developing countries: whose life is it anyway?' *International Journal of Educational Development* 19, 6:383–394.

Riddell, R.C. (1997) 'The changing concept of aid and development', in W.K. Cummings, and N.F. McGinn (eds) *International Handbook of Education and Development: Preparing Schools, Students and Nations for the Twenty-First Century*, Oxford: Pergamon Press.

Roberston, R. (1992) *Globalization: Social Theory and Global Culture*, London: Sage.

Robertson, S., Bonel, X. and Dale, R. (2002) 'GATS and the education service industry: the politics of scale and global re-territorialization'. Unpublished manuscript, University of Bristol, Graduate School of Education.

Robinson, C.D.W. (1994) 'Local languages for local literacies? Debating a central dilemma', *Language and Education* 8, 1–2:69–74.

Robinson, C.D.W. (1996a) *Language Use in Rural Development: An African Perspective*, The Hague: Mouton de Gruyter.

Robinson, C.D.W. (1996b) *Language Diversity and Accountability in the South: Perspectives And Dilemmas*, London: British Council Language and Development Seminar, mimeo.

Robinson-Pant, A. (2000) 'Women and literacy: a Nepal perspective', *International Journal of Educational Development* 204:349–364.

Robinson-Pant, A. (2001) 'Development as discourse: what relevance to education?', *Compare* 31, 3:311–328.

Rockwell, E. (1991) 'Ethnography and critical knowledge of education in Latin America', *Prospects* xxi, 2:156–167.

Rogers, A. (1992) Adults Learning for Development, London: Cassell.

Rust, V. D. (1991) 'Post-modernism and its comparative implications', *Comparative Education Review* 35, 4:610–626.

Rust, V. D., Soumaré, O., Pescador, O. and Shibuya, M. (1999) 'Research strategies in comparative education', *Comparative Education Review* 43, 1:86–109.

Sadler, M. (1900) 'How far can we learn anything of practical value from the study of foreign systems of education?' in J. H. Higginson (ed.) (1979) *Selections from Michael Sadler*, Liverpool: Dejall and Meyorre.

Said, E. (1978) *Orientalism*, London: Routledge and Kegan Paul.

Samoff, J. (1992), 'The intellectual/financial complex of foreign aid', *Review of African Political Economy* 53:60–75.

Samoff, J. (1993) 'The reconstruction of schooling in Africa', *Comparative Education Review* 37, 2:181–222.

Samoff, J. (1996a) 'Which priorities and strategies for education?' *International Journal of Educational Development* 16, 3:249–271.

Samoff, J. (1996b) *Analyses, Agenda and Priorities for Education in Africa. A Review of Externally Initiated, Commissioned and Supported Studies of Education in Africa 1990–1994*, Paris: UNESCO, Working Group on Education Sector Analysis/ Association for the Development of Education in Africa.

Samoff, J. (1999) 'Institutionalising international influence', in R. F. Arnove and C.A. Torres (eds) *Comparative Education. The Dialectic of the Global and the Local*, Lanham: Rowman & Littlefield.

Samson, S. (2001) 'A new pedagogy for training semi-literates to teach children, with special reference to Addis Ababa, Ethiopia'. Unpublished doctoral thesis for the University of Wales.

Sayed, Y. (2002) 'Democratizing education in a decentralised system: South African policy and practice', *Compare* 32, 1:35–46.

Schluter, M. and Lee, D. (1993) *The R Factor*, London: Hodder and Stoughton.

Schriewer, J. (ed.) (2000) *Discourse Formulations in Comparative Education*, Frankfurt am Main: Peter Lang.

Schriewer, J. with Holmes, B (eds) (1988) *Theories and Methods in Comparative Education*, Frankfurt am Main: Peter Lang.

Schuster, J.H. (1994) 'Emigration, internationalisation and the "Brain Drain": propensities among British academics', *Higher Education* 28, 4:437–452

Schweisfurth, M. (1999) 'Resilience, resistance and responsiveness: comparative and international education at UK universities', in R. Alexander, P. Broadfoot and D. Phillips (eds) *Learning from Comparing: New Directions in Comparative Educational Research, Volume One, Contexts, Classrooms and Outcomes*, Oxford: Symposium Books.

Schweisfurth, M., Davies, L. and Harber, C. (eds) (2002) *Learning Democracy and Citizenship. International Experiences*, Oxford: Symposium Books.

Sebah, J. (1999) 'Developing evidence-informed policy and practice in education'. Paper presented to the British Educational Research Association Conference, University of Sussex (September).

Shaw, M. and Ormston, M. (2001) 'Values and vodka: cross-cultural anatomy of an Anglo–Russian educational project', *International Journal of Educational Development* 21, 2:119–133.

Short, C. (2002) *Presentation by the United Kingdom Secretary of State for International Development at the Department for International Development South West Policy Forum*, 4 March 2002, Bristol.

Sifuna, D.N. (1992) 'Prevocational subjects in primary schools in the 8–4–4 education system in Kenya', *International Journal of Educational Development* 12, 2:133–145.

Skeldon, R. (1997) *Migration and Development: A Global Perspective*, London: Longman.

Sklair, L. (1999) 'Globalization: new approaches to social change', in S. Taylor (ed.) *Sociology. Issues and Debates*, London: Macmillan.

Smith, H. (2002) *Strengthening the Impact of Education on Poverty Reduction: Sector Wide Approaches*, Education Line, Spring Issue, Reading: Centre for British Teachers.

Smith, R.L. (2002) 'Lins perspective', *Educaid. Norwegian Cooperation and Basic Education*, 6, 2:1.

Soudien, C. (2002) 'Education in the network age: globalisation, development and the World Bank', *International Journal of Educational Development* 22, 5:439–450.

Stenhouse, L. (1979) 'Case-study and comparative education. Particularity and generalisation', *Comparative Education* 15, 1:5–11.

Stewart, F. (1996) 'Globalisation and education', *International Journal of Educational Development* 1, 4:327–333.

Stirrat, R. and Henkel, H. (1997) 'The development gift: the problem of reciprocity in the development world', *Annals of the American Academy of Political and Social Science* 554:66–80.

Street, B. (1984) *Literacy in Theory and Practice*, Cambridge: Cambridge University Press.

Street, B. (1999) 'Meanings of culture in development: a case study from literacy', in F.E. Leach and A.W. Little (eds) *Education, Cultures, and Economics*, London: The Falmer Press.

Stromquist, N.P. (1997) *Literacy for Citizenship: Gender and Grassroots Dynamics in Brazil*, Albany: State University of New York Press.

Stromquist, N.P. (ed.) (1998) *Women in the Third World. An Encyclopædia of Contemporary Issues*, New York: Garland.

Stuart, J. Morojele, M. and Lefoka, P. (1997) 'Improving our practice: collaborative classroom action research in Lesotho', in M. Crossley and G. Vulliamy (eds) *Qualitative Educational Research in Developing Countries*, New York: Garland.

Stuart, J.S. and Lewin, K.M. (eds) (2002) *Researching Teacher Education: The Multi-Site Teacher Education Research Project* (MUSTER). Special Issue of the *International Journal of Educational Development* 22, 3–4.

Sullivan, K. (ed.) (1998) *Education and Change in the Pacific Rim*, Oxford: Triangle.

Sutherland, M.B. and Cammish, N.K. (eds.) (1997) *Aspects of Gender, Education and Development*, Special Issue of *Compare* 27, 3.

Swainson, N. (1995) *Redressing Gender Inequalities in Education. A Review of Constraints and Priorities in Malawi, Zambia and Zimbabwe*, London: ODA.

Sweden, Ministry of Foreign Affairs (1997) *Partnerships with Africa: Proposals for a New Swedish Policy Towards Sub-Saharan Africa*, Stockholm: Ministry of Foreign Affairs.

Sweeting, A. (2001) 'Doing comparative historical education research: problems and issues from and about Hong Kong', in K. Watson (ed.) *Doing Comparative Education Research: Issues and Problems*, Oxford: Symposium Books.

Teasdale, G.R. (1998) 'Local and global knowledge in higher education: a search for complementarity in the Asia–Pacific region', *International Journal of Educational Development* 18, 6:501–511.

Teasdale, J.I. and Teasdale, G.R. (1999) 'Alternative cultures of knowledge in higher education in the Australia–Pacific region', in F.E. Leach and A.W. Little, (eds) *Education, Cultures, and Economics*, London: The Falmer Press.

Teddlie, C. and Reynolds, D. (eds) (2000) *The International Handbook of School Effectiveness Research*, London: The Falmer Press.

Thaman, K.H. (1993) 'Culture and the curriculum' in M. Crossley (ed.) Special Issue of *Comparative Education on Education in the South Pacific* 29, 3:249–260.

Theisen, G. (1997) 'The new ABCs of comparative and international education', *Comparative Education Review* 41, 4:397–412.

Thomas, E. (2000) *Culture and Schooling. Building Bridges Between Research, Praxis and Professionalism*, Chichester: John Wiley.

Thomas, R.M. (ed.) (1990) *International Comparative Education. Practices, Issues and Prospects*, Oxford: Pergamon Press.

Thomas, R.M. (1998) *Conducting Educational Research: A Comparative View*, London: Bergin and Garvey.

Tikly, L. (1999) 'Post-colonialism and comparative education', *International Review of Education* 45, 5/6:603–621.

Tikly, L. (2001) 'Globalisation and education in the postcolonial world: towards a conceptual framework', *Comparative Education* 37, 2:151–171.

Tikly, L. and Crossley, M. (2001) Teaching comparative and international education: a framework for analysis', *Comparative Education Review* 45, 4:561–580.

Tjeldvoll, A. and Smehaugen, A. (1998) *Scandinavian Comparative Education Research in Progress*, Oslo: Nordic Network of International and Comparative Education (NICE).

Tobin, J. (1999) 'Method and meaning in comparative classroom ethnography', in R. Alexander, P. Broadfoot, D. Phillips (eds) *Learning from Comparing. New Directions in Comparative Educational Research. Volume 1. Contexts, Classrooms and Outcomes*, Oxford: Symposium Books.

Tooley, J. (1999) *The Global Education Industry. Lessons from Private Education in Developing Countries*, London: Institute of Economic Affairs.

Tooley, J. and Darby, D. (1998) *Educational Research. A Critique*, London: Office for Standards in Education.

Torres, C.A. (1998) 'Paulo Freire'. Paper presented to the Tenth World Congress of Comparative Education Societies, Cape Town, South Africa.

Torres, C.A. (2001) 'Globalization and comparative education in the world system', *Comparative Education Review* 45, 4:iii–x.

Torres, C.A. and Mitchell, T.R. (eds) (1995) *Sociology of Education. Emerging Perspectives*, Albany: State University of New York Press.

Torres, C.A. and Puiggrós, A. (eds) (1997) *Latin American Education. Comparative Perspectives*, Boulder: Westview Press.

Trahar, S. (2002) 'Towards cultural synergy in higher education'. Paper presented at the Second Symposium on Teaching and Learning in Higher Education, 'Paradigm Shift in Higher Education', Centre for Development of Teaching and Learning, National University of Singapore, 4–6 September 2002.

Trethewey, A.R. (1976) *Introducing Comparative Education*, Oxford: Pergamon Press.

UNDP (1999) *Human Development Report 1999*, New York: Oxford University Press.

UNDP (2000) *Human Development Report 2000*, New York: Oxford University Press.

UNDP (2001) *Human Development Report 2001*, New York: Oxford University Press.

UNESCO (1957) *World Illiteracy*, Paris: UNESCO Publishing.

UNESCO (1971) 'Literacy and Adult Education in the Asian Region', *UN Bulletin for Education in Asia*, V. Paris: UNESCO Publishing.

UNESCO (1993) *World Education Report 1993*, Paris: UNESCO Publishing.

UNESCO (1995) *World Education Report 1995*, Paris: UNESCO Publishing.

UNESCO (1996) *Learning: The Treasure Within*, Report to UNESCO of the International Commission on Education for the Twenty-First Century (The Delors Report), Paris: UNESCO Publishing.

UNESCO (1997) *Adult Education in a Polarising World*, Paris: UNESCO Publishing.

UNESCO (1998a) *Our Creative Diversity. Report on the World Commission on Culture and Development*, Paris: UNESCO Publishing.

UNESCO (1998b) *World Education Report 1998*, Paris: UNESCO Publishing.

UNICEF (1989) *The State of the World's Children Report*, Geneva: UNICEF.

Usher, R. (1996) *Understanding Educational Research*, London: Routledge.

Vaizey, J. (1962) *The Economics of Education*, London: Faber and Faber.

Van der Eyken, W., Goulden, D., and Crossley, M. (1995) 'Evaluating educational reform in a small state. A case study of Belize, Central America', *Evaluation* 1, 1:33–44.

Verspoor, A. (1989) *Pathways to Change: Improving the Quality of Education in Developing Countries*, Washington, DC: World Bank.

Verspoor, A. (1991) 'Twenty years of World Bank support for basic education. Presentation and evaluation', *Prospects* xxi, 3:314–329.

Verspoor, A. (1993) 'More than business as usual: reflections on the new modalities of education aid', *International Journal of Educational Development* 13, 2:103–112.

Wallerstein, I. (1974) *The Modern World-System: Capitalist Agriculture and the Origins of the European World Economy in the Sixteenth Century*, New York: The Academic Press.

Ward, M. (2002) *Foreign Aid, Power and Elementary Education Reform in Pakistan from 1992–1999*. Unpublished PhD thesis, Norwich: University of East Anglia.

Warwick, D.P. and Osherson, S. (1973) 'Comparative analysis in the social sciences' in D.P. Warwick and S. Osherson (eds) *Comparative Research Methods*, Eaglewood Cliffs, New Jersey: Prentice Hall.

Waters, M. (1995) *Globalisation*, London and New York: Routledge.

Watkins, D.A. and Biggs, J.B. (eds) (1996) *The Chinese Learner. Cultural, Psychological and Contextual Influences*, Hong Kong: University of Hong Kong, Comparative Education Research Centre.

Watkins, D.A and Biggs, J.B. (eds) (2001) *Teaching the Chinese Learner: Psychological and Pedagogical Perspectives*, Hong Kong: University of Hong Kong, Comparative Education Research Centre.

Watkins, K. (1996) *The Oxfam Poverty Report*, Oxford: Oxfam.

Watkins, K. (2000) *The Oxfam Education Report*, Oxford: Oxfam.

Watson, K. (1973) *Educational Development in South-East Asia: an Historical and Comparative Analysis of the Growth of Education in Thailand, Malaya and Singapore*. Unpublished doctoral thesis for the University of Reading.

Watson, K. (1980) *Educational Development in Thailand*, Hong Kong: Heinemann, Educational Books (Asia).

Watson, K. (1982a) 'Comparative education in British teacher training institutions', in R. Goodings, M. Byram and M. McPartland (eds) *Changing Priorities in Teacher Education*, London: Croom Helm.

Watson, K. (1982b) *Education in the Third World*, London: Croom Helm.

Watson, K. (1988) 'Forty years of education and development: from optimism to uncertainty', *Education Review* 40, 2:137–174.

Watson, K. (1990) 'Information dissemination: the role of the International Journal of Educational Development, 1979–1989', *International Journal of Educational Development* 10, 2:95–114.

Watson, K. (1993a) 'Language, education and political power: some reflections on North–South relationships', *Language and Education* 6, 2–4:99–121.

Watson, K. (1993b) 'Rulers and ruled: racial perceptions and schooling in colonial Malaya and Singapore', in J.A. Mangan (ed.) *The Imperial Curriculum*, London: Routledge.

Watson, K. (1995) 'Redefining the role of government in higher education: how realistic is the World Bank's prescription?', in L. Buchert, and K. King (eds) *Learning from Experience: Policy and Practice in and to Higher Education*, The Hague: Centre for the Study of Education in Developing Countries (CESO).

Watson, K. (1996a) 'Educational provision for the 21st century: who or what is shaping the agenda and influencing developments?', *Southern African Review of Education* 1: 1–19.

Watson, K. (1996b) 'Banking on key reforms for education development: a critique of the World Bank review', *Mediterranean Journal of Education Studies* 1, 1:43–61.

Watson, K. (1998) 'Memories, models and mapping: the impact of geopolitical changes on comparative studies in education', *Compare* 28, 1:5–31.

Watson, K. (1999a) 'UNESCO's vision for education in the twenty-first century: where is the moral high ground?' *International Journal of Educational Development* 19, 1:7–17.

Watson, K. (1999b) 'Comparative educational research: the need for reconceptualisation and fresh insights', *Compare* 29, 3:234–248.

Watson, K. (1999c) 'Dependency v. partnership: the paradoxes of educational aid and development in an age of globalisation', University of Reading. Mimeo.

Watson, K. (1999d) 'Language, power, development and geopolitical changes: conflicting pressures facing plurilingual societies', *Compare* 29, 3:233–248.

Watson, K. (ed.) (2001a) *Doing Comparative Education Research. Issues and Problems*, Oxford: Symposium Books.

Watson, K. (2001b) 'The impact of globalisation on educational reform and language policy: some comparative insights from transitional societies', *Asia–Pacific Journal of Education* 21, 2:1–18.

Watson, K. and King, K. (1991) 'From comparative to international studies in education: towards the co-ordination of a British resource of expertise', *International Journal of Educational Development* 11, 3:245–253.

WCEFA (1990) *World Declaration on Education for All and Framework for Action to Meet Basic Learning Needs*, New York: Inter-Agency Commission for WCEFA.

Weiler, H. (1978) 'Education and development: from the age of innocence to the age of scepticism', *Comparative Education* 14, 2:179–198.

Welch, A.R. (1999) 'The triumph of technocracy or the collapse of certainty? Modernity, postmodernity and postcolonialism in comparative education' in R.A. Arnove and C.A. Torres (eds) *Comparative Education. The Dialectic of the Global and the Local*, Lanham: Rowman and Littlefield.

Welch, A.R. (2001) 'Globalisation, postmodernity and the state: comparative education facing the third millennium', *Comparative Education* 37, 4:475–492.

Wertsch, J. (1995) *Socio-Cultural Studies of Mind*, Cambridge: Cambridge University Press.

Whitty, G., Power, S. and Halpin, D. (1998) *Devolution and Choice in Education*, Buckingham: Open University Press.

Willan, B. (2002) 'Globalisation and human rights', *Royal Society of Arts Journal*, 1, 6:18–21.

Wilson, D.N. (1994) 'Comparative and international education: fraternal or Siamese twins? A preliminary genealogy of our twin fields', *Comparative Education Review* 38, 4:449–486.

Wilson, D.N. (2003) 'The future of comparative education in a globalised world', *International Review of Education* 49, 1: in press.

Wohlgemuth, L. (1999) 'Education and geopolitical change in Africa: a case for partnership', in K. King and L. Buchert (eds) *Changing International Aid to Education*, Paris: UNESCO Publishing.

Wolfensohn, J. (1995) *New Directions and New Partnerships*, Washington, DC: World Bank.

World Bank (1971) *Education Sector Working Paper*, Washington, DC: World Bank.

World Bank (1975) *Rural Development Sector Working Paper*, Washington, DC: World Bank.

World Bank (1978) *Review of Bank Operations in the Education Sector*, Washington, DC: World Bank (OED Report No. 2321).

World Bank (1980) *Education Sector Policy Paper*, Washington, DC: World Bank.

World Bank (1981) *Accelerated Development in Sub-Saharan Africa: An Agenda for Action*, (The Berg Report), Washington, DC: World Bank.

World Bank (1988) *The Educational Crisis in Sub-Saharan Africa*, Washington, DC: World Bank.

World Bank (1989) *Sub-Saharan Africa: From Crisis to Sustainable Growth*, Washington, DC: World Bank.

World Bank (1990) *Primary Education: A World Bank Policy Study*, Washington, DC: World Bank.

World Bank (1991) *Vocational and Technical Education and Training: A World Bank Policy Paper*, Washington, DC: World Bank.

World Bank (1994) *Higher Education: The Lessons of Experience*, Washington, DC: World Bank.

World Bank (1995) *Priorities and Strategies for Education: A World Bank Review*, Washington, DC: World Bank.

World Bank (1998) *World Development Report: 1998/99 – Knowledge for Development*, Washington, DC: World Bank.

World Bank (1999) *Education Sector Strategy*, Human Development Network, Washington, DC: World Bank.

World Bank (1999/2000) *World Development Report: Entering the 21st Century*, New York: Oxford University Press.

World Bank, Human Development Network (2001) *Constructing Knowledge Societies: New Challenges for Tertiary Education. A World Bank Strategy, Education Group Human Development Network*, Washington, DC: World Bank.

World Bank, Human Development Network (2002) 'World Bank strategy in the education sector: process, product and progress', *International Journal of Educational Development* 22, 5:429–437.

Young, R. (1997) 'Comparative methodology and postmodern relativism', *International Review of Education* 43, 5–6:497–505.

Zachariah, M. (1990) 'For a committed internationalism in the comparative study of cultures', *Compare* 20, 1:83–87.

Index

administration 4, 46–7, 69, 91, 119;
  constraints 88; framework 39;
  procedures 91; responsibilities 3;
  structures 29, 92
adult education 44, 76, 80, 89
aid 84–5, 88, 90–4, 96, 99, 100, 107,
  113–14; agencies 41, 46–7, 93, 95, 97,
  100–2, 108–10, 113; agenda 98;
  collaboration 98, 102; coordination
  95, 97; decrease in 113, 114;
  education 85, 90, 94, 96; fatigue 113;
  overseas aid 84, 91, 108, 112, 113;
  partnerships 95, 97, 99, 107, 111;
  policy 97, 109; relationships 101–2,
  111
analysis 12, 14, 51, 117, 119; cultural
  52; multi-level 18, 126, 138; units of
  131
assessment 59, 71–3, 82, 111, 119;
  society 71 see also evaluation

basic education 85–6, 89, 91–3, 95–6,
  100, 107–111; for girls 111
bilateral agencies 84–6, 88–9, 91, 95, 96,
  99, 115
Brandt Report 84, 89, 100–1, 113, 145
bridging 50, 70, 77, 83, 117, 121–3, 125,
  129–30, 132, 142; cultures and
  traditions 77, 83, 116, 122, 142

census figures 43; problems 43
China 3, 7, 15, 27, 39, 43, 45, 102, 118,
  129; TNC universities 106
Chinese 12, 13, 24, 130; context 76
class 63, 77, 82, 137; inequalities 137
colonial: ambitions 63; colonialism 29,
  60, 63, 65, 102, 124; education
  systems 60; empires 24; era 54, 66;
language 89; neo-colonial 75, 84, 89,
  94, 115; powers 60, 85; regimes 102;
  reverse colonisation 57; territories
  20, 60, 88–9
Commonwealth 29, 79, 96; partnership
  96
communities 71, 121; aid recipients 98;
  local 103–4; multi-cultural 124;
  pluralist 124
community education 9, 89;
  development 80; empowerment
  128; identity 103
comparativists 9, 15–16, 51, 59, 64, 75,
  116–20, 124, 128, 135
competitive league tables 2, 72–3, 119;
  motives 135
contexts xv, 3, 5–6, 9–10, 12,17, 39, 40,
  43, 48–50, 58, 62, 65–6, 71–3, 75, 77,
  82, 84, 92, 102, 106, 111, 115, 118–23,
  126, 129, 131–2, 136, 139, 142;
  cultural 14–15, 20, 22–3, 25, 33, 36,
  51, 74, 77, 130; different 93, 102, 115,
  136; economic 93, 123;
  environmental 46; global 119;
  historical 118; local 36, 39, 115;
  multicultural 47; national 14, 61;
  policy 120; political 93, 122;
  sensitive 51, 74, 76, 81–2, 97, 102,
  119, 129, 137, 139,142; social 122–3;
  socio-cultural 129; war-torn 79;
  Western 42
critical analysis 4; dualism 26;
  perspectives 52; reflection 4; review
  11; scholarship 71, 123; theory 51
cross-cultural: advances 141; analyses
  40, 81; bridging 122; collaboration
  115, 139; conflict 78; dialogue 2, 77,
  82, 130, 136; dimension 69, 134;

groups 77; implications 12; issues 7, 10, 130, 138; language complications 47; limitations 76; research 32, 47, 124, 139, 142; tensions 131; transfer of models 39, 131; understanding 79

cultural: analysis 52, 125; approach 25, 140–1; appropriateness 109; background 106; bias 48; borrowing 20, 22–3, 25, 29, 60; boundaries 140; circumstances 125; conceptions 129; constraints 88, 104; context 14–15, 20, 22–3, 25, 33, 36, 51, 55, 74, 77, 87, 119, 126–7, 130; dependency 51; dialogue 141; differences 33, 50, 63, 66, 102, 115, 123, 130–1, 136–7; dilemmas 139; dimension 77, 116; divisions 52; dominance 36; factors 55–6, 62, 68, 70, 82, 120–1, 124; identity 76, 141; imperialism 65; influences 77; integrity 21; movements 57; objectives 74; perspectives 8, 33, 52, 61, 69, 70, 76; philosophy 23; pluralism 30, 141; resistance 80; sensitivity 74, 80–2, 89, 132, 137, 139; studies 57, 68, 77, 117, 125; traditions 125

culture xi, xii, xiv 2–3, 6, 10, 17, 19, 27, 36, 48, 62–3, 65, 72, 74–7, 79–80, 82, 87–8, 115, 119–20, 122, 124, 126, 131–2, 138–42

curriculum 9,12, 22, 28, 40, 104, 108, 111; change 6; content 106; development 89; effect of TNCs 103; reform 105, 109; rewriting in USSR 37; sponsorship 106

debt burden 113–14; debt relief 114; debt service average 114

definitions 16–20

dependency theory 28–9, 47, 51, 59, 84, 89, 92, 98, 102

developed countries 8–9, 66, 95–6, 100, 120, 122, 125

developing countries 14–15, 45–7, 62–4, 66, 72, 78, 84, 86, 90, 92–4, 96, 99, 104, 109, 112–13, 115, 120, 122–23, 125, 132

development 15, 51, 59, 62, 70, 77, 81–90, 94, 97, 101–2, 114,116, 130, 133, 136–37, 139; agencies 5, 74, 84, 87, 93, 112, 115, 120; aid 96, 112, 120; alternative models 72; collaborative

112, 115, 121, 128–29, 136; cooperation undermined 107; economists 111; educational 120; initiatives 74; international 128; local ownership of solutions 101; mistakes 135; national 116; priorities 85, 91, 122, 129; problems 79; process 85, 100, 115, 124; research 98, 108; role of education 111; strategies 3, 124; studies 2, 66; theoretical and methodological 4; under-development 51

difference xi, xiv, 3, 8, 10, 49–50, 62, 65–6, 68, 74, 76, 82, 131, 133, 136, 139; diversity 9, 11–13, 29, 31, 33, 39, 49, 50, 56, 62, 65–6, 68, 76, 82–3, 112, 117, 130, 132, 134–8, 140, 142

Eastern Europe 5, 26–7, 61, 113–14; collapse of Soviet Empire 94, 112–13; external assistance 94; 'turbo' capitalism 72

economics 21, 57, 71; analysis 108; circumstances 125; competitiveness 72; control 66; development 43, 51, 85–88, 93, 101, 116; effect of SAPs 107; expansion through education 111; factors 55–6, 73; forces 55; foundations 59; growth 26–7, 87, 93, 113; imperialism 92; in globalisation 56, 103, 141; management 113; national 103; objectives 135; priorities 73, 139; privatisation 106–9; problems 91; rationalism 71; recession 94; reconstruction 85; reform 113; restructuring 93; stability 100; structures 107; TNCs' effects 104

education systems 14, 16, 59, 65, 72, 81, 85, 91–2, 99, 104, 106, 110–12, 120, 122, 134

enrolment 13, 40, 104; female 104; higher education 40; primary age 40, 45, 114; secondary school 45; statistics 42, 44; tertiary 45

evaluation 16, 72, 95, 119, 121, 137; capacity 3, 137; methodologies 137; performance indicators 72

examinations 108; assessment 59, 71–2; results 22, 59, 72

funders 8, 68, 84, 89–90, 97, 101; commissioning research 110;

developing countries lack 47; donor agencies 87, 89–92, 94–5, 98–101, 108, 113–14; donor coordination 97–8; donor governments' policies 98, 113; external funding agencies 41, 110–11, 121, 123; *see also* partnerships

geopolitical: changes 5, 10, 61; educational structures 78; global context 102; influences xv; relations 1, 5, 8, 48, 67, 71, 116, 134, 139; realities 50, 123

global 13, 25, 39, 59, 68, 115, 132, 138; agencies 73; agendas 83–4, 87, 107, 110; change 11; climate 135; community 103; competition 105; conflict 78; context 119; corporations 100, 103, 105; disparities 78–9, 84, 100, 106; division of labour 54; economy 67, 100, 103, 111–12, 139; education 59, 84, 88, 105, 109, 137; educational assistance 90; enterprises 75, 131; era 66, 123, 133; focus 50; forces 122–23, 130; framework 126, 140; impact 111; inequalities 78, 112; influence 59, 77; issues 118, 130; knowledge 91; language 78; literacy figures 87; marketplace 53, 76, 100, 104–7; poverty 107, 111–12; power 66; priorities 82; problems 108; research 60; 'solutions' 84; strategic priorities 111; theoretical insights 129; trading 104; trends 131; welfare 100

globalisation xi, xiii, xv, xvi, 1–5, 7–8, 10, 30, 34, 36, 48–55, 57–62, 66–8, 71–5, 77, 79, 82, 87, 89, 100–4, 106, 112, 115–16, 122–3, 126–42; higher education 22, 40, 109, 110; diversion to basic education 109–10; investment in 93

historical 10; analysis 51, 76, 82, 138; approach 20, 26, 35, 62, 125, 141; context 118; development 22; evolution 50–1; experience 9; factors 71; foundations 20; influences 77; insights 9, 22; perspective 4, 9, 88, 125; phases 4, 20–5, 29, 31, 50, 60, 76, 138, 141; research 68; review 71; shifts 50;

specificity 19; studies 68, 117; theories 16

history xiv, 3, 9, 11–13, 21, 29, 31–2, 52, 62, 66, 116, 125, 134, 136, 138; 'end of history' thesis 72; of education 21

human resource development 72, 84; skills 72–4, 82, 95, 103, 106; training 72–4, 82, 103; TNCs' influence 103, 106

identity 77, 82, 122, 124, 131–33, 137, 139, 141

IEA 1; findings 120; model 120, 131; studies 72–3, 119–20

international: agencies 31, 59, 66–7, 73, 75, 78, 87–9, 106, 109, 115–16, 122, 131, 135, 137; agendas 131–32; assistance to education 90; banks 103; consultancy 10; cooperation 19, 70; decision-making 127; development 50, 63, 71, 73, 75, 80–3, 92, 94, 115, 121, 124, 128, 136; dialogue xv; education 13, 116, 120–21, 124, 132; experience 6; fieldwork 32; orientation 16; perspectives 84; structures 127; transfer 3, 21, 23, 34, 57, 60–1, 66–8, 73, 75, 86, 102, 115, 120, 130, 141; trends 118; understanding 19, 55, 59, 79

IMF 85, 93, 103, 107–8, 113 investment in education 27, 29, 73, 88, 93, 111, 114, 120; imposition of SAPs 107; in stable countries 100

journals 24–5, 117, 139

language 87–8, 104, 124; differences 43, 73, 108; indigenous 88, 138; policies 3; problems 41–2, 47; rights 106; skills 47

learning 18, 68, 72, 76–7, 81–2, 87, 95, 119, 129, 131, 137; and globalisation 58; distance 111; forms of 10, 111; lifelong 2, 73, 80, 82, 111, 138; open 111; society 10, 68, 73; teacher interaction 22; theory 136

linguistic divisions 52; background 106; groups 109; plural societies 4, 47, 73; problems of communication 47 literacy 44, 85–7, 95–6, 98, 105, 108, 124; female 95, 98; functional 86; illiteracy 95; programmes 88, 108; rates of 87, 95

marginalisation 104, 107–8; countries 127; groups 79, 127, 131, 138; of local knowledge 108, 110
methodology 1, 4, 5, 7, 10, 19, 25, 31, 39, 67, 75, 81–2, 120, 126, 132, 138
migration 57, 65, 106; wars 106
MDGs 96, 114
modernisation theory 3, 27–8, 52, 63, 68, 102, 122; modernism 52, 63, 122, 127
multicultural forces 6, 73; aspirations 77; communities 124; contexts 47; groups 76; world 141
multidisciplinary field 7, 12, 15, 20, 30–1, 33, 38, 51, 58–9, 66, 74, 83, 117, 122, 124, 130, 134, 140; perspective 79; research 123; studies 19
multilateral organisations 54, 59–60, 68–9, 84, 86, 88–90, 96, 106, 108, 113, 115; partnerships 95

nation-state 51, 53–5, 57, 61, 66–7, 79, 91, 117, 122, 126–7, 132, 137; neoliberalism 6, 52–4, 57, 66, 71–2, 82, 102, 106, 116, 131, 137
non-formal education 2, 44–5, 80, 89, 91–3, 128
non-governmental organisations (NGOs) 15, 49, 80, 95, 101, 108, 110, 114–15, 124, 128; collaborative ventures 96, 98; definition 97; partnerships 95–7,101
North–South divide 54, 66, 72, 81, 84; inequality 101; knowledge gap 129; partnership 98, 100, 129, 139
Northern hemisphere 8, 37, 41, 46, 48, 54–5, 61, 66, 72, 78, 81, 84, 89, 97–8, 100–1, 109, 112, 115, 117, 129, 139; academic researchers 97; aid agencies 46, 89; research capacity 48; researchers in Southern hemisphere 46

official documents 37; bias in 37; statistical evidence 38, 42, 45
OECD 13, 35, 44, 79, 85, 88, 99, 106, 113

partnership 94–102, 108, 110–12, 114–15, 118, 128–9, 136, 139; donor-recipient 94, 99–100, 111, 115; local and external personnel 129; new partnerships 95, 100–1; Northern and Southern agencies 139; undermined by SAPs 107; with national governments 110
performance 120; performance indicators 72; performativity culture 72
philosophical approach xiii, 20, 32, 64, 70, 125, 137, 141
policy and practice 4, 5, 8–10, 14, 19–20, 23, 48, 51, 60, 62, 64, 67–9, 72–4, 77, 80, 86, 90, 93, 98–102, 115–16, 119–21, 124, 127–32, 135, 137, 141–2; agendas 73; aid policy 97, 102; context 120; dialogue 84; exchange 129; future 9; initiatives 60, 73; priorities 137; public 135; relevance 128; transfer 119; trends 78
policy-makers 6, 8, 13, 16, 25–6, 58, 72, 80–1, 93, 101, 109, 118–22, 125, 128, 135, 139; partnership 128; research 69; results 120; studies 57, 129
political factors xiv, 27, 55–6, 59, 77, 123, 141; accountability 113; advocacy 135; commitment 94; constraints 88; context 122; control 66; in globalisation 56; interpretation 119; intolerance 79; motives 129; movements 57; philosophy 26; politics 63; science 21, 57; transformations 124; unrest 106
poor communities 101, 104–05
population figures 43; age group 43; inaccuracy of 43
post-colonialism 4, 8, 52, 65, 68, 87, 89, 97, 121, 124–5, 138, 142; critique 8; debates 5; framework 48, 66; perspectives 6, 10, 50; theory 65–6, 77
poverty 86–7, 94, 100, 104, 106–7, 135; agenda 69; alleviation 46, 73, 82, 92, 107–8, 114, 138; and education 131; and wars 107; definitions 107; increase world-wide 100, 108; World Bank's role 112
primary education 2, 12, 22, 40, 45, 57, 64, 86–7, 89, 91–3, 95–6, 108–9;

spending per pupil 96; universal
(UPE) 43, 96, 108
priorities 70–1, 73, 78, 81–2, 85–6, 88,
94–5, 98, 101, 104, 106, 110, 116–20,
130–1, 135–9; educational 4;
research 5, 59, 66, 68; setting 93
professional cultures xii, xiii, 3–8, 31,
39–40, 49, 62, 72, 83, 111, 117–22,
129, 132, 134, 138–9, 142;
development 140

quality assurance 73, 136, 138

race 63, 65, 77, 82, 124, 137;
inequalities 137
reconceptualisation 4, 6–7, 10, 33–4, 61,
67, 69, 115–23, 128–32, 135–40, 142
of research problems 48; thesis 8,
12, 50, 70, 123, 142
reform 9, 14–17, 24, 28, 38–9, 46, 51, 59,
62–5, 68, 72–3, 76, 80–2, 87, 93,
108–13, 120–1, 126, 129–30, 136
refugees and migrants 2, 79, 131;
education of 79
research 3, 8, 52, 61, 77, 84, 92, 108, 110,
122, 127, 137–8, 142; activity 118;
agenda 5, 51, 66–71, 73–4, 77, 84, 92,
98, 131, 135; and development 103;
applied 132; approaches to 13, 141;
base 94; based 9; capacity building
127–28, 132, 137; centres 135;
collaborative 41, 74–7, 123, 127–8,
137; competitive 123; cross-national
120; cultures 121, 123;
dissemination 123, 129; educational
4, 8, 10, 50, 57, 64, 66–70, 77, 81–3,
109, 110–12, 115–18, 120–1, 125,
127–8, 130–1, 136, 139; empirical 4,
92, 123, 131; enterprise 120; focus
38, 61, 118, 126; frames of reference
131; framework 117–18; in
developing countries 45;
independent 109; initiatives 134;
instruments 69; issues 81; local
capacity 66, 77, 101, 110–11, 115,
128, 132; methods 33, 141;
orientation 1, 140; policy-oriented 7,
68, 124, 132; potential 118; priorites
5, 59, 66, 68, 71–2, 139; problem
oriented 118; problems 32, 48, 70,
116; process 80–1, 138, 142;
qualitative 52, 62, 64, 127; social 4,
5, 10, 71, 118, 125–6, 130; strengths

118; themes 70, 131; timescale 40;
training 118, 134, 140 researchers
16, 51, 58, 67, 97, 110, 119, 122–3,
125, 128, 132, 139; developing
countries 47; educational 118, 129,
133; external 101; local 75, 110, 128;
partnerships 128; practitioner 128;
social science 125; teams 41
Russia 2, 36, 102; collapse of 57, 68, 72,
94, 102, 112; falsifying records 37;
Kruschev 37; Lenin 27; Stalin 37;
USSR 8, 26–8, 37–8, 61

school 71, 89: achievement 6, 26, 119;
autonomy 6; choice 109; core
subjects 119; effectiveness studies 2,
72; elite 105; enrolments 44–5;
equipment 89, 92, 114; governance
111; health programmes 111; IEA
studies 72–3, 119; improvement
strategies 72, 109; leadership 69,
106, 109–10; league tables 119; local
community involvement 39, 109;
management theory 69, 109;
mapping 43; organisation 69;
performance 72, 119; publicly run
105–6; schooling 108; society
relationship 26; sponsorship 106;
systems 105, 109
secondary education 22, 87, 89;
schools' spending per pupil 96
SWAPs 108, 110–11
small states xi, 3, 29, 79, 91, 126–7, 131
socio-cultural analysis of global trends
3 change 70; contexts 6, 20, 62, 129;
dimension 60–1; perspectives 136
process 63; studies 125, 132
socio-political change 5, 68, 122, 126;
events 126
Southern hemisphere xiii, 1, 7–8, 20,
28–9, 46–8, 54–7, 61, 66, 72–4, 81, 84,
90, 95, 97–8, 100–2, 106, 108, 115,
117, 129, 137, 139; lack of research
capacity 47–8
statistics 13; achievement 111; data
34–5, 37–8, 43–5; distortion of 37;
government 37; information 35;
limitations 42; official 45; raw data
42
Structural Adjustment Programmes
(SAPs) 93, 100, 107–8; disastrous
effects 100, 107–8; increased
poverty 100, 107–8

substantive dimensions xii, xiv, 10,
    136, 138, 142; issues 138, 140
sustainability 81–2, 88, 92–3, 95, 99,
    101, 121

teachers 16, 71, 88–9, 108, 110, 138–9;
    learner interaction 22; numbers of
    13; professionalism 6; salaries 114;
    training 20, 22, 89, 109, 134, 140;
    training head teachers 109
teaching 18, 68, 77, 82, 119, 128–31,
    134, 140; resources 92, 96
technical and vocational education 9,
    22, 89, 91, 93, 100, 103
tertiary education 87, 89
time 80, 82, 122, 135; calendars 80;
    constraints 110; fixed timescale 108;
    frames 81, 92, 98
training 22, 72–4, 82, 93, 103; education
    management 93; financial
    management 93 transnational
    corporations (TNCs) 100, 103–5,
    131; company universities 106;

influence on countries 103;
    involvement in education 131
travellers' tales 12, 20, 60

uncritical transfer 5, 23, 60, 67, 89, 115,
    129–31, 135, 141
UNESCO 7, 13, 26, 35, 38, 40–4, 59, 73,
    84–8, 91, 96–7, 106, 108, 110
University 72, 89, 105; expansion 108;
    local research institutions 110;
    programmes 140; sponsorship106;
    teaching 134, 140

Western world 9, 13, 20, 25, 27–8, 74,
    76, 93, 101–2, 109, 113, 115, 130, 141;
    contexts 42; educational systems 60,
    92; functionalism 28; ideology 57,
    61, 113; imperialism 54;
    management 72; non-Western
    perspectives 61; values 89, 113, 134
World Bank 13, 26, 35, 37–9, 42, 44, 59,
    73, 78, 84–7, 90–4, 97, 99–100, 103,
    107–113